Ostraca from the Temple of Millions of Years of Thutmose III

Culture and History of the Ancient Near East

The titles published in this series are listed at *brill.com/chan*

Ostraca from the Temple of Millions of Years of Thutmose III

By

Fredrik Hagen

BRILL

LEIDEN | BOSTON

Library of Congress Cataloging-in-Publication Data

Names: Hagen, Fredrik, author.
Title: Ostraca from the Temple of Millions of Years of Thutmose III / by Fredrik
    Hagen.
Description: Leiden ; Boston : Brill, 2021. | Series: Culture and history of the ancient
    Near East, 1566-2055 ; volume 120 | Includes bibliographical references and
    index.
Identifiers: LCCN 2021004820 (print) | LCCN 2021004821 (ebook) |
    ISBN 9789004447554 (hardback) | ISBN 9789004447561 (e-book)
Subjects: LCSH: Excavations (Archaeology)–Egypt–Deir el-Bahri Site–Catalogs. |
    Temple of Thutmose III (Deir el-Bahri Site, Egypt)–Catalogs. | Ostraka–Egypt–
    Catalogs. | Egypt–Antiquities–Catalogs. | Inscriptions, Egyptian–Egypt–Deir
    el-Bahri Site–Catalogs.
Classification: LCC DT73.D45 H34 2021 (print) | LCC DT73.D45 (ebook) |
    DDC 932/.3–dc23
LC record available at https://lccn.loc.gov/2021004820
LC ebook record available at https://lccn.loc.gov/2021004821

Typeface for the Latin, Greek, and Cyrillic scripts: "Brill". See and download: brill.com/brill-typeface.

ISSN 1566-2055
ISBN 978-90-04-44755-4 (hardback)
ISBN 978-90-04-44756-1 (e-book)

For Rob Demarée, a model colleague

∴

Contents

Preface

This work was made possible, in the first instance, by Myriam Seco Álvarez, who entrusted me with the publication of the hieratic material from her excavation at the Temple of Millions of Years of Thutmose III at Thebes, where she has been directing a joint project between the University of Seville and the Egyptian Ministry of Antiquities since 2008. I am grateful to her for this opportunity, and for providing such a welcoming environment in Luxor. I would also like to express my thanks to all the team members who took part in the seasons when I was there (2016 and onwards), both for their hospitality and for their patience in introducing me to the various parts of the site that they were working on: Javier Martínez Babón (co-director), Manuel Abelleira Duran, Ibrahim Noureddine, Mohammed Sayed Temsah Osman, Mariá Franco González, Pauline Calassou, Florian Löffler, Reyes Somé Salazar, Immaculada Delage González, Javier Tre Garcia, Inés María García Martínez, Inmaculada Concepción Lozano Urbano, Roger and Liliane Seiler, and of course our host at the dig house, Abu Hagga Mohamed Abd Lahi. In addition to these colleagues I owe a special debt to the following: Augustine Gamarra Campuzano for numerous discussions of mudbrick technology and architecture, as well as the organisation of work crews; Mohammed Naguib Reda and Mahmoud Al Shafei for essential input on ceramics and pottery classification (all identifications of clay and pottery types are due to them); and Ahmed Amin for photography and much assistance, both in Luxor and Cairo.

The work would not have been possible without the kind support of our Egyptian colleagues both on-site and in various offices: Fathi Yassim abd el Karim (Director of Qurna), Ezz Kamal el Nubi (Chief inspector Middle Area), Ahmed Boghdadi (Inspector of the magazine on the site), Mahmoud Mohamed El-Aazab (Inspector during the 2018 season), Mohamed el Aazab (Inspector of the mission in Carter Magazine).

Our inspectors were all supportive and helpful, but Shaima Abdul Kareem in particular stands out in terms of both enthusiasm and an extraordinary talent for spotting joins in both ostraca and papyri, despite not being a philologist.

Financial support for the excavation work was provided by the Botín Foundation, Santander Universidades, the Cajasol Foundation, and the Gaselec Foundation.

Much of my own initial work was done in parallel with the project *Tomb Construction in New Kingdom Egypt* (funding for which was generously provided by the Velux Foundation in Copenhagen), and I am grateful to my colleagues on that project, Daniel Soliman and Rune Olsen, for many constructive discussions of the material. Similarly, I have benefited from feedback and discussion following presentations of material in several locations, including Basel, Cambridge, Leiden, Leipzig and Uppsala.

Material such as that presented here frequently poses philological challenges, both in terms of palaeography, syntax, and lexical semantics, and I have not infrequently solicited input from colleagues when encountering difficulties. Here I am particularly grateful to Malte Römer and Matthias Müller who both generously spent their time checking transcriptions and translations thoroughly, and made many helpful suggestions. For convenience and legibility I generally do not note each individual contribution in the text, but readers should be aware of the substantial nature of their comments—their willingness to help has improved this book considerably. Another colleague who provided comments on an individual text was Joachim Quack, who first drew my attention to the parallels in *The Opening of the Mouth Ritual* for L33. Finally, the two anonymous referees for this volume provided a number of additional references (and the odd suggestion for readings), as well as useful input on structure, for which I am grateful.

I have also benefited from the help of one of our MA students, Sika Skytte Odsbjerg Pedersen, who diligently coded the final hieroglyphic transcriptions and compiled the indices. Her keen eyes caught a number of slips and inconsistencies, and she also made some suggestions for alternative readings (noted separately in the commentaries). From the publishing side of things, Katelyn Chin and Erika Mandarino at Brill were a great help in the editorial process, and Cas Van den Hof handled the type-setting of this complicated book with both skill and patience.

Perhaps my largest debt of gratitude is to the grand old man of hieratic studies, Rob Demarée, who also in this case read through and provided valuable comments on my early draft transcriptions. I can think of few Egyptologists who are more generous with their time, and combined with his selfless sharing of material, as well as his readiness to help both younger and older scholars, he has long been a model of collegiality. I had intended to contribute to the Festschrift that was published in his honour a few years ago (Haring, Kaper and van Walsem 2014), but other commitments meant that I was unable to do so. I therefore dedicate this book to him as a modest—and much belated—'thank you' for all of his support and help over the years.

Figures and Tables

Figures

Tables

Notes on Organisation, Transliteration and Transcription

For convenience every ostracon published here has been given the siglum 'Ostracon T3', followed by a letter indicating genre (A = administrative, D = docket, L = literary, F = figurative) plus a two-digit number (abbreviated 'O. T3.A01'), with the sequence of the numbers assigned loosely on the basis of content. Where several fragments with individual excavation numbers have been joined—and most such joins were identified by my archaeological colleagues upon excavation, not by me—these are listed under a single siglum in the catalogue. In one case where an object had a literary extract on one side and a drawing on the other, the decision was made to include it in the catalogue under both literary texts and drawings, and so in practice there are two sigla associated with a single object (this is L15 which is the same object as F21).

The original excavation numbers, as presented under each individual entry below, consist of an excavation number separated by a slash ('/') from a string of numbers referring to the find coordinates. The latter give the position of the findspot by reference to the Y- and X-axis of the site map (Fig. 1), followed by a number indicating elevation, and the season it was found. So, for example, O.T3.A43, with a list of priests from the temple, has the numerical sequence 15670/910N6L215; this means that it was found in the grid denoted by 910 on the Y-axis and N6 on the X-axis, which corresponds to an area outside the enclosure wall to the north west, in layer 2, during the 2015 season (cf. *Archaeological context*, below). Some numbers incorporate other abbreviations, of which the following four occur in the catalogue: 'RM' stands for 'Ricke Magazine' (cf. A40, A49 and L01) and refers to material left by Ricke's excavation in the mid-1930s; 'SD' stands for 'Surface Debris' (cf. A38 and D16); 'T' plus a Roman numeral refers to one of the many tombs in the area (cf. A04 and F10 from 'Tomb VII', found in grids 960–970/S4), and finally 'R' refers to an area north of the enclosure wall (cf. A30 and L39).

Most ostraca are presented with photographs, facsimile drawings, transcriptions and a description. The descriptions are brief,[1] but in the case of ceramic ostraca I have tried to include information on clay fabric, pottery type, and date, where available. With material excavated over several seasons and stored in several locations, it has not always been possible to do so, but where the information is included I have been entirely dependent on colleagues who specialise in ceramics (primarily Mohammed Naguib Reda and Mahmoud Al Shafei), and all such descriptions of pottery is due to them alone. This information is not entirely uniform in the catalogue, which is due to changing circumstances on site, as well as over time—these objects were excavated over a period of almost ten years. I am not qualified to judge the accuracy of ceramic diagnostics, and have in most cases simply reported the written comments I got in reply to my questions regarding materiality. As a point of methodology, it is only fair to note that their comments were made without access to my own data on the text on the ostraca, and that my own readings and interpretations were made without access to their evaluations. In the vast majority of cases the two sets of evaluations were compatible, and occasionally even complementary: in my initial evaluation of L45—which has the name of one of the four sons of Horus, Qebehsenuef, in hieroglyphs—I had wavered between an interpretation of it as either a practice piece or a fragment of a ceramic canopic jar, but the comments from Mohammed Naguib Reda firmly identified it as the latter.[2] Conversely, A15 and L05 were both interpreted as either a New Kingdom or Late Period sherd, but the hieratic clearly identifies them as the former. However, it is perhaps not entirely surprising that there were also some discrepancies, where the comments on the materiality of the ostraca did not align with my own impressions of the contents. In one case (F12), the motif of a man with a fig leaf in front of the genitals seems to me to evoke a rather late date, if the iconography is indeed Christian (so perhaps Coptic Period?), whereas the date of manufacture for the sherd was 'probably' the Middle Kingdom. Here both might be correct, of course, with a very old sherd having been picked up and drawn on in a later period (cf. F16). More troubling is D02, which was identified as 'a body sherd of Marl jar, probably dated to the Late Period', but where the text clearly identifies it as a wine jar docket, the palaeography seems to belong to the 18th Dynasty, and the mention of a year 37 narrows it down to either Thutmose III or Amenhotep III. This is not to say that one type of evidence is necessarily more reliable than the other, but mistakes are easy to make, and a careful investigation of both materiality and text is neces-

---

1   Any reference to an ostracon being 'complete' or 'incomplete' refers not to the original object but to the integrity of the sherd after it had been inscribed, i.e. whether any text has been lost.

2   On the topic of methodology, and as a warning against relying too much on quick judgments, it is perhaps worth noting that Mahmoud Al Shafei, independently of Mohammed Naguib Reda, had described L45 as 'perhaps an Egyptian New Kingdom amphora' in his initial assessment.

FIGURE 1   Map of the mortuary temple of Thutmose III, with main elements marked. Note in particu-
            lar the side entrance on the right, through which the rubbish dump, immediately outside the
            enclosure wall, could be accessed.

sary when trying to understand the purpose and role of any individual object, including jars and manuscripts.

Translations and short commentaries have been included in most cases, mainly to improve accessibility for non-specialists. The comments are deliberately brief and the translations rather free, aiming to reproduce the sense of the Egyptian rather than a literal word for word translation. In the case of well-known literary compositions, I have for the sake of convenience followed the translations of Richard B. Parkinson in his *The Tale of Sinuhe and Other Ancient Egyptian Poems 1940–1640 BC* (1997).

The book follows the established Egyptological conventions in transliterating and transcribing hieratic:

[…]   in transcriptions or translations indicates missing text in the original, and any letters or hieroglyphs enclosed by such brackets have been restored by me; the ellipsis is not an indication of the length of a lacuna.

(…)   in translations indicates a word or phrase inserted by me for clarity but not present in the Egyptian.

⟨…⟩   in transcriptions and translations indicates an omission by the ancient scribe.

▨   (i.e. hatching) in the hieroglyphic transcriptions indicates damaged or illegible text in the original; in such cases the images and facsimiles can be consulted for the relevant traces.

At the request of the publisher, red ink in the original text is indicated in the translations by the use of **bold**, for typographical reasons, but in the case of transcriptions on the plates these have been reproduced in their original colours. All hieroglyphic text, both on plates and in-text, follow the direction of the original hieratic, i.e. from right to left.

The photographs reproduced here were taken specifically for this volume by Inés María García Martínez, during the 2019 field season.

In addition to transcriptions, facsimile drawings have been included for each ostracon. This decision has not been taken lightly—it represents a significant amount of extra work—but despite recent trends in similar catalogues to omit facsimiles (e.g. Demarée 2002; Burkard 2018), I believe such drawings may be useful (cf. Dorn 2011; Grandet 2017; 2010; 2006; 2003; 2000). For reasons of time I have produced the drawings digitally, rather than using the old-fashioned analogue method that I employed previously (e.g. Hagen 2011), and the minor inconsistencies in appearance in this book reflect a continual process of experimentation and learning.[3] Like all facsim-

iles my drawings are subjective in that there is invariably an element of conscious or unconscious interpretation, but what they lack in reliability they make up for by the introduction of details sometimes not captured by two-dimensional photographs of three-dimensional objects. Each drawing has been collated with the original object, under different lighting conditions and using various computer algorithms (including D-Stretch), and aims to reproduce the sum of the traces visible. This is perhaps most important in those cases where the reading is problematic, but readers may find them useful also when working with passages visible in the photographs themselves.

The textual commentary is kept to a minimum throughout, and I make no attempt at a historical synthesis in this volume. A full evaluation should ideally draw on the final archaeological report on the site itself, including an analysis of stratigraphy, construction, development, and other aspects that relate directly or indirectly to the interpretation of the texts, but it may take some time before this appears. However, such a synthesis would in any case be premature before the papyri are fully published—the ostraca and papyri are inextricably linked in terms of archaeological and social context, as well as content—although I hope to produce such a work once the relevant material has been made available. As the only substantially surviving temple archive of the New Kingdom it will surely repay close study, despite its fragmentary state.

The majority of the objects published in this catalogue were found quite recently, and in preparing them for publication I have tried to be as accurate and thorough as time has allowed. The demands of teaching and administration, as well as other research projects, has imposed limitations on this, but I hope that the transcriptions and translations are generally reliable, and that whatever inaccuracies and mistakes are left will not be judged too harshly. By a happy coincidence this book should be published around the same time as Malte Römer's much larger corpus of (primarily administrative) ostraca from the contemporary building works in the nearby Deir el-Bahri area, and together the appearance of these volumes will shed new light on the social history of the Theban West Bank, and in particular that of the 18th Dynasty monuments that still dominate its archaeological landscape.

---

3   There is as yet no standard way to produce digital facsimiles of hieratic, but the hieratic project directed by Ursula Verhoeven and

her team in Mainz has developed a method that is slowly being implemented also by others: my own work was unfortunately too advanced by the time I heard of their efforts, and I was unable to adopt their proposed method.

Abbreviations and Standard Reference Works

KRI   K. Kitchen, *Ramesside Inscriptions*. Oxford: Blackwells.

LÄ   W. Helck, O. Eberhard and W. Westendorf (eds.). 1975–
          1992, *Lexikon der Ägyptologie*, 7 vols. Wiesbaden: Har-
          rassowitz.

Urk. IV K. Sethe and W. Helck. 1906–1968. *Urkunden des
          ägyptischen Altertums, Abteilung IV: Urkunden der 18.
          Dynastie*. Berlin: Akademie-Verlag.

Wb.   A. Erman and H. Grapow (eds.). 1926–1963. *Wört-
          erbuch der ägyptischen Sprache*, 13 vols. Berlin and
          Leipzig.

Introduction

The so-called mortuary temple of Thutmose III, a type of institution called a 'Temple of Millions of Years' in Egyptian, is a large temple on the Theban West Bank, built to serve the cult of that king, as well as a local manifestation of Amun and perhaps also of Hathor (Legrain 1906: 184–185; cf. Laskowski 2006: 207–208; Troy 2006: 124–125). Its Egyptian name was Henket-ankh, and several powerful families in the area held priestly offices here, as evidenced by their tombs in the nearby necropolis (Haring 1997: 431–435). Its construction may have started as early as Thutmose III's co-regency with Hatshepsut, because the name of the temple is mentioned on the Chapelle Rouge of that Queen, but it undoubtedly continued for most of the king's reign, and one of the ostraca from Deir el-Bahri, published by Hayes (1960: 47–48), mentions building work there as late as year 49. The ostraca relating to building work that are published here for the first time probably fall within this period (see *Records of work*, below).

The physical remains of the temple as currently preserved are modest compared to similar temples nearby, but at the time of Thutmose III it would have been an important building in the landscape on the West Bank. It was here that the king chose to celebrate his triumphant return from the military campaign in the Levant in regnal year 22, at which point it must already have been an imposing structure, and jar labels published in this volume suggest that the *sed*-festival(s) of the king were also celebrated here. Despite its less than promising state of preservation, it was excavated several times, from the early explorations by Eugène Grébaut in 1889 (Daressy 1926), and the work of Arthur E.P. Weigall in 1905 (Weigall 1906, 1907), to the more systematic excavation by Herbert Ricke in 1934–1937 (Ricke 1939). Since 2008 Myriam Seco Álvarez and her Spanish-Egyptian team have been working at the site, both in excavating and restoring the temple and its enclosure wall (Álvarez 2015a; 2015b). In the course of their work, which significantly included excavation of the areas outside the enclosure wall, they discovered both ostraca and papyrus fragments in several locations, and the publication of this material was then assigned to me in 2015.

Upon my first arrival on-site, in November 2016, I was given access to approximately 230 pieces of pottery, limestone sherds, sandstone blocks and plaster pieces with inscriptions or drawings in ink, as well as a large number of papyrus fragments, then mounted in 14 frames of glass. Of these 230 or so objects, at least three (A40, A49

and L01) were probably already found during the excavations by Ricke in 1934–1937; the designation 'RM' (for 'Ricke Magazine') refers to a structure initially thought to have been built by Ricke but which is now thought to be from the earlier work of Weigall, and presumably used by both excavations for the storage or deposition of objects. The remainder of the objects had been discovered by Myriam Seco Álvarez' team over the course of several seasons of excavation, from 2008 and onwards. Unlike the objects found by Ricke, the latter group has a specific recorded archaeological context (see *Archaeological context*, below).

The objects may be divided up into different categories according to materiality and contents. The fragments of sandstone came from building blocks of the temple, and together with the plaster pieces they are best classified as graffiti rather than ostraca; in total they amount to around 30 individual pieces (Hagen, In preparation A). The remaining pottery and limestone sherds are ostraca in the traditional Egyptological sense, and they can be roughly classified as containing either drawings or text. The distinction is not always meaningful in view of the intensely visual nature of the Egyptian scripts, particularly in the case of hieroglyphs, and in some instances there are also overlaps where a single object carries both drawings and text. Nonetheless it provides one way of managing the material in a publication such as this, although it should be stressed that the same individuals—scribes and priests— were probably responsible for producing both types.

In general, I have tried to be relatively exhaustive in the inclusion of material here, and a reader may be inclined to ask what the purpose of publishing such fragmentary material is. The answer is simple: as one of the few temples where this kind of material has been found in the course of modern excavations, it is useful to have a foundation for evaluating writing practices both locally and more broadly in a comparative perspective. The latter point is particularly important for comparison with other modern excavations of hieratic ostraca, such as the Swiss work around the tomb of Ramesses X, where Andreas Dorn's publication (2011) has provided one example of how genres and categories can be mapped onto a large corpus of objects (mainly ostraca) to give an overview of writing activities associated with a work site. Additionally, the present publication presents something of a base-line which can be used to contextualise older finds of similar material, for example the hieratic ostraca found over a hundred years ago in the Ramesseum (Spiegelberg 1898), and the more recent finds from the same site (cf. *Archaeological context*, below).

Despite the attempt to be inclusive, there has naturally been a process of selection. Many of the ostraca are small fragments with no more than a few individual signs, and these have limited research value; it would be unjustifiable to publish them with a full record in a volume such as this. Such selection may be second nature to all field archaeologists, but perhaps not to the same extent to philologists, because it is fundamentally different from publishing, for example, museum collections of ostraca (e.g. Hagen 2011) where a selection has already been made in the acquisition process, whether they were originally bought on the market, donated by a collector, or excavated and allocated through a division of finds. Any number of smaller ostraca are likely to have been deliberately excluded during such procedures, so the range available for study is limited compared to those from a site excavated under carefully controlled conditions.

I have included a table at the end of the catalogue where such minor pieces are listed (Table 4), along with a couple of plates (98–99) which illustrate what some of this material looks like.

Despite this selection process there are a number of rather small pieces that have been given an entry in the catalogue itself. This is particularly true of literary pieces, where ostraca with just a couple of words preserved can sometimes be identified as a copy of a well-known composition. As witnesses these new manuscripts are rarely very informative, but they add to both the transmission history of the individual texts and to our knowledge of the literary canon of the New Kingdom, and so are afforded a regular catalogue entry despite their state of preservation.

In terms of scripts the excavation has found a single Coptic ostracon and two Demotic ostraca (to be published separately by other scholars), while the rest contain texts written in hieratic or hieroglyphs (or, in rare cases, something approaching the cursive hieroglyphic script), and these are the subject of this catalogue.

1 Administrative Documents

There are just over sixty ostraca that have been classified as administrative in the catalogue, covering a range of different types of texts that have been grouped together under 'accounts' (A01–23), 'records of work done' (A24–26), 'name-stones and name-lists' (A27–47), 'letters and messages' (A48–55), and 'varia' (A56–61): an overview of the most important texts are given below.

2 Accounts

The texts labelled as 'accounts' generally relate to the operation of the temple, in various ways. Many were clearly produced as part of the record-keeping of the temple in connection with the production or delivery of consumables offered in the daily cult, presumably as drafts or preliminary notes before being entered into more official accounts on papyrus, as is well attested in the earlier temple archives at Abusir and Lahun. At the temple of Thutmose III the papyrus archive is extremely fragmentary and so it is difficult to draw parallels between the use of the two media, but whereas the papyri seem mainly to consist of fragments of the daybook of the temple (Hagen 2018: 99–101), including lists of the daily offerings, many of the ostraca, such as the baking accounts, or the deliveries of geese, appear to be related to the recording of these resources in parallel with the cult accounts, as opposed to being drafts for the latter. In terms of accounting practices, the usual pattern of daily, weekly, monthly and yearly records were probably produced, although not all types are preserved among the surviving ostraca. An account (A05) for geese (?) and reeds (?) lists deliveries of these day by day, with two numbers listed per day: these presumably represent the daily quota of expected delivery followed by the amount actually delivered, as is common in accounting documents. In another account the precise commodity is not listed (A06)—although the high numbers might suggest fish or firewood, by comparison with the documents from Deir el-Medina—and here the scribe seems to have summarised weekly deliveries, i.e. per ten days.

Production of bread in the temple may have been monitored in a comparable way to that known from other institutions, and although there are no baking accounts comparable to the documents from the later palace archive of Seti I (Hagen 2018: 109–115), some ostraca (A01, A02, A08 and A10) may represent notes later used for the compilation of similar accounts on papyrus. Not surprisingly, the types of bread loaves and cakes mentioned in the ostraca also occur in the many lists of daily offerings in the papyrus material from the site (along with wine, vegetables, incense, etc.).

Several ostraca shed light on the complex logistics associated with the running of the temple, both in terms of production of commodities, deliveries of goods, and the distribution of consumables. One account (A04) lists wood belonging to (?) an *imy-st-ꜥ* priest of the fourth phyle, while others also mention phyles in connection with the distribution of offerings of fowl in connection with festivals (A11–12). One ostracon has an account of offerings made during the *wꜣg*-festival (A13), perhaps also meant as a preliminary note for later entry into the daybook of the temple kept on papyrus rolls. The latter is anonymous and presumably relates to the complete offerings in play, as opposed to ostraca naming the shares of individual priests (A11–12, 14; cf. A19); these are clearly more concerned with the reversal of offerings. As with most of the ostraca it is not possible to establish a firm chronology or sequence for the accounts, and the majority probably relate to the operation of the temple during or after the reign of Thutmose III, but one account which seems to deal with food for stone masons (A23) might be relatively early, perhaps from the building of the temple (see *Records of work* and *Letters and message*, below, for other examples of documents relating to this early phase).

The temple stores will have consisted of other goods in addition to consumables for festivals, and one ostracon (A17) mentions various types of planks and beams of wood, some perhaps boat parts, being delivered to the 'storehouse' (*wdꜣ*). The presence of wood—a relatively high-value commodity in the Egyptian context—as part of the temple holdings is not surprising (cf. A18), given that most large temples maintained a fleet of ships for trade and grain transport.

3   Records of Work

A small but intriguing group of texts relate to keeping track of building work in the temple, presumably from the main building phase under Thutmose III, even if they are not dated (and admittedly many temples were probably, in practice, building sites to a greater or larger extent for much of their existence). One (A24) mentions work on the pylon (*bḫn*) of the temple, in a format well attested in contemporary work records: a dated list of men working in various locations in the temple, with an overview of the types of work done. Another fragmentary text seems to be of the same basic type (A25), while one last text (A26) lists two people who are off sick, followed by a date and a note about two men being brought from Deir el-Bahri (the latter shows that this was not simply a name-list recording absences). There are obvious parallels to such texts from the contemporary construction sites at Deir el-Bahri (Hayes 1942; 1960; Römer 2017a; 2017b; 2014), from the nearby Ramesseum (e.g. recording the delivery of stones, or the plastering of doorways: Kitchen 1991; for the decoration work see *KRI* II, 671–672), or from the temple of

Ramesses II at Abydos (Pouls Wegner 2009), but it is not a very common category of record and so provides welcome evidence of administrative practice surrounding the building of the large mortuary temples.

4   Name-Stones and Name Lists

Several of the ostraca classified as 'name-stones' or 'name-lists' are simple limestone flakes or pottery sherds containing one or more personal names, sometimes also with titles (A27–30, 32–42), where the original purpose is difficult to reconstruct; my use of the term 'name-stone' here does not imply that the objects are identical to the pieces described by the same term that come from tomb construction sites like those published by Hayes (1942: 45–51), or to the late Ramesside examples published by Burkard (2018). In the latter case they appear to have been deposited inside the pyramid superstructure of a tomb, perhaps as a way for workers on the project to be commemorated by having their names built into the structure, but there is nothing to suggest a votive interpretation for those from the temple—perhaps they represent markers or tokens of some sort related to administrative practices (compare e.g. Hayes 1942: 25, nos. 99–115, which occasionally have dates as well as one or two personal names). There are some fragmentary lists of *wꜥb*-priests, at least two (A31 and A43) which seem related to administration, but also one (A 45) which is on the back of a limestone stela, the original purpose of which could be either administrative or related to the dedication or production of the stela.

The most complete list of priests, A43, has them grouped according to phyle (parts of at least three phyles survive), and even if it is partly broken it seems to suggest that each phyle consisted of ca. 14 individuals (as recorded for the first phyle). Despite the uncertainty of some readings, this is not without historical interest in that it might give a rough estimate of the size of the priesthood associated with one royal mortuary temple during the 18th Dynasty. Naturally the precise numbers may have varied over time, and it is risky to generalise on the basis of a single institution—there is significant variation in the physical size of these Temple of Millions of Years, after all—but it may be worth comparing the number with other temples. At the mortuary temple of Senwosret II at Lahun, for example, there were, in addition to the permanent personnel like the 'governor and overseer of the temple', and 'the chief lector priest', also a monthly crew of one temple scribe, one 'chief of the phyle', one regular lector-priest, one embalmer, one *imy-st-ꜥ*-priest, three *ibḥ*-priests, and two *wꜥb*-priests of the king, in addition to eight lay members of staff like doorkeepers and porters (Borchardt 1903: 114). At that temple, the monthly phyles of ten priests are attested both in generalised distribution lists (that note the numbers of shares for each position) and in name-lists of priests actually on duty. Is a direct comparison with the temple of Thutmose III valid? Certainly the two temples are of a similar type, in that both are dedicated to the cult of a king, but the Lahun temple, although not much is preserved of it, seems to have been significantly smaller than that in Thebes. More speculatively Posener-Kriéger (1976: II, 573–574) calculated a total size of the priesthood of the mortuary temple of Neferirkare, at the time of the late Old Kingdom, that would correspond to about 22 men on monthly duty. Again the type of temple—dedicated to the royal cult—is comparable to that of Thutmose III, but it is much smaller. Sauneron (2000: 54) suggested, partly based on the same data but also evidence from later periods, that 'mid-size temples' had about 10–20 priests per phyle. A significantly higher number of priests were suggested by Haring (1997: 79–81) for the larger temple of Medinet Habu in the Ramesside Period. His two estimates, based on the number of shares seemingly underlying the calculations of the offering-lists on the walls of the temple, were of 150 and 166 individuals, but as he admits there are many unknown factors in his calculations, not least the issue of how the shares would have been divided. As he notes (1997: 80), the famous Lahun papyrus published by Borchardt (1903) shows a significant difference between the shares due to the chief administrator of the temple compared to that of a regular priest (a relationship of 5:1), and even the base-line number of shares (150 or 166) for the temple is not entirely certain. Added to this is the potential unreliability of monumental inscriptions as a source for economic data in view of their idealising nature (Haring 1997: 35), so firm conclusions are difficult to come by. The relatively modest number of priests listed as belonging to the first phyle on A43 is a sobering reminder of the speculative nature of attempts at calculating the resources of ancient Egyptian institutions, but if one were to extrapolate in this one case, and assume that each of the four phyles had a similar number of priests, the total number associated with the temple on an annual basis—excluding permanent members of the priestly staff like the ḥm-nṯr-priest(s)—would be in the region of just under 60 priests. This would not be all of the personnel of course, but it is not currently possible to estimate the number of support staff like bakers, potters, craftsmen, and so on, and in any case numbers are likely to have fluctuated over time.[1]

5   Letters and Messages

Some of the ostraca listed here are very fragmentary, or are very short, so that their classification is uncertain (A48, 49–50, 52), but among the certain examples are several that are noteworthy. A51 is interesting for its sense of urgency, but the message itself is obscure. A more revealing example is A53, a message from a certain scribe called Amenhotep, said to be of Deir el-Bahri, who writes to a 'stone mason' (ḥrtiw-nṯr) called Ahmose. This well-preserved message is asking for stone masons to be sent, presumably to assist in some building works of Thutmose III, and mentions an individual—of some authority, judging by the context—called Benermerut, who can possibly be identified with the famous Overseer of the House of Gold and the House of Silver, and Overseer of All Works of the King, under the same king. This high-ranking official is already known to have been involved in the construction works at Deir el-Bahri from the ostraca published by Hayes (1960: 46), and the message of A53 specifically outlines how groups of masons were recruited from several contemporary building sites elsewhere on the Theban West Bank. The locations include Deir el-Bahri and the mortuary temple of Thutmose III, which should provide respectively four and two masons, and the two remaining pairs where requested from two named masons, one called Userhat and the other being the Ahmose who is addressed in the opening line. The findspot of this message at the temple is thus explained by the fact that those working here were also asked to send two masons to the scribe Amenhotep, but the precise events that led to it being brought here are less clear: the message is not addressed to people at the temple directly—perhaps it was simply left here once whoever was rounding up the groups of masons had picked up the final two from the temple? In any case it elaborates on the way in which skilled workmen were circulating among work-sites in the area, as already hinted at by the contemporary Deir el-Bahri ostraca published by Hayes. One of the latter (O. Eg. Exp. 23001.108) has

---

[1]   For a discussion of the kind of personnel associated with Theban

mortuary temples, see Haring (1997: 5–7, 47–50). The size of the senior permanent priesthood of Henket-ankh is also difficult to establish. In the list of personnel of the temple of Thutmose III drawn up by Haring (1997: 431–435), the only titles attested are a 'first' (i.e. the high-priest) and a 'second' ḥm-nṯr-priest, but one unpublished papyrus fragment also mentions a 'third' and a 'fourth' ḥm-nṯr-priest in what seems to be a list of rights to shares of offerings. The date of this fragment is broadly 18th Dynasty, and could reflect a situation shortly after the founding of the temple: the lack of later corroborating sources from tombs or statues of temple staff might then suggest a gradual decline in temple offices as well as resources (this general process in relation to mortuary temples is clearly illustrated by the Wilbour papyrus).

an administrative note dated to year 49 of Thutmose III, where workers are listed according to the locations where they work ('in this place', 'outside on the columns', and 'on the roof outside'), and at the end of the list are three workers (Sen, Neby and Mersuamun) who are said to be 'in Henket-ankh', i.e. at the mortuary temple of Thutmose III (Hayes 1960: 47). Their titles and tasks are not recorded, but they are included in the total at the bottom of the column along with the other workers and so clearly belonged to a crew which was assigned to the temple construction at Deir el-Bahri.

Another well-preserved letter is A54, from a builder called Senna to his superior, Senenmut. The latter is likely to be the famous steward under Hatshepsut based on the mention of the erecting of pavilions for him and another high official, the (unnamed) Overseer of the South, at the end of the message. Why the ostracon was brought to the temple is not explained (perhaps Senenmut was present here in person, overseeing some of the work?), nor is there much context for the message itself. A final short message contains orders relating to offerings for the *wȝg*-festival (A55).

6   Varia

The texts grouped under this heading are often difficult to classify. The first (A56) contains three recipes for what appears to be mudbricks, listing ingredients like clay, soil, straw, and sand, followed by different fractions. The precise volume that these fractions refer to is not stated, but presumably they all relate to a single measure, whether that is a *hȝr* or something else. I assume the different recipes would result in a raw material with different material properties, perhaps reflecting the area of usage for the bricks manufactured based on the respective recipes. It is worth noting that Myriam Seco Álvarez and Agustín Campuzano in an article on the mudbricks used in the construction of the temple, published several years before this ostracon was known, drew attention to different mixtures being observable in the bricks: '... the same mud brick maker was supplied with at least two different sources of mixtures that are distinct in the composition of the mud as well as in the proportions of the straw' (Seco and Campuzano 2015: 66). The other ostraca in this section include one which may refer to some scribes (A57), one with something that might be an identity mark (A58), one with some measurements ('8 cubits, 5 palms, and 2 fingers', so c. 460 cm), and one with a line of text that seems to relate to baking, perhaps instructions or production notes (A60).

7   Literary Compositions

The literary canon of the New Kingdom is based primarily on Ramesside data from Deir el-Medina, but it is corroborated by the limited finds of literary ostraca and papyri from elsewhere in Egypt. Evidence from before this, from the 18th Dynasty, is statistically much rarer, but also seems to support the notion that there existed a group of texts that were considered part of the core scribal curriculum (Hagen 2019: 265–275; 2020). The literary graffiti from tomb N13.1 at Assiut confirm, broadly speaking, this picture of a set of core texts in the late Second Intermediate Period and early 18th Dynasty, whatever the precise social context of these dipinti may have been (e.g. Verhoeven 2013; 2015: 143–150). Despite the fragmentary nature of much of the material from the temple of Thutmose III, it is clear that many central works of this literary canon are represented among the ostraca, although unfortunately the poor state of preservation means that it is frequently difficult to assign individual objects to the 18th or 19th Dynasty. The specific compositions attested are very much in line with what one would expect based on the already known literary world of Thebes in the New Kingdom.

The Instruction of Amenemhat I is attested with no less than eleven copies (L01–10, and L20 which also has a few lines from *Khety*), most of which contain passages from the opening lines of the text. This matches the general pattern of transmission in literary ostraca where the first few stanzas of any given text are found more often than other parts. It is well established that this composition is the most frequently copied of this canonical group of texts (Hagen 2012: 84; Gasse 1992), and the ostraca from the temple of Thutmose III confirms this pattern.

The second most frequently copied text in the ostraca from the temple is *Kemit*, perhaps the literary text most strongly associated with scribal education in the New Kingdom (Kaper 2010), which is represented in six copies (T3.L11–16). Here the hands range from relatively practised (L15) to rather inexperienced (L11–13), and it includes an unusual limestone fragment (L13), perhaps originally from a stela or wall relief but now in a rectangular form, with a few words in columns along the sides of the rectangle. There has been some debate about the purpose of copying this text, as well as the precise phase of copying during training (Hagen 2012: 99). It has been considered something done by beginning students, but also as part of the curriculum only assigned to more advanced students: it is almost invariably written in an old-fashioned hieratic using lined columns, a format and script that in the New Kingdom would have been quite far removed from the writings produced during the every-day activities of

TABLE 1   A list of papyrus manuscripts with three core texts of the Ramesside literary canon: *The Instruction of Amenemhat*, *The Instruction of Khety*, and *The Hymn to the Nile*

Manuscript	Compositions	Approximate date
P. Sallier II	*Amenemhat—Khety—Hapy*	Ramesside
P. Anastasi VII	[lost] *—Khety—Hapy*	Ramesside
P. Chester Beatty V (? frags. only)	[lost]*—Khety* (?)*—Hapy*	Ramesside
Tablet Louvre E8 693	[none]*—Khety—Hapy*	Ramesside
O. DeM 1204	*Amenemhat—Khety—*[none]	Ramesside
P. Berlin 23.045	[lost] *—Khety—Hapy*	Saite?

a scribe. The many copies in inexperienced hands could then be simply be an indication of a lack of familiarity with this register of the script even among relatively advanced students, rather than signalling the work of a beginning student with little overall experience of (regular) hieratic. Presumably it was learning the script and format that was the most important motivation for its use in scribal training: although the full text of *Kemit* includes elaborate letter formulae, these are essentially outdated by this stage and never used by New Kingdom scribes. The second half of the composition contains a number of verse-lines that are thematically linked to both wisdom instructions and autobiographies, which may have made it suitable for copying by scribal students, but on balance it is probably the script that was the main learning outcome. Familiarity with it would have broadened a student's grasp of the registers and formats of Egyptian scribal culture, and in a temple context a scribe or priest would have been likely to come into contact with other texts sharing some of these visual characteristics, both in terms of narrowly religious papyri with Coffin Texts, Book of the Dead, and ritual papyri, but perhaps also literary classics like *The Instruction of Khety* or *The Instruction of Amenemhat I* written in a similar way.[2] It is no surprise then that students were copying *Kemit* at the temple as part of their training—if anything the skills

they acquired by doing this would be more relevant to life in the temple than in most other institutions.

The Instruction of Khety survives in five copies (L17–21) from the recent Spanish-Egyptian excavations directed by Myriam Álvarez-Seco, and these are complemented by O. Cairo CG 25217 which was found at the temple as early as 1889 (Daressy 1901: 47).[3] The latter is a relatively large fragment (c. 20 × 18 cm) with five lines of text on the outside (*Khety* § 13.1–6), and six lines of one or more unidentified compositions on the inside.[4] One fragment (L20) has a single line of *Khety* at the top, followed by the end of three lines of *Amenemhat*. The combination of these two compositions on a single manuscript is not uncommon, and they appear to have been closely linked in the literary tradition, both in terms of transmission on ostraca and on papyrus manuscripts. They are the most frequently attested literary texts among the ostraca from Deir el-Medina where, respectively, over 150 and 200 copies have been found (Hagen 2012: 84, fig. 1). In fact Quack (2003: 183–184) has argued that *The Instruction of Amenemhat I, The Instruction of Khety*, and *The Hymn to the Nile* may have been thought of as a tripartite group of texts in the Ramesside Period and beyond, and has pointed out that the number of manuscripts that may have had all three of them is probably greater than often assumed (Table 1).

This grouping of these three texts on a single manuscript, both on papyrus and ostraca, is not attested before the Ramesside Period, but the phenomenon is probably a

2   Admittedly the hieratic used for *Kemit*—a text widely copied outside temple contexts too—is not precisely the same script as the cursive or linear hieroglyphs used for many religious texts, but they are relatively close visually speaking, and both are written in columns: familiarity with one would no doubt facilitate working with the other (e.g. the movement of the hand writing vertically). There are several fragments in cursive hieroglyphs among the papyri from the temple of Thutmose III: a preliminary investigation suggests the presence of at least one roll with *The Daily Temple Ritual*, as well as several (as yet) unidentified religious texts, in this format. For wisdom instructions copied—unusually—in this script and format, see Hagen 2012: 99, pls. V–VI; 2019: 263–264, and for the possible link to temples, see Parkinson 2019: 119.

3   This would appear to be the only hieratic ostracon found during Grébaut's excavation in 1889 (Daressy 1926); at least the *Journal d'entrée* does not record any others (cf. *Archaeological context*, below).

4   The first line on the inside, in large uncial characters, mentions '[Amun]-Re king of the gods'. Below this is another illegible text of five lines, according to Daressy (1901: 47), who goes on to present a transcription of four lines of a literary text, with verse-points and a date ('Month 1 of Shomu, day 14+'). Several of these lines begin *in-iw*, 'Is it the case that …'; this side is inaccessible as currently displayed, and I have not seen it personally. The provenance listed by Jäger (2004: xlviii–lii; 'Deir el-Medina') is erroneous.

consequence of the centrality of these texts in the literary tradition, and in scribal training, even in earlier times like the 18th Dynasty.

The Instruction of a Man for his Son is attested by a single ostracon (L22) that has an extract from the beginning of that text (§Prolog-1.5). Its presence here is in line with its status as part of the literary canon of the period, as evidenced by the considerable number and diversity of manuscripts (papyrus, leather rolls, ostraca, writing boards), a status that appears to go back to at least the Second Intermediate Period (Hagen 2020: 27 n. 74). *The Hymn to the Nile*, another composition that is known to have been part of the literary canon, is also attested in one copy (L23).

Among the 'Various literary texts' there are several ostraca with the name of Thutmose III, sometimes along other royal or divine names (L25–29): these are only "literary" in a loose sense—perhaps practice pieces for scribal students?—but they do not fit into any administrative category and so are listed here. One fragment of a model letter on writing equipment being delivered to Karnak temple (L30), with verse-points in red, is interesting in that it is a parallel to Papyrus Chester Beatty V (= BM EA 10685), part of the library of the scribe Qenherkhepshef from Deir el-Medina (Hagen 2019: 277–281). This is the only known parallel to the model letter from the papyrus, and confirms its use in a didactic context: a message concerning the delivery of various inks and pens to a temple may have had obvious thematical relevance to those training others in scribal skills at Henket-ankh.

Ritual texts are generally not very common on ostraca, but there is one ostracon from the temple that seems to contain a passage from *The Opening of the Mouth Ritual* (L33). This is not identical to the sources published by Otto (1960), but Joachim Friedrich Quack, who first identified it as belonging to that text, informs me that there are other more similar sources in the material he is working on for the new synoptic edition. As one of the most central rituals of Egyptian religion it is hardly surprising that it was present in the temple, and in fact recently a papyrus fragment of an illustrated version of the ritual was excavated inside the temple—presumably a small remnant of the original temple library (to be published in Hagen, *Papyri from the Temple of Millions of Years of Thutmose III*). The ostracon itself might relate to the transmission of the text in a didactic context, but the hand is competent, so it could also be an *aide-memoire* for a ritual performance, although it would only have contained an extract of the ritual as a whole.

Three ostraca preserve the opening formula of wisdom instructions ('Beginning of the wisdom instruction ...');

these could represent the beginning of a more substantial copy of a composition from that genre, or perhaps a simple exercise in writing this common formula: there are similar examples from the Ramesseum (Spiegelberg 1898: pl. 1, nos. 3 and 4; Leblanc 2004: pl. 12A). There are several other literary ostraca which I have been unable to identify. Some may belong to religious texts (L40, 44, 47), others may perhaps be from wisdom texts (L41, L43), and one rather curious example (L42) has a regular date formula, 'Regnal year 34, Month of Akhet, day 7', followed simply by the line 'The land brightened, and the sun rose'. The classification of it as a literary text rests on this second line, which has a certain poetic ring to it, but it need not have belonged to a formal composition—perhaps it represents a spontaneous creation by a literate individual in the temple?

One item which is included here even if it is not technically literary—it may strictly speaking not be an 'ostracon' at all—is L45. This is probably a fragment from a canopic jar, mentioning one of the four sons of Horus, Qebehsenuef, written in hieroglyphs. Unusually it was first written in red ink, and then overwritten in black ink, which is a practice often associated scribal training, but either way it is clearly not literary in the restricted sense of *belles lettres*.

It is often posited that the large New Kingdom temples on the Theban West Bank had scribal schools attached to them (e.g. Leblanc 2004; Barbotin 2013). Explicit evidence for this is surprisingly evasive, however, and often scholars have simply inferred the function of an area as a school based on the presence of ostraca with literary texts (Hagen 2012: 78–79). Whatever one thinks of this model of scribal education, there can be no doubt that training in writing skills took place in and around temples, presumably organised by personnel associated with the institution, but the precise nature of this—in groups, or individually, formal or informal—is debated. The situation in temples of later periods of Egyptian history is somewhat clearer, at least in theory. *The Book of the Temple*, a manual for the organisation of the ideal temple surviving in at least 50 copies from the Roman Period (Quack 2005), includes a section on the training of priests where education is said to be the responsibility of an 'Overseer of teaching' (*ỉmy-r sbꜣ.w* or *ỉmy-r sbꜣ.yt*). According to this text, each of the four phyles of a temple should have one such teacher, and his duties included the teaching of reading, recitation/singing (presumably of hymns and ritual texts), general rules for behaviour in the temple (lit. 'standing and sitting', 'entering and exiting'), and for the daily ritual performances (Quack 2002: 161–164). This priestly education appears, at this point in Egyptian history, to be restricted to the children of *ḥm-nṯr* priests, of lector-priests (*ẖry-*

ḥb), and of 'high-ranking *wꜥb*-priests' (*wꜥb.w ꜥꜣ.w*). Beyond this basic education, in principle only the children of *ḥm-nṯr* priests could advance to four higher levels of training. The first level included learning to read divine writings (lit. 'god's words'), as well as knowing the customs and mythical importance of the various regions or nomes of Egypt, and how to conduct oneself at the royal palace. The second seems partly to refer to the transmission of rituals by respecting tradition, as well as the interpretation (*wḥꜥ*) of religious texts. The curriculum of the third level was focussed on medical literature, while the fourth dealt with divination in relation to eclipses, and the 'literature of the Embalming-house'. Despite the extraordinary importance of *The Book of the Temple*, and whatever its date of composition may be (all manuscripts are from the 1st and 2nd Century AD, but Quack 2016: 268 thinks parts of it 'goes back to an older archetype'), it might be unwise to project this degree of formalisation back into earlier periods of Egyptian history, and there are signs that the situation may have been quite different previously (see in general Brunner 1957: 17–27 for the New Kingdom). For example, the later examination procedures for trainee priests are not attested in earlier periods (Quack 2002: 162, with references and discussion of Brunner 1957: 22, 30), but perhaps more importantly, in those cases where it is possible to look at the textual transmission within a New Kingdom temple based on ostraca, as at the Ramesseum, the temple of Merenptah, or the temple of Thutmose III, it is clear that people who were engaged in practicing their writing skills—whatever the precise nature of the educational process—were copying classical literary works, of which a significant proportion was wisdom instructions. This is very different to the picture painted by *The Book of the Temple* (Quack 2002: 170–171), if the two can be compared: admittedly the later source may not be comprehensive in its coverage of the curriculum, and training in literacy in New Kingdom temples need not have been restricted to, or exclusively focused on, priestly education in a narrow sense.

Whatever the case may be, the literary material from the temple of Thutmose III shows clearly that some ostraca were copied by untrained hands, as in the case of some *Kemit* copies (L11–14), but there are also fragments with the same composition written in very well-trained hands (L15), either by advanced students or perhaps by teachers. Such a range of handwriting is also present in other corpora of ostraca from Theban temples, such as that of Merenptah, as noted by Müller (2014: 146; for a recent discussion of the issue see Jurjens 2020). A number of the literary ostraca also have dates, written in red ink, under the text itself (L03, L18, L42, L48, L53), a feature which some

have linked to scribal exercises (McDowell 1996; 2000), but here too the hands are competent, and such dates can also be related to copying outside a didactic context (Hagen 2012: 94).

The literary ostraca thus provide a welcome glimpse of the literary world of this temple, a glimpse which is particularly important because the publication of the associated papyrus fragments is unlikely to shed much light upon this aspect of temple life (perhaps some 95% of these fragments are administrative). It is not unusual to have a situation where only a vague outline of the literary texts available to the ancient scribes in any given location can be established. The poor odds of survival for papyrus generally, and especially in areas close to the cultivation where institutions are likely to be located, means that it is rare to be able to reconstruct the history of literary transmission on the basis of papyrus manuscripts alone. The nearby village of Deir el-Medina is a case in point: here, despite the exceptional discovery of a private library of papyrus rolls, there are numerous literary texts only attested in the village through small extracts on ostraca, with no surviving papyrus manuscripts of the same compositions (Hagen 2012: 93). Along the same lines, Jochem Kahl (1999: 291) once attempted a reconstruction of the texts available to scribes at Assiut based on the inscriptions in local tombs. The ostraca from the temple of Thutmose III in other words provide an idea of the kinds of literary texts that would have been available to local priests, presumably as part of the temple library as well as privately held copies of papyrus manuscripts,[5] and which were used in the training of temple scribes or priests.

8   Figured Ostraca

There are some figured ostraca in the material, but many of them are so fragmentary that it is often difficult to identify the motifs: some 21 are included here. The quality of the drawings, where it is possible to judge, does not approach that of the more accomplished material from other sites on the Theban West bank (cf. the material published by Vandier d'Abbadie 1936–1959, Gasse 1986, Peterson 1973, Brunner-Traut 1979 and more recently Dorn 2011: I, 77–129). The only ostracon from the temple of Thutmose III that might be a partial exception to this has a relatively good and detailed drawing of a pectoral in red and black

---

5   No substantial remains of a temple library of the New Kingdom has ever been found (for a discussion of the relevant evidence see Hagen 2019: 251–255), but the presence of classical literature in such contexts, in the form of wisdom instructions (*sbꜣyt*), is suggested by a Ramesside book-list published by Fischer-Elfert (2016).

ink (F01), but as with the textual material the evaluation of the quality of the figured ostraca is not straightforward because the comparative material may not be entirely representative. Published collections of figured ostraca are the result of selection processes (in acquisition practices and/or publication focus) that would doubtlessly have excluded the majority of the examples included here, so representativeness is a major issue when trying to contextualise such groups of fragmentary material: the evaluation of any category of material culture has to be carried out with a reference to all relevant objects, not simply those having been judged worthy of a private or museum collection.

In short, the figured ostraca contain several groups of motifs:

- Human figures: a male (royal?) head (F02), a standing man with a stick (F03), and a figure with a kilt (F07). Another ostracon has a royal (or divine?) figure with a feathered crown (preceded by a cobra figure, also with a crown: F15). The male (?) standing figure on F12 has what appears to be a fig leaf in front of his crotch, which suggests a rather late date (Coptic period?).
- Divine and mythological figures: a sphinx (F10), perhaps Anubis in the form of a reclining jackal (F14), the above-mentioned cobra (F15), an ureaus (on the back of a copy of *Kemit*; F21 = L15), some unidentified seated gods (or kings?) in a shrine (F16), and Sobek as a crowned crocodile (F17).
- Animal motifs: an ibis (incised in pottery after firing, so perhaps to be interpreted as a mark of ownership: F04), perhaps a cow (F11), and some stylised crocodiles (F17).

In addition to this there is a single example of a plant, showing a red branch with black leaves, which is accompanied by some stylised hieroglyphs (a *ḏd*-pillar and a *wȝs*-sceptre; F09); this is also one of the few figured ostraca with colour. Most of the remaining figured ostraca contain lines and geometric shapes and patterns that I have been unable to identify (F05–F08, F18–19).

9 Dockets and Other Objects

Not all the objects listed in this volume are ostraca in the traditional narrow sense. One such example is L45, which as noted above might be part of a canopic jar (its archaeological context was no different to the other ostraca, however: it was found in general debris outside the enclosure wall on the north-west side). Another example is inv. no. 7521 (see Table 4) which might be a corner fragment of a limestone writing board, or perhaps even a graffito from a wall block; the surface is smooth and polished, and

the edges worked into a regular shape. Similarly difficult in terms of classification is A45, which is a rather broad and heavy limestone fragment carrying several lines of hieratic in black ink (names of *wꜥb*-priests) on one side, but which has finely carved raised relief on the other, showing an offering scene. This object presumably once was part of a stela that stood in the temple, but when or why the hieratic was added is unknown; was it simply a local priest or scribe who picked up the fragment to jot down an administrative note—in which case it may well be classified as an ostracon of sorts—or were the names inscribed on the back while the stela was still standing, perhaps to commemorate some of the priests serving in the temple?

Another category of objects which does not correspond to ostraca in the traditional sense are the hieratic dockets from storage jars.[6] Where the contents can be established, most come from wine jars (D01–13), some are from jars that contained fowl (D14–17) or date-beer (*srm.t*; D18), and some are uncertain (D19–23), but their function is rather different from 'ostraca' and most catalogues of such material avoid using this term to describe them. The number of dockets (23 in total) seems remarkably low, given the size as well as the period of operation of the temple, and also the considerable consumption in the daily cult of commodities like wine, fowl and oil, to mention only those categories which appear frequently in corpora of dockets from other sites.[7]

At the roughly contemporary palace of Amenhotep III at Malqata, for example, some two kilometres south of the temple of Thutmose III, excavations in the early decades of the 20th Century yielded almost 1400 dockets (Hayes 1951: 36). This material, succinctly summarised by Hayes, still awaits a full publication, in part due to the tragic death of C.A. Keller, who had been working on it (McGovern 1997: 69), but recently Niv Allon of the Metropolitan Museum of Art has resurrected the project. The striking contrast in volume when compared to the temple of Thutmose III is perhaps in part illusory: the vast majority (84%) of dated dockets from Malqata relate to the celebrations of the three Sed-festivals of that king in years 30, 34 and 37, and not to the regular operations of the palace.[8]

---

6 A convenient overview of the main corpora of New Kingdom dockets can be found in Hayes (1951: 37–38); more recent literature has been incorporated in the text below.

7 It may be worth noting here that this is not based on an abstract estimate of what is assumed to have been offered. The absence of monumental offering calendars at the temple of Thutmose III, compared to the extensive versions preserved at the Ramesseum and Medinet Habu, is hardly surprising given the extremely fragmentary state of the architecture at the site, but the papyrus archive demonstrates a significant level of offering of such goods on a daily basis.

8 Perhaps the explicit marking on many of the Malqata jars of the con-

The use of dated dockets outside these exceptional festivities is in fact rather modest: some 134 examples distributed over thirty years of activity. Clearly not every docket ever present will have been found during the excavations,[9] but this still only equates to a handful of storage jars with dockets per year, for a palace-city which, at least during peak periods of activity, would have involved hundreds of inhabitants catering to the royal household. At the temple of Thutmose III, as at other sites, hieratic dockets on storage jars were probably the exception rather than the rule; perhaps only one or two in any given consignment would have been labelled this way.

Perhaps, as Hayes suggested (1951: 39, 83) in his analysis of the Malqata material, storage jars—at least those which had not been used for oil—may have been widely re-used and their original dockets erased over time. From Amarna there is at least one example of a wine jar re-labelled for the storage of meat (Petrie 1894: pl. xxiii, no. 43), and Leahy (1985: 65–66) argued that the 'striking' concentration of wine jar labels from the Workmen's Village at the same site was probably an indication of the re-use of wine jars, rather than an unusually high level of consumption of this relatively prestigious commodity. In support of this interpretation, he drew attention to Deir el-Medina, which seems comparable to the Amarna Workmen's Village in many respects, where Janssen (1975: 350–352) suggested that wine was only rarely consumed, based on his work on the extensive administrative papyri and ostraca from this site. The latter's comments, however, were made in the context of a study of prices, and although correct in terms of the material analysed by him, they do not take into account the 2000 hieratic dockets that had been found at Deir el-Medina. These were not widely known when Janssen wrote, and even today only some 500 have been published (Koenig 1979, 1980), but the important preliminary observations by Tallet (2003: 255–278) are worth bearing in mind: a full three quarters of these dockets concern wine, and he suggests the apparent discrepancy (i.e.

between the rare mentions of wine in the administrative ostraca and papyri and the number of wine jar dockets) is due to wine not being part of the regular rations but rather special deliveries in connection with festivals (2003: 268).

Bouvier's (1999–2002, 2003) work on the jar labels from the Ramesseum also provides an interesting if somewhat limited point of comparison for the dockets from the temple of Thutmose III. Of the c. 2700 jar labels listed by him, all but 21 relate to wine, while the others contained fat (ꜥḏ), oil (nḥḥ, mrḥt), honey (bit) and incense (snṯr). The sheer number of labels is noteworthy in itself, and perhaps speaks to the economic importance of that temple vis-à-vis that of Thutmose III, but despite the considerable number of labels they are in no way a representative sample of the jars stored in the temple. For one thing they all come from a set of magazines in the north-western corner which was evidently the wine store (Bouvier 2003: 31), and jars with other commodities were undoubtedly stored elsewhere; and for another the dates, where preserved, are not evenly distributed, with 96% of dated wine labels, for example, coming from years 1–10 (presumably of Ramesses II: Bouvier 2003: 182–183; Tallet 2003: 257). More jar labels, significantly including a higher proportion of ones mentioning fat, oils, incense and honey than in the already known corpus, have been found in their thousands during the last decades of excavation under the directorship of Christian Leblanc, but a full publication of this material is still in preparation (Bouvier 2003: 31–32, n. 247; cf. Koenig 1992, and El-Hegazi and Koenig 1993–1994 for preliminary reports). Once the material has been processed and analysed this is likely to provide the benchmark for further work on the production and storage of consumables administrated by New Kingdom temples: it looks unlikely that other temples will yield anything approaching comparable numbers.

The preliminary report on the ostraca and jar labels from the mortuary temple of Merenptah by Matthias Müller notes that the majority of the non-literary ostraca from that site are in fact jar labels (Müller 2014: 145),[10] and although it is not clear to me why the situation there would be so different from that at the temple of Thutmose III, there may also be some differences observable for other types of texts in these two groups of ostraca (cf. *Distribution of texts*, below).

In conclusion, the inclusion of any given object in this catalogue, then, has in practice more to do with materiality than function: all are texts or drawings in ink, of which

---

tents being 'for the *sed*-festival', produced by a variety of individuals at different locations throughout Egypt, indicates a system of obligation to provide consumables for these occasions. The accounting and control mechanisms for this system would then explain, to a large degree, the need for such marks in these rather unusual cases; regular deliveries for everyday consumption may not have necessitated the same level of detailed information on the individual jars.

9   As with the dockets of the Ramesseum (see below), the number and distribution of the different types of dockets may also reflect the uneven excavation record of the site. In addition to the wine jars from the palace area, there was a noteworthy concentration of dockets that mention meat, almost 300 in total, which were found in a corner of the courtyard of the nearby temple of Amun, built some hundred metres north of the palace (Hayes 1951: 36 n. 10, 83 n. 54).

---

10   I am grateful to Matthias Müller for sharing his forthcoming catalogue of the Merenptah ostraca and for discussing the material with me.

the vast majority—but certainly not all—correspond to what are normally termed 'ostraca' in Egyptological literature.

10 Distribution of Texts

In conclusion, the overall distribution of types of texts on the ostraca from the temple of Thutmose III can be compared to other similar groups of material. The ostraca, 207 in all (Table 2), from the temple of Merenptah, for example, were summarised as follow by Müller (2014: 145):

TABLE 2   A table showing the distribution of contents among the ostraca from the mortuary temple of Merenptah

Type	Number of ostraca
Literary texts	22
Letters (model and real)	3
Administrative texts	6
Jar labels	40
Names	6
Figurative ostraca	9
Unidentified	121

AFTER MÜLLER 2014: 145

If one divides the total number of Thutmose III ostraca, 273 in all, between the same categories, the numbers look as follows (Table 3):

TABLE 3   A table showing the distribution of contents among the ostraca from the mortuary temple of Thutmose III. The numbers include those without a separate catalogue entry (cf. Table 4)

Type	Number of ostraca
Literary texts	55
Letters (model and real)	9
Administrative texts	33
Jar labels	23
Names	21
Figurative ostraca	21
Unidentified	113

These numbers are necessarily approximate in that classification is partly subjective: the list of priests on A43 for example, is here classified as a list of names but it is clearly also related to administration. Similarly, I have listed ostraca with one or more royal or divine name(s) as 'literary', although such a broad definition may inflate the numbers for that category artificially, depending on one's criteria for categorisation. In addition to these issues of classification, several of the 'unidentified' ostraca in the table at the end of the book could in principle have been assigned to 'literary' or 'administrative' on the basis of script, which might further affect the statistics.

Nonetheless the numbers may allow for a cursory comparison between two relatively similar sites: both are royal mortuary temples, in close proximity, that were operating, in part, during the same period of time. The numbers show clearly that the distribution of text types in the surviving material from the temple of Thutmose is somewhat different to that from the temple of Merenptah. There appears to be proportionally more literary texts from the former (c. 20% against 10% from Merenptah), but this is no doubt affected by my classification of ostraca with an individual royal and or divine name as 'literary', and so should not be over-emphasised. More interestingly is that the temple of Thutmose III has a significantly higher number of administrative texts (12% against 3%), a difference which remains even if one includes name-lists (yielding a combined total of 20% against 6%). However, as with the literary ostraca, one should be careful not to attach too much importance to these numbers given the subjective nature of the classification according to genres. In any case, the extent to which this apparent difference in distribution reflects a difference in writing practice or simply an accident of preservation must remain an open question.

11 Archaeological Context

It is relatively rare to have a recorded archaeological context for hieratic ostraca, at least in a detailed sense, because most of the surviving ostraca in institutional collections were acquired on the antiquities marked. There are some exceptions, including the large collections at the Egyptian Museum and the IFAO in Cairo which stem, primarily, from the excavations at Deir el-Medina and associated sites like the Valley of the Kings and the Valley of the Queens, but their precise archaeological context is now mostly lost (Haring 2020: 97–102). The publication of several hundred ostraca from the recent Swiss excavations near the tomb of Ramesses X is a happy exception to this state of affairs: here the find-spots were recorded and could be analysed in detail (Dorn 2011: I, 33–73). There are other groups of New Kingdom ostraca with a recorded context in a broad sense—the 18th Dynasty ostraca from construction sites at Deir el-Bahri, for example, or the (still unpublished) ostraca from the work of Reisner at Deir el-Ballas—but their exact findspots can only rarely be reconstructed.[11] In terms of comparative material from Theban mortuary temples the most well-known group is undoubtedly that from the Ramesseum which was published by Spiegelberg over a hundred years ago (1898), a find that is complemented by hieratic ostraca being found by the ongoing French excavations there under the directorship of Christian Leblanc. A concentration of these ostraca, especially literary ones, in the south-west corner of the temple, has been thought to represent a school (Leblanc 2004; Barbotin 2013; but cf. Hagen 2012: 78–79). In addition to this there is a group of ostraca which were found by the German excavations at the mortuary temple of Merenptah in the early 1970s and 1990s which are being worked on by Matthis Müller (2014). At the time of writing neither the (new) Ramesseum ostraca nor the Merenptah ones have been fully published, but once they are accessible it may be possible to analyse the archaeology of ostraca production in temples in more detail, and in the case of the Ramesseum group the modern excavations may even enable a more detailed recontextualization of the older find published by Spiegelberg.

Having a recorded find-spot for the ostraca from the mortuary temple of Thutmose III is in other words rather unusual, but unfortunately the data are not very revealing. The maps in Figs. 2–5 are schematic representations of the distribution of the different categories of ostraca and dockets across the site. Each category of ostraca is provided with a separate map; literary texts in Fig. 2, administrative in Fig. 3, dockets in Fig. 4, and figured ostraca in Fig. 5. The size of the circles corresponds to the number of such ostraca found in that excavation square, and each contains the relevant sigla in black letters and numbers. Readers should be aware that the findspots are approximate, and that the placement of the circles do not indicate precisely where, within any particular excavation square, the ostraca were found—the maps are simply meant to provide a convenient overview of their distribution.[12] In a couple of cases two or more joining fragments were found in separate excavation grids, and the numbers are then noted on the map, in the respective findspots, with a letter suffix added to the siglum (e.g. L45 in Fig. 3, where 'L45a' was found in grid 1010/N4 and 'L45b' in grid 1020/N2).

Not surprisingly, the vast majority were found outside the enclosure wall: the area inside had been turned over repeatedly, including by the two large-scale excavations by Weigall (1906, 1908) and Ricke (1939) in, respectively, 1905 and 1934–1937, and indeed three of the ostraca published here were discovered (and stored in the on-site magazine) by Ricke (A39, A48, and L01). Ostracon Cairo 25217 (Daressy 1901: 47), which was found during Grébaut's excavations at the temple in 1889 (Daressy 1926: 14), shows that even earlier explorations had turned up some hieratic material, and in view of this archaeological activity it was only to be expected that new material would mainly come from areas left untouched by previous excavations; in practice this meant the areas outside the enclosure wall. Of these areas, the ancient rubbish dump immediately to the right of the northern side-entrance (the area corresponding to 910–950/N5–N8 on the maps), which had been excavated by neither Ricke nor Weigall, was particularly rich in ostraca, with a number of both literary and administrative texts (Figs. 2, 3).

The area to the left of the same side entrance, in particular towards the north-western corner of the enclosure wall (grids 960–1020/N4–N8), yielded a concentration of literary ostraca, although here too there were some administrative texts. At first sight this concentration of literary texts might seem noteworthy, but in fact this area contained spoil heaps from the previous excavations of the temple, meaning that the archaeological context is secondary (or even tertiary). It is in other words not possible to identify this area as a place of instruction or teaching. Although I remain somewhat sceptical of identifying any location as a "school" based simply on the presence of literary texts in the archaeological record (Hagen 2012: 85–86), it seems self-evident that scribal training took place in connection with the temple. The extent of this, much less

---

11   For the Deir el-Bahri ostraca, cf. the preliminary reports by Malte Römer (2017a, 2017b, 2014), who will publish the corpus in the near future. The material from Deir el-Ballas, some of which has previously been worked on by Stephen Quirke and which is currently being prepared for publication by Niv Allon, can partly be related to specific parts of the site (notably houses 'B' and 'C' near the north-western corner of the North Palace; Lacovara 1997: 10 n. 68, 15). However, these ostraca, which were recovered by the Hearst expedition and which are currently at the Museum of Fine Arts in Boston, is complemented by a group in Berlin and Strasbourg (Parkinson 2009: 174–175), and these cannot be linked to a secure archaeological context because they were bought on the Luxor antiquities market by Ludwig Borchardt (M. Müller, 'Ein Ostraka-Archiv aus Deir el-Ballas', paper presented at the Binsen-IV conference in Mainz, 9 December 2019).

12   A small number of ostraca are not shown in Figs. 2–5: these include those rediscovered in Ricke's on-site magazine (A39, A48, L01), one docket (D20) whose incomplete inventory number proved impossible to recover, one ostracon with an 'R'-number (L39) which was found outside the enclosure wall to the north, and A53 which was found outside the pylon (grid 840/S3), an area which for technical reasons could not be included on the map.

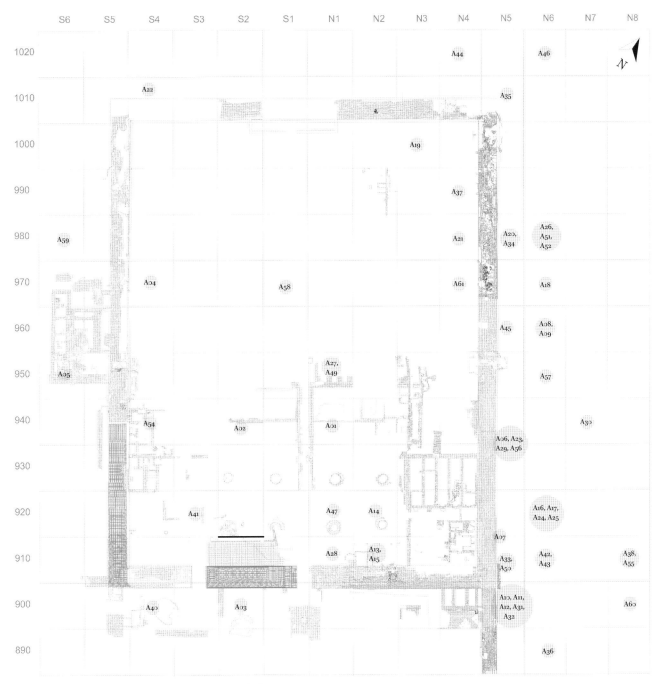

FIGURE 2   Map of the temple with the findspots of administrative ostraca

its organisation, remains unclear, but the literary ostraca certainly give an impression of the kinds of texts and genres that were accessible to those associated with the temple.

The dockets show the clearest distribution of all the categories (Fig. 4), where most sherds were found in the ancient rubbish dumps near the north-eastern corner of the temple, outside the enclosure wall. A couple of exceptions are D18 (the only one mentioning *srmt*, or date-beer) from outside the southern enclosure wall, near the corner (grid 1000/S6), and D19 (unknown commodity, but pos-

sible wine), from an area just inside the enclosure wall to the left of the main entrance (grid 910/S2). Finally, two wine jar dockets were found just to the left of the side entrance, whereas the rest were found to the right of this entrance. This pattern is not surprising given the nature of the deposit: presumably what we are seeing is simply workers throwing out empty or broken jars as part of the general debris.

The map of figured ostraca (Fig. 5) shows, like that of the literary and administrative material, that the majority were found outside the enclosure wall on the north side of

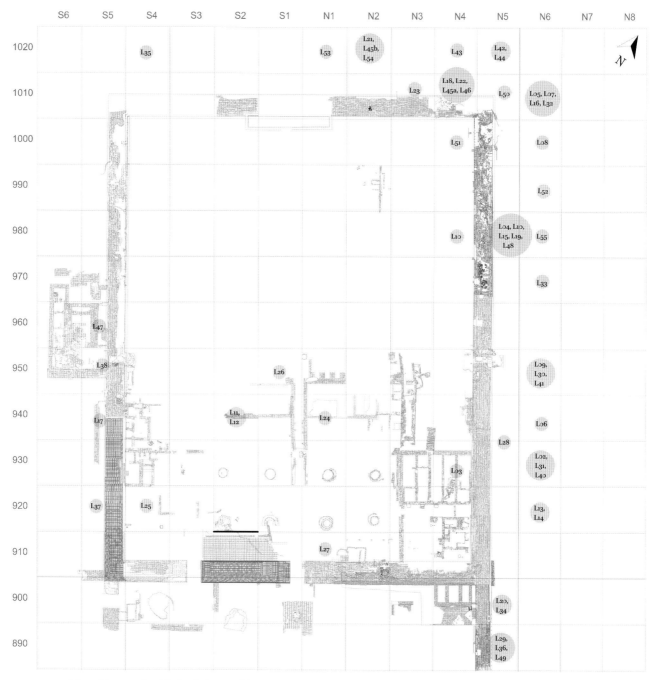

FIGURE 3   Map of the temple with the findspots of literary ostraca

the temple, but with a few also having been found on the south side, and even a handful inside the temple precinct.

As mentioned above the presence of a single hieratic ostracon from the temple in the *Catalogue général* of the Egyptian Museum in Cairo, published in 1901, shows that earlier excavations here also turned up hieratic material. CG 25217—which at the time of writing (October 2019) is on display at the Museum in the gallery dedicated to writing and literature—is the only published example, but it naturally raised the question of whether there might be more material at the museum of a similar nature. With the kind help of Marwa Abd Elrazek of the Registrar, Collection, Management, Documentation Department of the Egyptian Museum I was able in October 2019 to consult both their database and the old *Journal d'entrée* volumes of the relevant periods, and as far as I can see there are no more ostraca recorded as entering the Museum from this site. The entries immediately above CG 25217 (= JE 28871) relate to objects from Rizaqat, and the one below was bought on the market in Luxor (no dealer mentioned), and then follows a series of objects found at Medinet Habu.

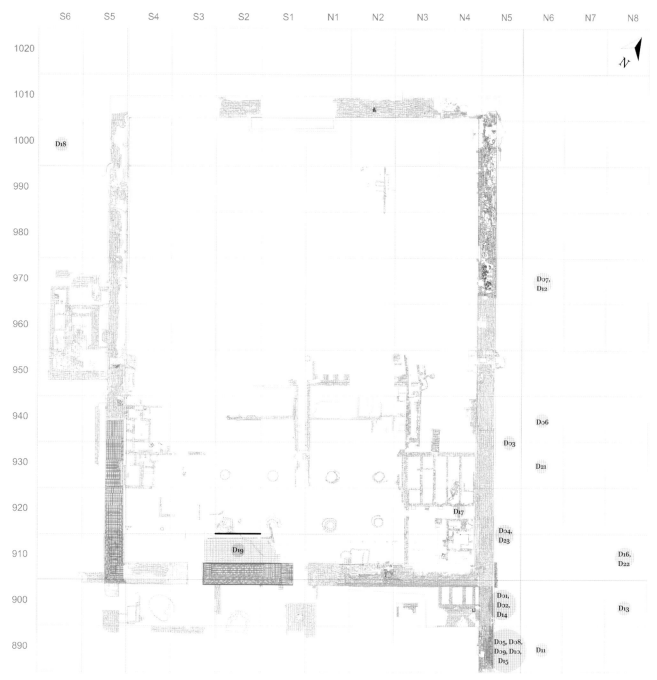

FIGURE 4   Map of the temple with the findspots of jar labels

The only other relevant entry is from 1938 when "a lot of ostraca" is recorded as having been provided by Ludwig Borchardt—presumably acting on behalf of Ricke—from excavations at the mortuary temple of Thutmose III (Temporary Register 14.6.38.1). This "lot" consisted of 20 pieces of pottery, 19 of which have traces of ink and were retained by the museum, but inspection of the photograph of this group in the database showed that the ink is largely disjointed lines on various sherds, presumably either abstract shapes or an unidentifiable motif, and their fragmentary state means that I have excluded them from this cata-

logue.[13] These ostraca do not seem to have much scientific value, but their presence at the museum is interesting

13   There is also a group of largely unpublished 18th Dynasty administrative papyri at the museum, most of which seem to be catalogued under JE 21367, and which may be relevant to the hieratic documentation from the temple of Thutmose III, if only for comparative purposes. Some were scheduled to be included in Golénischéff's projected second volume of the *Papyrus hiératiques* in the *Catalogue Générale*, and can be found on plates 50 (CG 58048–9), 51 (CG 58050–1), 69 (CG 58074; cf. Ali 2000), 70 (CG 58076–7), 71 (CG 58078; cf. Ali 1997), 72 (58079–81), 73 (58082–3), and 74–75 (CG 58088) of the loose sheets that were

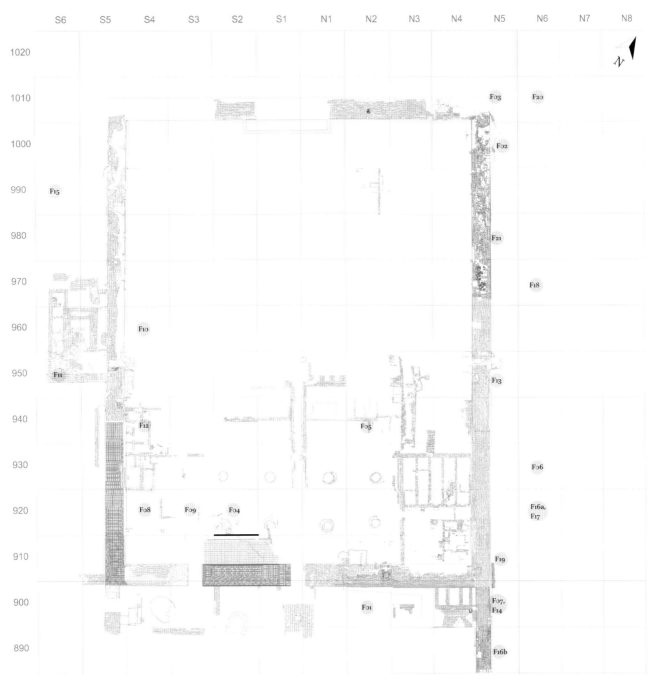

FIGURE 5   Map of the temple with the findspots of figured ostraca

from the perspective of prioritisation of finds—perhaps one would be justified in assuming that if a number of well-preserved and informative ostraca had been found by Ricke, then they would also have been sent to Cairo, or stored in the on-site magazine.

shipped along with the first volume. Their contents make it probable that they belong to a temple archive: one heading from year 1 of an unnamed king reads 'His majesty, l.p.h., commanded that offerings be established for his father Amun-Re, ⟨Lord⟩ of the Thrones of the Two Lands, in his festival of the valley', followed by a list of offerings (CG 58088).

A final word of warning may be in order. Readers will see a frustrating number of question marks in both transcriptions and translations, for which I apologise—despite my best efforts (as well as the kind assistance of colleagues), the material has defeated attempts at decipherment in several cases. No doubt some of these could eventually have been solved, given enough time and attention, but I have decided to prioritise a reasonably quick publication. Whether this volume strikes the right balance between speed and accuracy will be for others to judge, but that it represents a compromise will be obvious to all.

Catalogue

1   Administrative Texts

1.1   *Accounts*

T3.A01 (pl. 1)

Excavation number: 9096/940N1L109

Description: A pottery sherd with four fragmentary lines of hieratic in black ink, and numbers in red.

Contents: A list of different amounts of various types of bread.

Translation:

(x+1)   [...]

(x+2)   *psn*-bread: 30

(x+3)   *šꜥy.t*-cakes: 30

(x+4)   [...]-bread: 40

(x+5)   [...]

Notes:

(x+2) *psn*-bread, not infrequently written without the *n* as here, is one of the most well-attested types of bread both in offering lists and other contexts; it was a round and relatively flat bread, and is often listed alongside *bit*-bread and *šꜥy.t*-cakes (Schwechler 2020: 45–63, no. 12; *Wb.* 1, 549.18–21; Grandet 1994: II, 93 n. 339).

(x+3) For this type of cake, which is one of the most common in offerings lists, see Schwechler (2020: 104–117, no. 22; cf. Grandet 1994: II, 91 n. 332). It seems to have been made from flour and ground earth almonds, sometimes flavoured with honey, and then fried in fat in a shallow pan (Davies 1943: II, pl. 49); it was produced in a wide variety of physical shapes (Schwechler 2020: 114–117). There is a title 'šꜥy.t-baker' as well as 'chief šꜥy.t-baker', which Verhoeven (1984: 123, 157) has suggested might imply a more complicated production method than regular bread. In any case it appears to have been associated with feasts and special occasions, rather than everyday life.

T3.A02 (pl. 1)

Excavation number: 9164/940S2L910

Description: A body sherd of medium Nile clay, from a New Kingdom jar, with the beginning of seven lines of hieratic.

Contents: A list of different types of bread.

Translation:

(x+1)   [...]

(x+2)   *psn*-bread [...]

(x+3)   *šꜥy.t*-cakes [...]

(x+4)   *psn*-bread [...]

(x+5)   *š.t*-bread (?) [...]

(x+6)   *bit*-bread [...]

(x+7)   [...]

Notes:

(x+5) The word is clearly written differently from *šꜥy.t* (cf. line x+3 above), and presumably relates to another type of baked goods. There is a rare type of bread called *šꜣt.t*, mainly attested in the Old Kingdom, but this is normally written 𓏞𓊃 (Schwechler 2020: 103–104; *Wb.* 4, 414.9). Malte Römer (pers. comm) suggests that it might also be a continuation from the previous line of something like [*ps*]*š.t*, 'division'.

(x+6) The *bit*-bread was a staple of institutional bread production, and figures prominently in offerings lists, where it is often the first type of bread listed (Schwechler 2020: 15–24; Grandet 1994: II, 93 n. 338). Its precise form is unknown, but an oval or conical shape is implied by the most common determinatives, and it could be made from both emmer wheat (*bd.t*) and barley (*it*). In terms of use in temples it was presented to the divine images both during the daily tempel ritual and during festivals.

T3.A03 (pl. 1)

Excavation number: 9245/900S2L810

Description: A body sherd of a large New Kingdom storage jar, with the end of two lines of hieratic.

Contents: Numbers only.

Translation:

(x+1)   [...] 100[+] 85

(x+2)   [...] 60 (?) [...] Remainder (?): 8

Notes:

(x+2) At the beginning of the line there is a group that looks like 80, but with an additional vertical stroke that clearly does not correspond to a number—could 90 be meant?

T3.A04 (pl. 2)

Excavation number: 9369/TVIICL111 (found in grid 970/S4)

Description: A limestone ostracon with three lines of hieratic in a classic 18th Dynasty hand; complete on all sides. It was found in the disturbed top layer of Middle Kingdom tomb no. VII, in the southern area of the temple area.

Contents: An account of wood.

Translation:

(1)   Wood, 2 pieces of 12 cubits.

(2)   It is the property of the *imy-*

(3)   *st-ꜥ* priest of the fourth phyle.

Notes:

(2) The reading of *imy* is certain based on the traces. The presence of an *imy-st-ꜥ* priest in a royal mortuary temple is no great surprise because they belong to the monthly rota of *phyles* (Kees 1958: 50, s.v. 'Assistent'). They are attested from the Old Kingdom (Pantalacci and Lesur 2012: 315 n. c), throughout the New Kingdom (Helck 1960–1970: I, 51; *KRI* VI, 447.4), and well into the Roman period (Quagebeur 1971: 269–270; Vittmann 1983: 238), but their precise function is not entirely clear, even if they are sometimes explicitly linked to the presentation of offerings. The literal meaning ('he who is in the position of the arm'?) is not very revealing, but perhaps 'ritual assistant' or similar might capture the meaning (Shalaby 2012: 375). The 18th Dynasty evidence was collected and discussed by Thomson (1998: 217–220), and the information presented there may imply that each phyle had only one such priest, as seems also to have been the case in the Middle Kingdom (e.g. Borchardt 1903; cf. Kees 1953: 50). I read the expression as a whole as *ꜥḥꜥ pw n pꜣ imy-st-ꜥ*, which would be a rather unusual formulation for an account, but I can see no other plausible interpretation.

(3) Certain ordinal numbers could, at least from the 12th Dynasty to the late New Kingdom, be written with horizontal strokes, in the same manner as dates (Möller 1927: I, 63 n. 3; II, 60 n. 2; cf. Wreszinski 1908 for a late example), and so the number is here read '4' rather than '5'. This is also more plausible from a historical perspective as there were four and not five phyles at this point, although admittedly the phyle system in New Kingdom temples is not well attested by documents of practice (most examples come from monumental inscriptions), and the literature is limited (e.g. Helck 1982: 1044; Spencer 2010: 259–260). A04 is one of relatively few mentions of the phyle system in the ostraca from the temple (see also nos. A11, A12 and A43). The writing of the *-nw* ending with plural strokes (📷) seems slightly unusual, but cf. the Middle Kingdom P. UC 32191—a festival list from the mortuary temple of Senwosret II—for another example (Collier and Quirke 2006: 92–95, fold-out transcription line 2; I am grateful to a reviewer for this reference).

T3.A05 (pl. 3)

Excavation number: 15012/950S6L112

Description: An indeterminate pottery sherd with traces of four lines of hieratic in an administrative hand. Complete except for the bottom part (= day 18).

Contents: A weekly account of various commodities (per-

haps *isrw*, 'rushes' or 'reeds', and *r*, 'geese'?), with dates and numbers. Deliveries are both above (day 11) and below (day 12) the expected quota, but with some days entirely missing.

Translation:

(1)   Day 10. Day 11: 40. Delivered: 68.

(2)   Day 12: Reeds (?), 80. Delivered: 68.

(3)   Day 14: Ditto, 80. Delivered: 80.

(4)   Day 17 (?): *r*-geese (?) [...] 40. Deliv[ered ...]

Notes:

(1) The area in the upper right hand corner is a little smudged, but the scribe appears to have added the day sign (⊙) above the number 11. Naturally there were no deliveries on day 10 which was the weekend. I do not know what the sign in upper left-hand corner represents.

(2) The reading of the commodity is not clear: could 📷 be 'reeds' or 'rushes' (*Wb.* 1, 32.5–8)?

(4) The delivery may relate to geese; I read 📷, but with no great confidence. The following group is likewise obscure. If the reading is correct, this is a type of goose often cited in connection with temples and offerings (*Wb.* 2, 393.1–6; cf. Grandet 1994: II, 19 n. 82, with references; Bailleul-Lesuer 2016: 43–45, 52 table 1; 316–317, 543 table 25). An anonymous referee suggested reading this as a *ḥri*-bird (*Wb.* 3, 146.14), which might also be possible—another potential occurrence of this word is in in T3.A12, line 4 (below), but this too is quite tentative, and the writing is notably different in the two cases.

T3.A06 (pl. 4)

Excavation number: 15090/930–940N5L113

Description: A rim sherd of a restricted bowl of medium Nile clay, probably of the New Kingdom, with traces of three lines of hieratic in an administrative hand.

Contents: An account of deliveries (?) per week.

Translation:

(x+1)   (Day?) 1. [...]

(x+2)   (Day?) 10. 1785. 2000+ [...]

(x+3)   3rd month.   (Day?) 20. 3400. 160. 5. 5. 2000+[...]

Notes:

(1) The mark in the "margin" to the right of the first line is curious—could it be a very abbreviated ⌃, 'delivered'?

T3.A07 (pl. 4)

Excavation number: 15452/910–920N5L413

Description: A hard rock (not limestone) with two lines of hieratic; perhaps complete. The width and weight of this is unusual compared to limestone ostraca, making it slightly unwieldy.

Contents: A baking account (or order?).

Translation:

(1) Large *bit*-loaves, at baking value 30:

(2) 45 baked (loaves)

Notes:

(1) The definition of a baking (or brewing) value in connection with baking and brewing is well attested for both bread and beer (e.g. Verhoeven 1984: 99–100; Pommerening 2005: 174–194), and the calculation of production based on this *ps.w*-value was a central part of the accounting arithmetic of the Egyptian scribe: it normally refers to the amount of loaves expected from one *ḥḳꜣ.t* (c. 4.8 litres) of grain. A depiction of a procession of offering-bearers from the temple of Ramesses II at Abydos shows men carrying four trays of *bit*-loaves, and here the headings mention four different sizes of loaves, with baking values of 5, 10, and 20 (Scwechler 2020: 21). The final number is lost but may well have been 30, as in this ostracon, if the relative sizes of the loaves depicted are to be trusted (obviously the larger the baking value the smaller the loaf). I assume the scribe separated the number '40' at the end of line 1 from '5' in line 2 because of the uneven surface, and that they should be read as a single number.

T3.A08 (pl. 5)

Excavation number: 15462/960N6L113

Description: A body sherd of a marl clay jar, with the end of four lines; the writing looks more like charcoal scratches than ink.

Contents: An account, but only numbers are preserved.

Translation:

(x+1) [...]

(x+2) [...] 10 [...]

(x+3) [...] 12, 11+ [...]

(x+4) [...] 5 1+[...]

(x+5) [...] 2 2

Notes:

(x+4) The number is written as five strokes, instead of the usual hieratic sign for '5'.

(x+5) The four strokes here are grouped together in pairs and could perhaps be read as both '2, 2' and '4'.

T3.A09 (pl. 5)

Excavation number: 15466/960N6L113

Description: A pottery sherd from a flat-based dish, made from medium Nile clay (NB2), with a range of jottings.

Contents: Difficult to say—some of the individual signs appear to be numbers ('300' appears twice), but their distribution, and the considerable number of other signs that I cannot decipher, hinders interpretation. Perhaps it is simply a notepad with more or less arbitrary scribbles. It is similar to the much smaller fragment 15431 (listed in the table at the back of the book).

T3.A10 (pl. 6)

Excavation number: 15503/900N5L114

Description: A limestone ostracon with two lines of hieratic. The ostracon is unusually wide and heavy.

Contents: A text dealing with bread loaves.

Translation:

(1) [...]

(2) [...] *bit*-loaves: 25.

T3.A11 (pl. 6)

Excavation number: 15510/900N5L214

Description: A limestone flake with four lines of hieratic in a rather cursive hand; complete at the top and right-hand edge.

Contents: A list of offerings in connection with one or more festivals.

Translation:

(1) [...] of the fourth (?) phyle for the [...]

(2) 10 birds. Peres (?): 5 *r*-geese.

(3) 10 *r* (?)-geese. The *wꜥb*-priests at the first festival [...]

(4) [...] Nebnakht (?): 2 *r*-geese.

Notes:

(1) The top of the number is faint, leaving a simple vertical stroke. This can hardly be '1' (which is written *tpy*, cf. A12 below), so is probably another example of '4' with the horizontal writing of an ordinal number (cf. A04).

(2) The illegible word in the middle can either be a personal name (on the model of line 4), as I have favoured in the transcription, or another commodity. The *r*-geese are well attested as being part of the temple economy, and Thutmose III states in his *Annals* that he 'created for him (i.e. Amun) flocks of *r*-geese in order to fill the *hrmw*-enclosure, as daily offerings' (*Urk.* IV, 745:2–3; cf. Bailleul-Lesuer 2016: 276–282).

(3) The word for 'geese' at the beginning of the line is written slightly differently to the examples above, but I cannot think what else it might be. Orthographically the determinative of *ḥb* should be ⟳, although palaeographically it looks more like ⊙.

(4) The name seems relatively clear but is lacking a determinative, although admittedly this could be missing in the break.

T3.A12 (pl. 7)

Excavation number: 15546/900N5L214

Description: A limestone flake with four lines of hieratic in a typical 18th Dynasty administrative hand on the front; the back is empty. The ostracon is complete on all sides.

Contents: A list of offerings given to the first phyle.

Translation:

(1) The first phyle. Given to Pahemu:

(2)   2 ḥtꜣ-bird, 1 sr-goose, 80 ꜥšꜣ-birds. Exchanged:

(3)   Inpu: 10 ꜥšꜣ-birds. Wab: 10 ꜥšꜣ-birds.

(4)   That which is with Mahu: 7 ḥrt-birds (?).

Notes:

(2) For the ḥtꜣ-bird, a species not precisely identified, see Bailleul-Lesuer (2016: 318–319) and Grandet (1994: II, 97 n. 386; 'espèce indéterminée'; *Wb.* 3, 342.1), and for the sr-goose, see Bailleul-Lesuer (2016: 316–317; cf. *Wb.* 4, 191.16), who identifies it as the greylag goose (*Anser anser*). The ꜥšꜣ-bird is also an unidentified species of bird, perhaps a duck or dove (Bailleul-Lesuer 2016: 347–348; *Wb.* 1, 229.11). The meaning of 'exchanged' here is elusive to me: are Inpu and Wab getting these birds instead of what they should have gotten? Or is it related to some informal arrangement (e.g. repayment of debt) between Pahem and his colleagues? In any case I take *Wꜥb* to be a personal name, rather than the title.

(4) The reading of the final type of fowl is not certain, perhaps ḥr(.t)? A ḥr.t-bird is attested in the Ramesseum onomasticon (just before kk, 'hoopoe'; Gardiner 1947: I, 9), and the *Wb.* also cites a single example of another unidentified bird mentioned in a Ramesside model letter called ḥrỉw (*Wb.* 3, 146.14; Caminos 1954: 349), and finally there is a type of duck (?) attested in the Old Kingdom written ḥrṯ (Hannig 2003: 879).

T3.A13 (pl. 8)

Excavation number: 15602/910N2L1014

Description: A limestone ostracon with nine lines of hieratic in an 18th Dynasty administrative hand; complete on all sides.

Contents: An account of offerings in connection with the celebration of a wꜣg-festival.

Translation:

(1)   The wꜣg-festival:

(2)   Large šꜥy.t-bỉt-cakes: 2. Small ones: [6?]

(3)   Dates, bowls (?): 22

(4)   Various bread of the divine offerings: 70, total: 100.

(5)   Beer, ds-jars: 13, total 15 [...]

(6)   'Flour-cakes' in white-bread shape: 8, total 10.

(7)   White-bread of the offerings: 8, total 10.

(8)   Vegetables, bundles: 5

(9)   Ditto, bunches: 5 (?)

Notes:

(2) For the specific variety of šꜥy.t-cakes mentioned here, see Schwechler (2020: 115). As the edge has broken away there is a missing numeral here: if the total of 100 two lines below are summarising lines 2–4 then it should be 6. The traces are incompatible with this, and are perhaps rather to be interpreted as a reed-leaf in šrỉ, 'small loaves'.

(3) I do not know what the word after bnr, 'dates', might be, and its transcription is doubtful: šꜣwꜣ seems unattested, but there is a later word for some kind of bowl written ○▭ (*Wb.* 4, 401.2–3). Dates are often measured in mḏꜣ ([hieroglyphs]), which might be a type of container specifically used for pressed dates (Grandet 1994: II, 100 n. 405; cf. Janssen 1975: 474), or alternatively in ẖr, 'sacks' (Grandet 2010: 55, no. 10168; 2017: 101, no. 10357), ds-jars ([hieroglyphs] ; Janssen 1975: 474; Grandet 2006: 27, no. 10019), or mḥ.t-plates ([hieroglyphs] ; Grandet 2010: 48, no. 10162; 2017: 35, no. 10303). Dates can further appear as both 'fresh' (wꜣḏ) and 'dried' (šw), and can be distributed in unspecified 'large' or 'small' portions (Grandet 2010: 57, no. 10171), as well as in 'cut bunches' (? ḥnk; Grandet 1994: II, 100 n. 406; cf. Gardiner 1941: 158 n. 1), and dried ones are normally measured in ꜥ-bowls ([hieroglyphs] ; Grandet 1994: 275, 297). However, none of these words seem to match the hieratic here.

(5) The final number here and in the two lines below are clearly arrived at by adding two in each case; why this calculation was made I do not know.

(6) The word (d)kꜣ.w literally means 'flour', but is also attested in the New Kingdom as a type of cake, sometimes made with honey (KRI V, 129.16), and often listed next to various other cakes and bread loaves (*Wb.* 5, 8.3–5, cf. 5, 494.15–495.5; Helck 1960–1970: 840). It can apparently be made in different shapes, including [hieroglyphs], 'bnbn-shape', [hieroglyphs], 'ḥnw-shape', and [hieroglyphs], 'sḥn-shape', as well as 'in white-bread shape', as in this case. The latter shape is also found in lists of goods both on papyrus (P. Boulaq 11, col. 2, line 14; Peet 1935–1938: 190; cf. P. Cairo JE 21367; unpublished but cf. TLA documents DZA 30.309.100; 30.308.850), and in monumental form (Medinet Habu; KRI V, 120.5–8): the latter significantly includes a visual unit marker that is used to represent a category of 'cake' (as opposed to bỉt-loaves and other types of bread; cf. e.g. Nelson 1934: pl. 139). The Medinet Habu offering calendar further shows that there where different sizes based on 'baking-values' (ps) of 4, 8 and 10. As Ben Haring has pointed out (1997: 60, cf. 110), there is a shift in the monumental orthography of this word, from dkw to k(ꜣ)w, between the reigns of Ramesses II and III, at least in the inscriptions from their mortuary temples at Thebes. The title 'kꜣw-baker' appears repeatedly in the 18th Dynasty administrative accounts on the back of P. St. Petersburg 1116A (vso. 45, 110, 121, 194; Golenischeff 1913; cf. *Wb.* 5, 8.4). The term is not listed as a separate type of cake or bread in Schwechler's book on bread terminology, but is mentioned briefly under 'white-bread' (t-ḥḏ; Schwechler 2020: 190–191).

(7) The common 'white-bread' is ubiquitous in New Kingdom offerings lists—see Schwechler (2020: 183–200, no. 41).

(9) The determinative of *ḥrš*, 'bunch' is incompatible with the expected ⌘, but there are examples with the coiled rope (⌘) which is perhaps just possible palaeographically (unlike ⌘ which can also be used: Grandet 2010: 94, no. 10209).

T3.A14 (pl. 9)

Excavation number: 15627/920N2L314

Description: A limestone sherd with nine lines of hieratic in an administrative hand of the 18th Dynasty, written in red ink; largely complete except for a small piece that is missing from the lower right.

Contents: An account of offerings given by or to various priests? Several key words I cannot identity, so the interpretation of this text is unclear.

Translation:

(1) **List of *rr* (?)**
(2) **and *r*-geese from the offering table.**
(3) **The *wꜥb*-priest Mer[mer?]: 1. Wine, *mn*-jars: 1. Vegetables (?): 1**
(4) **The *imy-st-ꜥ* priest Amenhotep: *rr* (?) and goose (?): 1.**
(5) *ḥtꜣ*-duck: 1. *rr* (?) [...] 1 *dbn* (?).
(6) **The *wꜥb*-priest Tjenen (?): *rr* (?), 1 *ḏꜣḏꜣ*-vessel (?), heaped: 1**
(7) *rr* (?), *nmst*-jug: 1
(8) **Ditto (i.e. *wꜥb*-priest) Mery: [?], 1. *šꜥy.t*-cake**
(9) **of white-bread shape: 1**

Notes:

(1) The opening lines poses a problem: one expects a word for 'list' or similar, but I do not have great faith in my transcription. The commodity (?) seemingly written ⌘ is equally problematic: it appears also in lines 4–7 below, and seems to be measured in both a *ḏꜣḏꜣ*-vessel (l. 6) and in a *nms*-vessel (l. 7). If it can indeed be 'heaped' (cf. l. 6) then it might be a dry and/ or grainy substance.

(2) The preposition is clearly *ḥr* (*wdḥw*), which I translate as 'from (the offering table)', presumably as a reference to offerings given to the individuals named below.

(3) I take ⌘ to be part of the personal name after the title '*wꜥb*-priest', rather than a second title. There are only three personal names beginning with *imy-r* in Ranke (1935: 25.18–20), none of which match the traces.

(4) For the priestly title, see A04 above; I cannot make sense of the final stroke of this line.

(6) The personal name is partly erased: traces would suit ⌘, perhaps the common name *tnn* (Ranker 1935: 391–392); Römer (pers. comm.) notes that there is a stone mason with this name who is mentioned on O. Eg. Exp.27056, l. 14 (unpublished), and who was active under Thutmose III (year 40+). The final circular sign I interpret,

following a suggestion by Malte Römer, as the sign often employed to mean 'heaped' in descriptions of volume of dried goods (as opposed to ⌘, meaning 'level'; Spalinger 1987: 309–310). The determinative of *ḏꜣḏꜣ*, 'jar' I suppose is a mistake made by association with the common word *ḏꜣḏꜣ*, 'head', otherwise that word has no determinative.

(8) I take the traces at the beginning of the line, where a small piece has broken off in antiquity, to be the 'ditto' sign (⌘), but it could also be the remains of the three strokes of the water sign of the full title. I have not been able to identify the commodity following the name; the first sign looks vaguely like ⌘.

T3.A15 (pl. 7)

Excavation number: 15639/910N2L1114

Description: A body sherd of a jar of Nile clay, probably of the New Kingdom ('or Late Period'), with four lines of hieratic on the outside; complete apart from the top, but perhaps no more than two lines missing. In view of the hieratic the earlier of the two dates suggested by the ceramicist is presumably the correct one.

Contents: An account listing just over a week's worth of deliveries of fowl.

Translation:

(x+1) [...] Day [...]
(x+2) Day 5 or Day 6: 2 birds.
(x+3) Day 7: 1 bird. Day 8: 2 birds.
(x+4) Day 9 or Day 10 or Day 11
       Delivered   Delivered

Notes:

(x+2) The word *nfr*, is here, and in line 4, interpreted as 'or' (*Wb*. 2.257), on the suggestion of Römer, rather than the more common 'good' (the latter is well attested in calendars of 'good' and 'bad' days, but this makes little sense in the context of an administrative document dealing with the prosaic topic of deliveries of fowl).

(x+3) The writing of the number '8' with the standing strokes (as opposed to the horizontal ones normally used for dates) seems somewhat unusual.

(x+4) The sign ⌃, which has been added below the line under 'day 9' and 'day 10', normally designates deliveries in administrative documents (Helck 1974: 61). This suggests that the document deals, at least in part, with actual deliveries and not simply expected quotas.

T3.A16 (pl. 10)

Excavation number: 15654/920N6L414

Description: A body sherd of a jar of medium Nile clay, with several lines of hieratic (in at least two columns) on the outside, as well as the ends of two lines on the inside.

Contents: An account.
Translation:

	(Outside col. I)	(Outside col. II)
(x+1)	[...]	That which is under the authority of
(x+2)	[...] 1	Nebamun: 4.
(x+3)	[...] 1	
(x+4)	[...] 1	
(x+5)	[...] 1	Kheryheb (?): 1

	(Inside)	
(x+1)	[...] 3 cubits.	
(x+2)	[...] the writings (?)	

Notes:

(1, x+4) The name Kheryheb ('Lector priest'?), if this really is the correct reading, is unattested, but there are parallels for names based on titles, e.g. Pahemnetjer ('The ḥm-nṯr priest'; Ranke 1935: 115.16). The first group seems plausible, but admittedly the reading assumes—based on the relatively clear determinative ⌐ before the seated man—that there is an orthographic mistake in the writing of ḫb without a ḥ.

T3.A17 (pls. 11–12)
Excavation number: 15661/920N6L414
Description: A limestone flake with five lines of hieratic on the front, and three on the back; complete on all sides.
Contents: An account of various types of wood delivered to the temple magazines, including some ship parts.
Translation:

Front
(1) Month 3 of Akhet, day 7. Entered into the storehouse:
(2) Acacia, planks: 4. Coniferous wood, roller: 1.
(3) Sycamore, planks: 20.
(4) That which under the authority of the door-keeper.
(5) Total: 27. Plank of acacia: 1. Sycamore, planks: 3. Beams (?): 1.

Back
(1) Acacia, rib: 1.
(2) Coniferous wood, hull plank: 1
(3) Ditto, large balk: 1

Notes:
Front
(1) The heading used here is reminiscent of the caption to a scene showing wine being brought into a storehouse from the tomb of Rekhmire (TT 100), which reads 'Bringing wine to the storehouse [of the temple]' (sꜥk.t irp r wḏꜣ; Davies 1943: II, pl. 50). The phrasing on the ostracon is also comparable to the Ramesside grain account on the back of P. Sallier IV (= BM EA 10184, vso. 7.4, 10.4), where sacks of grain are delivered to another type of storehouse ('Entered into the magazine'; sꜥk r pꜣ mḫr; Gardiner 1937: 93–94; Caminos 1954: 353, 358), so perhaps this is a standardised accounting phrase. The specific 'storehouse' or 'magazine' (wḏꜣ) mentioned here might correspond to one of the magazines in the north-eastern corner of the site (half of which was converted into the residence of the high priest of the temple at some point in the Ramesside Period: Seco Alvarez and Babón 2015: 383–391).

(2) For the identification of šndt-wood as acacia (Acacia nilotica) and ꜥš as a coniferous wood (probably Abies cilicica), see Germer (1985: 7, 90–91). In this line, as in many below, the form of the wood is simply said to be ḫt, 'piece' or 'plank', but in the case of ꜥš the form of the wood is given as stꜣt. Etymologically related to the root stꜣ, which is used in words relating to physical activities dealing with dragging, pulling or stretching (Wb. 4, 351–354), it seems to denote some kind of roller. One of my reviewers draws attention to what may be the same word in a 12th Dynasty stela (Sadek 1980: 84, no. 143, l. 14), where amethyst was 'dragged on sledges and loaded onto ⌐' (iṯḥ ḥr wnš, ꜣtp ḥr stꜣ.t), and the 18th Dynasty dockyard papyrus in the British Museum which lists a ⌐ in the context of ship-building (Faulkner 1962: 255, with reference to Glanville 1931/1933: 11; both translate 'roller').

(3) For nht as sycamore (Ficus sycomorus), see Germer (1985: 25–27).

(4) The final signs of the title are rather faint, probably because the ink was running out.

(5) At the beginning of the line, to the right of the margin of the other lines, is the annotation 'Total: 27'. I assume the scribe meant for this to summarise lines 1–5, and that it was written here simply for reasons of space (the ostracon seems complete). Needless to say the sum does not match the total number of pieces of wood listed, regardless of how one counts: there are 30 if one adds all the numbers, 25 if one only adds the numbers in the lines above, and 28 if one only counts the 'planks/pieces', and the three additional pieces of wood on the back would complicate this even further. The reading of the final type of wood is problematic: ḥꜣ (cf. Wb. 3.12; part of a chariot) is only a guess as the crucial first sign is unclear.

Back
(1) The wg-plank (Wb. 1, 376.7–8) is often used in shipbuilding, where it specifically refers to the ribs of a ship (Jéquier 1911: 62–63): it occurs repeatedly in the contemporary accounts of the royal dockyard published by Glanville (1931: 105–121; 1933: 7–40, esp. p. 34).

(2) The *dph*-plank is also used in ship-building, and it has been suggested that it is a Semitic loan word with the meaning 'broad', perhaps referring to the hull planks (Hoch 1994: no. 578). The word is otherwise apparently only attested in a Ramesside papyrus in Turin (Janssen 1975: 380).

(3) As Janssen (1975: 370–371) noted, *šʿd* refers to a square piece of wood from which various types of planks could be produced.

T3.A18 (pl. 13)

Excavation number: 15674/970N6L115

Description: A body sherd of a New Kingdom jar of marl clay (A4), with four lines of hieratic on the outside, in an 18th Dynasty administrative hand; perhaps complete on all sides. The individual signs are much abbreviated, making it difficult to read despite the relatively well preserved ink.

Contents: An administrative note, perhaps relating to the cutting of wood.

Translation:

(1)   That which is going to be cut (?):
(2)   [...] large beams (?) [...]
(3)   [...] 5 105
(4)   Delivered: 10. Total: 20

Notes:

(2) The transcription of the whole line is doubtful, especially the beginning. Perhaps read *sꜣy ꜥꜣ*, 'large beams' at the end?

(3) I cannot read this line. Römer (pers. comm.) suggests, with some reservations, *itḥ inr* 5–105, 'dragging stones 5, 105', with a reference to one of his contemporary ostraca from Deir el-Bahari (O. Eg. Exp. 23001.208, vso. x+2), while Müller (pers. comm.) thinks it might possibly be read *iw -st ḥr*; perhaps others will be able to solve it.

T3.A19 (pl. 13)

Excavation number: 20852/1000N3L316

Description: A body sherd from an imported jar (similar fabric to 20879), with two lines of hieratic on one side; seemingly complete.

Contents: A note of festival rewards due to the high priest.

Translation:

(1)   The festival rewards of the high
(2)   priest: 80.

Notes:

(1) The relatively rare term [hieroglyphs], *ḥn.t*, 'festival rewards' or similar (*Wb.* 3, 289.17) also occurs in the Elephantine offering list of Thutmose III, where one of the headings, perhaps related to the 'Appearance of Sothis' festival (on 3

Shomu 28), reads 'That which is for festival rewards (*ḥn.t*) for this festival: wine, 1 *mn*-jar [...]' (*Urk.* IV, 828.9). Another occurrence of the word is in the Amada stela of Amenhotep II, where it is stated that 'He (the king) established festival-gifts (*ḥn.t*) anew for his fathers the gods' (*Urk.* IV, 1294.9–10). Gardiner (1916: 106) suggested 'expenses' or 'festival outlay' in his commentary on *Sinuhe* B275, and more specifically the sense seems to be goods handed out as gifts or rewards in connection with festivals. I interpret this as an unidentified commodity (bread?) allocated to the high-priest of the temple, rather than his contribution to the festival offerings.

T3.A20 (pl. 14)

Excavation number: 21160/980N5L117

Description: A piece of limestone with one line of hieratic in red ink, rather broad and heavy; complete.

Contents: A weight.

Translation:

(1)   Deben: 17.

Notes:

(1) For the use of such objects at Deir el-Medina, normally silex rather than limestone as in this case, with indications of weight, see most recently the discussion by Dorn (2011: 143–145). 17 *deben* would correspond to approximately 1547 grams; it proved impossible to weigh the stone on site, but it seemed roughly the right weight (comparable to a 1.5 litre bottle of water).

T3.A21 (pl. 15)

Excavation number: 21268/980N4L317

Description: A marl clay pottery sherd from the neck of a decorated jar of the early- to mid-18th Dynasty, with two lines of hieratic.

Contents: An account of rations.

Translation:

(1)   [...] Rations: *psn*-bread: 310+ [...]
(2)   [...] people (?) [...]

T3.A22 (pl. 15)

Excavation number: 21472/1010S4L118

Description: A small marl clay pottery sherd from a Memphite amphora of the New Kingdom, with a single line of hieratic in black ink.

Contents: An account (?).

Translation:

(1)   Wine, *mn*-jars: [...]

T3.A23 (pl. 16)

Excavation number: 15075/930–940N5L113

Description: An indeterminate pottery sherd with the

ends of two lines of hieratic in black ink on the front, and traces of three lines on the back.

Contents: Administrative text; perhaps rations for stone masons.

Translation:

Front

(x+1)   […] stone masons.

(x+2)   […]*mw*-jars: 4.

Back

(x+1)   […]

(x+2)   *p<ꜥ>t*-cakes: […]

(x+3)   *šꜥy.t*-cakes: […]

Notes:

(Front, x+2) The commodity is clearly a liquid, based on the determinative at the beginning of the line, but I am not sure about the type of jar: 🏺 seems certain at the end.

(Back, x+1) Müller (pers. comm.) suggests that the traces might match ⌐.

(Back, x+2) This is presumably *pꜥ.t*-cakes (*Wb.* 1, 503.12; cf. Spalinger 1985: 193 n. 14; Caminos 1954: 204), although the TLA does not seem to record this specific spelling (without the *ayin*).

1.2   *Records of work*

T3.A24 (pls. 17–18)

Excavation number: 15657/920N6L414

Description: A limestone ostracon with two columns of hieratic text in black ink, with a dividing line between the columns. It appears to be complete at the top, bottom and left-hand edge, but a substantial piece has broken away on the right-hand side, leaving only the end of the lines of column I.

Contents: An administrative text recording construction work being carried out on the pylon and other parts of the temple. The first column lists groups of individuals, perhaps work crews, while the second contains details of the work done.

Translation:

Column I:

(1)   [Month X of Season Y] final day. (On) this day:

(2)   […]: 6 (?) [men]

(3)   […]-bringers: 7 men

(4)   […] 8 men (?)

(5)   […] 5 men (?)

(6)   […] inside: 6 men

(7)   […]

(8)   […] 2 men

(9)   […] Total: 25 men.

Column II:

(1)   Totality of work done on this day:

(2)   Namely, doing building-work on the pylon

(3)   and its courtyard (?). Doing building-work

(4)   on the side and its

(5)   inside. Doing building-work on the

(6)   great stairway (?), from

(7)   top to

(8)   bottom.

(9)   Placing the *sbw*-planks for

(10)   the roof (?).

Notes:

(I.1) The traces of the first signs would be compatible with ⟅. The heading presumably refers to the same day as the following column, perhaps originally introduced by a date. This is followed by a record of work crews in different locations or under the authority of different individuals (cf. the following lines). Similar lists in the contemporary ostraca from the building of the temples at Deir el-Bahri includes headings like 'Muster of this day', or 'List of workers' (*snhy n hrw pn*; *rḫt bꜣkw*; Hayes 1960: no. 17), but the traces here are not compatible with these phrases.

(I.2) The structure of the information in the following lines seems to be a location followed by a number of men who are working there, but the traces at the end of line I.2 are difficult to match with a number, partly because the ink is rubbed off in places (could it be '6'?).

(I.9) I find it difficult to relate the possible readings of numbers with the total number of workers given in the final line. In any case it seems clear from line six that the groups of workers are listed at least in part by location.

(II.1) The first sign of the heading is difficult: Demarée suggests 𓏴 (*dmḏyt*), as in line I.9.

(II.2) The meaning of the term *ỉwꜥ*, the reading of which seems certain (cf. lines II.3 and II.5), presumably refers to some kind of building activity seeing as it relates to the pylon and its constituent parts (its 'side' and its 'interior'). It is also used to describe the work on the 'great stairway', and it is therefore tempting to associate it with construction work using mudbricks:

ỉwꜥ pꜣ bḫn ḥr ḥꜣf (?)	(building) the pylon and its courtyard (?)
ỉwꜥ pꜣ gꜣb ḥnꜥ pꜣy=f ḥn	(building) the side and its interior
ỉwꜥ tꜣ wꜣ.t ꜥꜣt rd	(building) the great stairway

The word *bḫn* in the context of temple architecture is most plausibly to be interpreted as a pylon (Wilson 1997: 326–327), despite lacking the feminine ending (*Wb.* 1, 471.10–11). The absence of the ending may partly be explained by the similarity to the masculine word *bḫn* (*Wb.* 1, 471.6–8) which is used of fortified military installations and large houses, and partly by the script. In New Kingdom hieroglyphic texts the word for 'pylon' (*bḫn.t*) is normally written with the *.t*-ending, but in Ramesside hieratic it is not infrequently omitted, at least in the plural (Grandet 1994: 14 n. 64; KRI VI, 411.11, 13, 16, 412.6–7; cf. Gardiner 1947: II, 204*; 19; 1948: 34).

(II.3) The reading of the sign 🖋 is problematic. I have tentatively followed a suggestion by Römer and transcribed 🖋 (*h*, *Wb.* 2, 470.1–5), a word meaning 'courtyard' or similar. As he notes one might expect something like *wsḫ.t* instead, but I have no better suggestion, and the word is attested in 18th Dynasty texts, albeit normally with the house determinative.

(II.4) At the end *pȝ* is certain, and *yᵢf* plausible. The term *gȝb*, var. *gbȝ* (*Wb.* 5, 163.13) may refer to the side of a room or structure, as in P. Westcar 8.18–20 which mentions the western and the eastern side of a 'columned hall' (*wȝḫy*); an earlier occurrence is in P. Reisner III (H 24; Simpson 1969: 33, pl. 16), an account which also deals with construction work on various parts of a building, probably a temple, where the 'western side' is mentioned (I am grateful to one of my reviewers for this reference).

(II.6) I read *ᶜȝt* but not with any great confidence, which yields something like *tȝ wȝt ᶜȝt rd*, perhaps literally something like 'the large and stepped way', but precisely what this refers to I do not know: could it be the ramps that lead up from the pylons to the interior of the temple?

(II.8) *iwtn*, 'ground' or 'earth' (*Wb.* 1, 58.5–10) is here clearly used in the technical sense of 'ground level'.

(II.9) For *sbw*, a type of plank or board (*Wb.* 3, 432.18) that might be collected by a temple as part of its dues, see P. Chester Beatty V (= BM EA 10686), rto. 8.5 (Gardiner 1935: I, 49; II, pl. 26; and cf. Caminos 1954: 345; 1963: 33). It has been suggested that this is a phantom word, and that the signs 🔤 should be read simply *s* (Görg 1980: 160–161); the word would then identical with *sȝw*, 'planks' (*Wb.* 3, 419.14–17).

(II.10) The word almost looks like 🔤, but this would be an otherwise unattested type of building. I have suggested instead 🔤, presumably as a variant writing of *hȝyt*, 'roof' (*Wb.* 2, 476.12–13), even if the writing is a bit odd for the 18th Dynasty. One of my reviewers suggests the reading 🔤 as an alternative, i.e. *wᶜbt*, 'workshop, embalming place' (*Wb.* 1, 284.1–7), which is also possible.

T3.A25 (pl. 19)

Excavation number: 15658/920N6L414

Description: A limestone flake with five lines of hieratic; complete at top and right.

Contents: An account of work.

Translation:

(1) [... Month X] of Akhet (?), day 27. Those who are going out on this day:

(2) [...] 15.

(3) [...] day [2]7. Again, the crews (?) who will push ahead (?) [...]

(4) [...]

(5) [...]

Notes:

(3) The reading of parts of the line is unclear. The sign group after *whm* must refer to the subject of *r thm* but I do not know what it might be. One of my reviewers suggests *mnf.t*, 'troops' (*Wb.* 2, 80.1–5), which is perhaps possible—in any case the word must refer to a group of workers. The lack of determinatives obscures the specific meaning of *thm* here, but it normally implies a pushing or stepping motion; attested activities include puncturing, the destruction of enemies, the driving of cattle, and 'stirring' in cooking (*Wb.* 5, 321.6–322.6).

T3.A26 (pl. 20)

Excavation number: 7894/980N6L116

Description: A limestone fragment with four lines of hieratic; probably complete except for a small flake that has come off the surface in the lower left-hand corner.

Contents: A note on the absence of personnel, and the recruitment of workers from the building sites at Deir el-Bahri.

Translation:

(1) Merymaat: sick.

(2) Nanasuy: sick.

(3) Month 1 of Akhet, day 3. Recruiting 2 men from Djeseru in order

(4) to make them [...]

Notes:

(1) The signs at the end extend over the ridge at the top, proving that the top of the ostracon is complete as preserved—there were no lines above. Römer (pers. comm.) notes the presence of the name Merymaat on two unpublished ostraca from Deir el-Bahri: O. Eg. Exp. CO 30 (line x+13) from the final decade of the reign of Thutmose III, and O. Eg. Exp. 27057 (line 5), from the reign of Hatshepsut. Neither source mentions a title, but the former could be a mason (*ḥrtiw-nṯr*).

(2) The name is otherwise unattested, but despite the faintness of the ink the reading seems certain. At the end there is no room for the full phonetic writing of *mr*, 'sick', but an abbreviation after the full writing in the line above is not surprising.

(3) The reading of the place-name is plausible in view of the first sign, but there may be a sign missing as a small flake has broken away from the surface here, and ◡ is written quite high up. For the movement of work-forces between sites on the Theban West Bank, see also O. Eg. Exp. 23001.108 (Hayes 1960: 47, no. 21) from Deir el-Bahri, where three individuals (Sen, Neby and Mersuamun) are said to be 'in Henket-ankh', i.e. in the mortuary temple of Thutmose III.

(4) The final signs of the line are faint and illegible to me: the determinatives and the grammatical construction suggest an action verb at the end.

1.3   *Name-Stones, and Lists of Names and Titles*
T3.A27 (pl. 21)
Excavation number: 9079/950N1L208
Description: A limestone flake with two lines of hieratic, seemingly complete.
Contents: Mentions a stone mason.
Translation:
(1)   The stone mason
(2)   Amenhotep

T3.A28 (pl. 21)
Excavation number: 15188/910N1L611
Description: A small rim sherd from a New Kingdom restricted bowl with a red band, with a single line of hieratic; probably complete.
Contents: A name.
Translation:
(1)   Mahu

T3.A29 (pl. 21)
Excavation number: 15215/930–940N5L113
Description: A body sherd, probably of a Canaanite jar, with a single line of hieratic, probably complete.
Contents: A name.
Translation:
(1)   Hati

T3.A30 (pl. 21)
Excavation number: 15217/R4/5L613 (found near grid 940/N7)
Description: A body sherd of an Egyptian jar of medium Nile clay, red slipped in and out, with a single line, probably complete.
Contents: A name and title.
Translation:
(1)   The scribe Khaia (?)
Notes:
(1) I read the personal name as Khaia (Ranke 1935: 265.6),

but it could perhaps also be [hieroglyphs], on the pattern of *ḥꜥ* + divine name (Ranke 1935: 263.8–10, with Onuris and Anubis); the latter suggestion I owe to my student Sika Pedersen.

T3.A31 (pl. 22)
Excavation number: 15498/900N5L214
Description: A limestone flake with five lines of hieratic, distributed over two columns. The second column is written upside-down in relation to the first, with an uninscribed area between them. The ostracon may be complete in terms of width, judging by the layout, because the beginning of the lines at the bottom lines up with the ends of the lines above, but clearly there are fragments missing at the bottom.
Contents: Two lists of *wꜥb*-priests.
Translation:

    Column I
(1)   The *wꜥb*-priest Hekanefer
(2)   The *wꜥb*-priest Minnakht [...]
(3)   The *wꜥb*-priest Amenemope

    Column II (upside-down)
(x+1)   [...]
(x+2)   The *wꜥb*-priest [...]: 2
(x+3)   The *wꜥb*-priest [...]

T3.A32 (pl. 23)
Excavation number: 15628/900N5L214
Description: A small piece of flint with a single line of hieratic on one side; this is written on a thin chalk deposit covering the flint on this one side.
Contents: A personal name (?).
Translation:
(1)   Wehemdjedet (?)
Notes:
(1) If this is a personal name, which seems likely, it appears to be unattested elsewhere, although Ranke (1935: 83.14–23) lists several names constructed with *wḥm* as the initial element. Alternatively, it might be an order: "Repeat what I have said".

T3.A33 (pl. 23)
Excavation number: 15633/910N5L114
Description: An indeterminate pottery sherd with a single line of hieratic on the outside.
Contents: Presumably a personal name, but difficult to read.
Translation:
(1)   Hauiam (?)
Notes:

(1) I have no great faith in my transcription here; if it is a personal name then it is not in Ranke.

T3.A34 (pl. 24)

Excavation number: 15675/980N5L315

Description: A small body sherd of an Egyptian jar with cream slip, probably New Kingdom, with the beginning of a single line of hieratic on the outside. The hand is careful and deliberate, perhaps even literary in register, and its classification as an administrative note therefore not certain.

Contents: A title (?).

Translation:

(1) The chief guardian (?) [...]

Notes:

(1) One of my reviewers suggested reading [sign], ḥꜣ, instead of [sign], sꜣw, which is palaeographically possible (and might then yield a phonetic writing of ḥry ḥꜣw.t, 'chief of offering tables', or similar), but the following traces are not compatible with the expected *aleph*.

T3.A35 (pl. 24)

Excavation number: 20698/1010N5L215

Description: An indeterminate pottery with traces of a single line of hieratic on one side. Perhaps largely complete except for a small piece broken off at the beginning of the line.

Contents: A personal name (?).

Translation:

(x+1) [...]emshakemu

Notes:

(x+1) The signs are relatively clear, but would not match an Egyptian word, so this is presumably a foreign name.

T3.A36 (pl. 24)

Excavation number: 20968/890N6L116

Description: A small rim sherd of a New Kingdom restricted bowl, of medium Nile clay, with one line of hieratic; complete.

Contents: A personal name.

Translation:

(1) Kenamun

Notes:

(1) The determinative is written very elaborately with two separate strokes, almost like [sign], but the name is only attested in the masculine.

T3.A37 (pl. 25)

Excavation number: 7984/990N4L1517

Description: A limestone fragment with two lines of hieratic; complete.

Contents: Title and name of an individual.

Translation:

(1) The scribe Payamun (?)

(2) ...?

Notes:

(1) Despite the clarity of the ink, I find this ostracon very difficult to read. It might be a faulty writing of something like pꜣy⸗i ⟨it⟩ imn, 'My-father-is-Amun', which is a name pattern attested with other divine names (Ranke 1935: 420.4, with Khonsu). Palaeographically it might be possible to instead read the final group as [sign], but this is also problematic given the next line.

(2) The first sign might be the archaic form of the determinative of the name on the preceding line, above an n ([sign]). Following this is something that could be also be a name, but apart from the initial sign, which is probably the city sign ([sign]), I do not know what to make of it. Perhaps something like [sign]? But this is highly doubtful and the tiw-bird in particular is difficult to reconcile with the hieratic. If this is a name then it is not attested elsewhere, but there is an Old Kingdom name Niuti(u) written [sign] or [sign] (Ranke 1935: 169.5–6), which might be related. Römer suggests that instead of the double reed-leaf one might read the sign [sign] as [sign]; either way I can make little sense of this.

T3.A38 (pl. 25)

Excavation number: 21530/910N8SD18-1

Description: A large pottery sherd, probably from a Canaanite jar, with a handle; the outside bears a short inscription in black of a single line.

Contents: Name and title of an individual.

Translation:

(1) The scribe Si (?).

Notes:

(1) The writing of the name is very faint, and the reading not quite clear ([sign], Ta, is perhaps also just possible). Römer (pers. comm.) informs me that there is a draughtsman called Si, son of Yrt ([sign]), mentioned on O. Eg. Exp. 23001.189 (line x+4), from the final decade of the reign of Thutmose III.

T3.A39 (pl. 26)

Excavation number: 9035 RM (Ricke Magazine)

Description: A body sherd of a New Kingdom jar with two fragmentary lines of hieratic, in a rather big hand, on the convex side.

Contents: Mentions two individuals by name and title.

Translation:

(x+1) The royal scribe and overseer of the House of [...]

(x+2) The royal scribe Kha[...]

Notes:

(x+1) To the right of the first line the sign ⨍ is written on its own, probably in the same hand but slightly smaller than the other signs; above this there are faint traces of link that might correspond to a previous line.

T3.A40 (pl. 26)

Excavation number: 9083/900S4L108

Description: A body sherd of a Levantine jar with some residue material, with two fragmentary lines of hieratic in black ink; incomplete at top and left hand side.

Contents: A list of personnel.

Translation:

(x+1)   The water carrier [...]

(x+2)   The scribe Neferrenpet.

T3.A41 (pl. 27)

Excavation number: 9270/920S3L111

Description: A body sherd from a New Kingdom (?) jar of medium Nile clay, with the beginning of four lines of hieratic; very cursive, probably late Ramesside.

Contents: List of names (?).

Translation:

(x+1)   Ptahem[...]

(x+2)   Khonsu (?) [...]

(x+3)   Montu[...]

(x+4)   Tekhy (?)

T3.A42 (pl. 28)

Excavation number: 15668/910N6L215

Description: A flat pottery dish two columns, each with three lines of hieratic, written on the outside.

Contents: A list of personal names and amounts (of bread?).

Translation:

	Col. I.	Col. II
(1)	Nehemredy: 2	Kaemwaset: 1
(2)	May son of Nebimose: 2	Hay ⟨son of?⟩ Seneb (?): 1
(3)	[...] 1	Si: 1

Notes:

(I.1) An otherwise unattested name.

(II.1) The bull sign is a qualified guess, but the phonetic signs are clear. Römer (pers. comm.) notes that the name also occurs in O. BM EA 43269 (line 1), from the fourth decade of Thutmose III, and in BM EA 41224 (vso. line 1).

(II.2) The interpretation of this line is difficult: Hay is a common name, and the little dot after the phonetic signs suggests that the name ends here, but the expected 'son of' is not present. The transcription of the final name is little more than a guess. Alternatively one might read Hayseneb, which would make this too an unattested name (cf. line I.1).

T3.A43 (pls. 29–34)

Excavation number: 15670/910N6L215

Description: A limestone flake with several columns of hieratic on both sides, with dividing lines. It is complete at the top and the left-hand side, with a couple of small pieces missing in the top right and bottom right-hand corners. The writing frequently curves around the edge of the ostracon on the left side, not all of which is visible in the photographs, but the facsimiles include these additional signs. The hand on the back is larger, and some of the signs here, especially on the bottom half, appear to be shaped slightly differently from the ones on the front, but probably still within the range of variation that could be expected from a single scribe.

Contents: A list of wꜥb-priests grouped in phyles.

Translation:

Front

Col. I

(1)   The first phyle:

(2)   The wꜥb-priest Nebamun. The goldsmith Nebamun: 2. Total: 2

(3)   The wꜥb-priest Amenmose, ditto: 6. [...] 1.

(4)   The wꜥb-priest Seniem[...]

(5)   The wꜥb-priest Menkheperre.

(6)   The wꜥb-priest Weben.

(7)   The wꜥb-priest Seba.

(8)   The wꜥb-priest Mery (?).

(9)   The wꜥb-priest Ahmose. The goldsmith and applier (?) Sahekek (?).

(10)   The wꜥb-priest Nesu.

(11)   The wꜥb-priest Amenhotep. The goldsmith and applier (?) Menkhet (?). The wꜥb-priest Nebenta.

(12)   The second phyle:

(13)   The wꜥb-priest Nehsheri (?).

(14)   The wꜥb-priest Menkheperre. The goldsmith and applier (?) Pawahdjay (?).

(15)   The wꜥb-priest Amenemhat.

(16)   The wꜥb-priest Amenemheb.

(17)   The wꜥb-priest Hekanefer.

(18)   The wꜥb-priest Amenhotep. The goldsmith Abdy: 2.

(19)   [The wꜥb-priest] Amenemhat.

(20)   The goldsmith Safy (?): 1.

Col. II

(x+1)   [The wꜥb-priest ... Sen]na (?)

(x+2)   [... lost ...]

(x+3)   [... lost ...]

(x+4)   The *wʿb*-priest Kha.

(x+5)   The *wʿb*-priest Iny.

(x+6)   The third phyle:

(x+7)   The *wʿb*-priest Amen⟨em⟩hat.

(x+8)   The *wʿb*-priest Amenhotep.

(x+9)   The *wʿb*-priest Amenhotep.

(x+10) The *wʿb*-priest Sapair.

(x+11) The *wʿb*-priest Amenmose.

(x+12) [The *wʿb*-priest Amen?]emhat.

Back

(1)   The *wʿb*-priest Amenem[hat?]

(2)   The *wʿb*-priest Nebmeru⟨t⟩ef

(3)   The *wʿb*-priest [...]. The goldsmith Ka: 2.

(4)   The *wʿb*-priest Amen[tjau?]. Ditto: 2.

(5)   The *wʿb*-priest [...].

(6)   The *wʿb*-priest Meru. Ditto Seneb. Remainder (?): 1.

(7)   The *wʿb*-priest Amenemheb.

(8)   The *wʿb*-priest Amenhotep.

(9)   The *wʿb*-priest Nebamun. The goldsmith [...]

(10) The *wʿb*-priest Nebmerutef.

(11) The *wʿb*-priest Sapair.

(12) A gold necklace (?)

Notes:

(I.1) The headings for the groups of priests here and below (I.12, II.x+3) do not seem to be related to the horizontal dividing lines (between lines 8/9, 9/10 and 15/16). The first phyle includes a total of eleven *wʿb*-priests, and four individuals who appear to be goldsmiths (lines 2, 3, 9 and 11).

(I.2) The end of the line is difficult. The sign after the first mention of the name Nebamun is probably the same group found in various lines below (I.9, I.11, I.14, I.18, I.20, and vso. 3), which I have transcribed as ⟨sign⟩ and interpreted as the title *nby*, 'goldsmith'. In this case as in most other examples the sign is followed by a personal name:

a)   *nby Nb-imn*: 2 (I.2)

b)   ditto [illegible name]: 2 (I.3)

c)   *nby bs Sȝ (?)-ḥkk* (I.9)

d)   *nby bs Mtḥtȝ (?)* (I.11)

e)   *nby bs Pȝ-wȝḥ-dȝ (?)* (I.14)

f)   *nby ʿbdy*: 2 (I.18)

g)   *nby Pȝ-[..]-fy* (I.20)

h)   *nby Kȝ*: 2 (vso. 3)

i)   ditto (= *nby*) ditto (= *Kȝ*): 2 (vso. 4)

k)   ditto (= *nby*) *Snbw*: 1 (vso. 5)

l)   *nby* [illegible name] (vso.8)

Despite the lack of a name determinative in some of these examples (I.18, I.20 and vso. 3), the most plausible interpretation of the sign ⟨sign⟩ is as a title, although the

orthography (without phonetic complements or determinatives) is admittedly rather abbreviated for a hieratic text. Römer (pers. comm.) reports an example from the contemporary ostraca from Deir el-Bahri where the title is abbreviated ⟨sign⟩ (O. Eg. Exp. 23001.223, vso. line x+5), which contrasts with the fuller form ⟨sign⟩ in another of his unpublished 18th Dynasty ostraca (O. BM EA 47921, line 2). The connection between *wʿb*-priests and goldsmiths might initially seem obscure, but both positions are closely linked with temples, and people who hold both titles are attested: one Theban tomb owner records two sons who are both '*wʿb*-priests and goldsmiths of the temple of Amun' (cf. DZA 2490470, from 'Theben. Grab Wb. Nr. 23').

(I.4) The reading of the name is uncertain: the initial elements (⟨sign⟩) are relatively clear, but the traces following do not match any of the names on this pattern in Ranke (1935: 308.20–21).

(I.5) Not surprisingly there are more than one priest named after Thutmose III (cf. I.4). Either of these might be identical with the *ḥm-nṯr*-priest of the same name mentioned in the tomb of Puyemre (TT 39, temp. Thutmose III; Davies 1922–1923: II, pl. 64), or the *wʿb*-priest and 'scribe of the divine offerings' named Menkheperre(seneb) in TT 87 (Minnakht, temp. Thutmose III; *Urk.* IV, 1178.11; 1205.11–12), but the name is likely to have been very common among the families in the area, especially those with ties to the temple priesthood.

(I.7) The phonetic value of the star sign in this name is not certain: both *sbȝ* and *dwȝ* are possible (Ranke 1935: I, 303.9; 398.11; II, 386).

(I.8) The first group of the name might be ⟨sign⟩, but it looks slightly different to the other instances of this group (cf. vso. 2, 6 and 9); other possibilities include ⟨sign⟩, ⟨sign⟩, or similar. All these would yield attested names. There is a mention of a *wʿb*-priest of Menkheperre of Henket-ankh called Mery on a stela in the Fitzwilliam Museum in Cambridge (inv. no. E.ss.27; cf. Martin 2005: 91–92), but even if the reading on A43 is correct, this is a very common name so the identification is not certain.

(I.9) I read the element following *nby* as ⟨sign⟩, perhaps with a technical sense of a goldsmith specialising in applying gold leaf or similar, presumably derived from the root meaning of *bs* as 'introduce' or 'usher in'. The personal name *ḥkk* is attested, but the sign in front—which I read as ⟨sign⟩—is uncertain.

(I.10) There is *wʿb*-priest of the temple called Nesu who is mentioned on a stela in Cairo (CG 34117; Lacau 1926: 170, pl. 53), as well as on a limestone fragment of a throne found at the temple (Weigall 1906: 134 no. 22)—this may well be the same individual, given that the Cairo stela specifically describes him as a 'wꜥb-priest of the first phyle', i.e. the same phyle that he is ascribed to on the ostracon.

(I.11) Other wꜥb-priests of the temple by the same name are mentioned in I.18, II.x+8, II.x+9 and vso.8; assuming that they are different individuals, any one of them (or none) might correspond to the wꜥb-priest Amenhotep of the temple mentioned on an 18th Dynasty statue in Rhode Island (*Urk.* IV, 1502.12). The phrase 'The wꜥb-priest Nebenta' was added underneath the line. This name is not attested, but there are names on the same pattern, e.g. Nebenkemet (⸢⸣; Ranke 1935: 185.14) or Nebentaneb (⸢⸣; Ranke 1935: 185.15).

(I.12) Assuming nothing is lost at the bottom of the ostracon, the second phyle lists at least nine wꜥb-priests and three goldsmiths, but the traces at the top of column II suggest that at least another three lines are missing, bringing the potential total for the second phyle to eleven or twelve priests.

(I.13) The reading of the personal name is due to Demarée; the description 'younger' (*šrï*) is not certain.

(I.14) For the reading of *nby*, see above. Because of the lack of space, the scribe has placed the personal name immediately below the line. The reading is complicated by some scratches on the surface of the stone. The initial part of the name (*Pꜣ-wꜣḥ*) seems certain and is a common New Kingdom name (Ranke 1935: 103.19), but the final signs do not appear to match a known name—*dꜣ* is no more than a qualified guess.

(I.17) A wꜥb-priest 'of the royal *ka* of Thutmose III in Henket-ankh' named Hekanefer is also found on some funerary cones (Davies and Macadam 1957: nos. 393–394), which might concievably be the same individual; the cones also include the title *ïmy-r sbꜣ.w*, perhaps 'overseer of teachers' or 'overseer of gates' (cf. Haring 1992: 434).

(I.19) A narrow splinter appears to have come off the right hand edge here, probably not more than a centimetre or two. The traces at the beginning suggest that wꜥb was written without the water signs, presumably due to a lack of space here (for another example of the title without the water signs, see A45, l. x+5, but there presumably omitted by mistake).

(I.20) The traces here are faint, and written partly around the edge of the ostracon; one expects a personal name after the title 'goldsmith', but the traces are difficult to reconcile with any known name; 'Safy' may be the most plausible transcription.

(II.x+1) Only the final part of the name is preserved, but based on the layout of the following lines, perhaps a rather short name. Senna (⸢⸣) is simply a qualified guess, and there are of course numerous names ending in *-nꜣ*.

(II.x+4) A wꜥb-priest and lector-priest of the temple named Khay is mentioned in the tomb of one of the High Priests of the temple (TT 31, of Khonsu; Davies 1948: 20–21, pls. 15–16), but given the late date of the tomb (temp. Ramesses II) this is unlikely to be the same individual.

(II.x+5) Römer (pers. comm.) draws attention to the fact that the absence of the phonetic complement ⸗ in the writing of *ïn* would be unusual, and that other possibilities include reading ⸢⸣ or ⸢⸣; however both of these would be unattested.

(II.x+6) The third phyle lists at least 6 wꜥb-priests on the front: more names may be lost at the end because a fragment appears to have broken off here. Whether this phyle continued on the back, or whether that list is for the fourth and final phyle, is impossible to determine; there is no heading mentioning the fourth phyle on this ostracon.

(II.x+7) The scribe has omitted the determinative at the end; abbreviated writings occur in several lines below (cf. e.g. the omission of *p* in the next two lines in the name Amenhotep, the missing *aleph* in Sapair, and the missing determinative in the final line), presumably because of the limited space available.

(vso.1) The traces at the top suggest the title 'wꜥb-priest', followed by the personal name 'Amenem[hat?]'. It is difficult to say whether this should be interpreted as the continuation of the list of the third phyle begun on the other side, or if it is in fact a separate list of members of the fourth phyle: the number of names on the back in total amount to eleven wꜥb-priests and two goldsmiths, which is comparable to the numbers listed for the first and the second phyle on the front, so I am inclined to believe that this side contains the fourth phyle. On this interpretation the broken-off fragment mentioned above would probably have contained another three or four wꜥb-priests belonging to the third phyle; there would certainly have been room for this if the fragment originally extended as far as the lower edge of the ostracon.

(vso.2) The orthography of the name is different from vso. 10 below; there is certainly no space for ⸢⸣.

(vso.3) The determinative of the name Ka is missing, but the interpretation of it as a personal name seems certain (cf. I.2 for details on the structure of such entries).

(vso.4) The traces after Amen[...] are very faint, but perhaps compatible with ⸢⸣; this would yield Amentjau, for which Ranke (1935: 31.18) has a single 22nd Dynasty example, and he notes that it may be a variant of the name Amenpaitjau known from the Tomb Robbery papyri (Ranke 1935: 27.10). Another possibility, suggested by Römer (pers. comm.), might be to read Amen[wau] (Ranke 1935: 24).

(vso.6) I assume the final part of the line ('Ditto Seneb. Remainder (?): 1') belongs to line 6 because of the position of the ditto sign, even if the rest of the line curves upwards and might therefore be taken to belong to line 5. The final name is clearly Seneb, but the penultimate sign is curious: Römer suggests ⌇ *dꜣ.t*, 'remainder', with similar forms among his ostraca (O. Eg. Exp. 23001.77, vso. line 1; BM EA 41655, lines 3 and 8, and BM EA 47921, vso. Line 4); this form with the diagonal tick is otherwise listed only as Ramesside by Möller (1927: 35 no. 391).

(vso.9) The name of the goldsmith is illegible, but the space available is limited so it would have been short.

(vso.12) The reading of the last line is problematic. The final signs might be *dbḥ.t*, a word which can be a type of jewellery (*Wb.* 5, 442.4), yielding something like 'gold: (one) *dbḥ.t*-necklace'. Alternatively, if it is to be understood like the other entries with the gold sign above, then it could be a title here too, followed by a personal name: 'the goldsmith Debehet' (compare Ranke 1935: 399.13–16).

T3.A44 (pl. 27)

Excavation number: 15677/1020N4L115

Description: A small limestone flake with two lines of hieratic on one side; probably complete.

Contents: A message (or name)?

Translation:

(1) The officials

(2) *in* (?) *ḫmnw* (?) *mitt*

Notes:

(2) The ink is clear but I am not convinced of the accuracy of the transcription of the first three signs, and cannot venture a guess as to their meaning.

T3.A45 (pl. 35)

Excavation number: 7727/960N5L116

Description: This is a limestone fragment probably from a stela, and so its classification as an "ostracon" is somewhat arbitrary—it partly depends on when the hieratic text on the back was inscribed (before or after the destruction of the original object), and for what purpose. If it was inscribed in connection with the production of the stela then it might list those responsible for commissioning it, but it could equally have been used as a simple ostracon after the stela was broken. The raised relief on the front preserves the left side of a standing human figure, perhaps the king, holding a *ḥs*-jar from which water is being poured onto an offering table. In front of the offering table is a partly preserved sitting figure (Amun?) with an ankh-sign in one hand, and with the other raised across the chest; the left-hand side of the body, as well as the torso and head, are missing. The

hieratic text on the back consists of traces of the beginning of six lines of hieratic, in black ink, in an administrative hand.

Contents: A list of personal names.

Translation:

(x+1) [...]

(x+2) [ ] The *wꜥb*-priest [ ]

(x+3) The *wꜥb*-priest Mery

(x+4) The *wꜥb*-priest Hatiay

(x+5) The *wꜥb*-priest Meryu

(x+6) [...]

Notes:

(x+2) There are traces of some signs before ⌇.

(x+5) In the writing of the title of Meryu ⌇ appears to have been omitted.

T3.A46 (pl. 35)

Excavation number: 21414/1020N6L118

Description: A small Nile clay pottery sherd from a New Kingdom jar, with two lines of hieratic on the outside and illegible traces of another line on the inside.

Contents: Names.

Translation:

(1) [...] Khnummose, Ma[...]

(2) [...]nakht(?) [...]

T3.A47 (pl. 36)

Excavation number: 21433/920N1L413

Description: A small limestone flake with one line of hieratic. The flake appears complete on all sides (the back is empty). There are traces of a glue-like substance with sand stuck to it around the edges and on the back, as if it had been deliberately attached to something.

Contents: Mentions 'servants' or 'workers'.

Translation:

(1) The workers.

Notes:

(1) Presumably this is an abbreviation for *nꜣ sḏm⟨w⟩-⟨ꜥš⟩*, 'the workers', and the plural is clearly intended despite the lack of plural strokes after the noun. Römer (pers. comm.) cites several examples of *sḏm* being written for *sḏm-ꜥš* in his contemporary material from Deir el-Bahri, both in titles and as a noun (e.g. O. Eg. Exp. 23001.166 + 168, lines 5 and 6; Eg. Exp. CF 6, line 9; BM EA 51833, lines 11 and 12; O. DAI 56, line 6; O. Leiden I 430, line 1; cf. O. Senenmut 69, line 1; Hayes 1942: pl. 14). One of my reviewers tentatively suggests that it may have been affixed to a vessel or box, 'as in later demotic, functioning as an organizational label system for the records'.

1.4 *Letters and Messages*

T3.A48 (pl. 36)

Excavation number: 9036 + 9138 RM (Ricke Magazine)

Description: A rim sherd from a New Kingdom beer jar, with three faint lines of hieratic, written on the convex side. There are traces of a band of decoration at the top, with a simple pattern made by the removal of small pellets of clay.

Contents: There is very little text preserved, but perhaps a message.

Translation:

(x+1)   [...]
(x+2)   [...] that you may make offerings (?)
(x+3)   [...] I will [...]

Notes:

(x+2) Müller (pers. comm.) alternatively suggests 'until you make offerings'. The horizontal stroke above the line probably belongs to 𓊩, as is common in Ramesside hieratic (cf. Möller 1927: II, no. 268).

T3.A49 (pl. 37)

Excavation number: 9080/950N1L208

Description: A limestone flake with a single line of hieratic: appears to be complete.

Contents: Perhaps a short message or marker concerning a commodity (provisions?) for Deir el-Bahari.

Translation:

(1)   Provisions (?) for Djeseru

Notes:

(1) The reading of the first group is not certain. If the transcription of the first group is correct then this short text concerns *wḥꜤ.w*, 'provisions' (*Wb.* 1, 350.10), a category of victuals also known from the Annals of Thutmose III (*Urk.* IV, 656.8); for a docket with this term see Pendlebury (1951: pl. xciv no. 250). Römer (pers. comm.) cites another example from ostracon BM EA 43271 (vso., line 1). Other alternatives might be to read the city group (𓊖 ?), although I am not sure what the meaning would then be (surely there is no 'city' at Deir el-Bahri); or, as Römer suggests, it might be the sun disc as the final element of a personal name. However, the space before the first signs in ink suggests that nothing in missing here, so one expects a self-contained phrase. A reviewer suggested to read it as the bread sign (𓏐), which is also possible.

T3.A50 (pl. 37)

Excavation number: 15486/910N5L214

Description: A rim sherd from a bowl of medium Nile clay, with the remains of three lines of hieratic on both the outside and the inside.

Contents: The classification of this ostracon is problematic, but perhaps an administrative letter or message, rather than a literary text.

Translation:

Outside:

(x+1)   [...]enta for Sen-Djehuty [...]
(x+2)   [...] about it [...]
(x+3)   [...]

Inside:

(x+1)   [...]
(x+2)   [...] work [...]
(x+3)   [...] Merisu for Sen-Djehuty [...]

Notes:

(x+1) The interpretation of the preposition *n* is problematic. It could be part of an abbreviated letter-formula (NN ⟨writes⟩ to NN), as on A53 below, or it could indicate possession, in the sense of responsibility ('on behalf of') in the context of the organisation of work. The latter I owe to a suggestion by Römer (pers. comm.). He further cites the following attestations for the name Sen-Djehuty in the Deir el-Bahri corpus: (1) an overseer of the granary of Amun, in O. Eg. Exp. 23001135 (line x+3), from the fourth decade of Thutmose III, and O. Berlin P. 19615 (line 2), from year 43. This is the well-known individual mentioned by Helck (1958: 388, 498). (2) two examples where there is no title preserved: O. Eg. Exp. 23001.122 (a name stone), and O. BM EA 47903 (line x+3).

(vso. x+3) Here interpretation of the *n* is plausibly that of responsibility and not the address formula, given its position within the text, as pointed out by Römer (pers. comm.); he also cites an example of the name Merisu on O. BM EA 41218 (line 1), and suggests that this may be an abbreviation for Merisuamun, who is mentioned on O. Eg. Exp. 23001.108 (vso., line 25) where a Merisuamun is said to be 'in Henket-ankh', i.e. in the temple of Thutmose III (Hayes 1960: 47, no. 21).

T3.A51 (pl. 38)

Excavation number: 20922/980N6L116

Description: A body sherd from a jar made of medium Nile clay, with the beginning of five lines of hieratic on one side. Incomplete on all sides except right-hand edge.

Contents: A message.

Translation:

(x+1)   [...]
(x+2)   [...] which are in the [...]
(x+3)   And hurry very much! You should receive [...]
(x+4)   Do not delay (?) [...]
(x+5)   this document [...]

Notes:

(x+3) The reading ꜣs is certain, but the traces of ⟶ are very faint.

(x+4) The expression *m ir di ꜥḥꜣ* is well attested with the meaning 'Do not cause (NN) to lack/wait', but the determinatives seem also to be influenced by ⌂⟶⧲ *ꜥḥꜥw*, 'lifetime', which might yield something like 'Do not pass your life …'. In view of the urgency of the message, as expressed in the line above, the former interpretation seems more likely.

T3.A52 (pl. 38)

Excavation number: 20923/980N6L116

Description: A body sherd probably of an oasis jar, with two lines of hieratic on one side; the hand is quite elaborate, perhaps even literary in style.

Contents: A message, or perhaps a literary text?

Translation:

(x+1)   [...] We will cut the cord [...]

(x+2)   [...] good [...], and those who are before you [...]

Notes:

(x+1) The first sign looks like ⧸ but without a context it is difficult to be sure.

(x+2) I owe the reading of the final group to Demarée.

T3.A53 (pls. 39–40)

Excavation number: 15855/840S3L717

Description: A limestone sherd with seven lines of hieratic in black ink on one side and five lines on the back, in an 18th Dynasty administrative hand. Complete on all sides.

Contents: A message about the recruitment of labourers for an unspecified building project involving workers from several different locations, including the mortuary temple of Thutmose III, Henket-ankh. The letter was presumably written elsewhere (perhaps Deir el-Bahri?) and then sent to the mortuary temple where it was found. Some aspects of transcription and syntax are difficult but there is a clear sense of urgency (cf. the triple *sp-sn* in lines 5–6) which may be the reason behind some of the mistakes in the text.

Translation:

Front

(1)   The scribe Amenhotep of Djeseru to the stone mason

(2)   Ahmose. Send two stone masons to me

(3)   in the morning, at Khaakhet.

(4)   Look, it is Benermerut

(5)   who has written about it!!!!!!

(6)   Look, the stone mason

(7)   Userhat

Back

(1)   is providing two additional stone masons;

(2)   two further stone masons will come

(3)   from the temple of Menkheperre (Thutmose III);

(4)   and another four stone masons will come from Djeseru;

(5)   In total: 10

Notes:

(2) The ink mark above the number is simply an accidental blot. The sense of *imi ir n=i* is clearly 'send me' or 'assign to me'. The stone mason Ahmose is also attested in the Deir el-Bahri ostraca that Malte Römer is preparing for publication (O. Eg. Exp. 23001.46, vso., line 5; O. BM EA 47908, vso., line 1); the latter of these is a message written to 'the Overseer of the House of Silver, Benermerut', who is also mentioned in this text (see note to line 4 below).

(3) The reading *nw m dwꜣ r ḥꜥ ꜣḥ.t* is certain. The first is a designation of time, and *r ḥꜥ ꜣḥ.t* defines the location. Römer (pers. comm.) notes the appearance of *ḥꜥ ꜣḥ.t* in O. Eg. Exp. 23001.72 (vso., line 5), and draws attention to a building called 'Amun-kha-⟨em⟩-akhet Maat-ka-re (= Hatshepsut)' (*imn-ḥꜥ-⟨m⟩-ꜣḥ.t-Mꜣꜥ.t-kꜣ-rꜥ*), often abbreviated to ⧈, which Brovarski argued refers to 'the central sanctuary at Deir el-Bahri with its outer bark room and inner sanctuary' (1976: 73; but cf. Helck 1960–1970: I, 93, who interprets it as a possible mortuary temple for princess Neferura). In the famous list of Theban temples in the tomb of Puyemre (TT 39) it notably occurs between Djeser-djeseru and Henket-ankh, whereas the comparable list in Rekhmire's tomb (TT 100) omits it (Davies 1922–1923: I, 94–95; II, 79–80).

(4) Benermerut is presumably to be identified with the Overseer of the House of Gold and the House of Silver of that name, who was also Overseer of Work of Amun (*imy-r kꜣ.t n imn*) and Overseer of All Works of the King (*imy-r kꜣ.t nb.t nt nsw*), active under Thutmose III in year 45 of his reign (Bryan 2006: 87; Helck 1958: 401, 509). He was involved in the contemporary building works at Deir el-Bahri, as the ostraca published by Hayes (1960: 46) show, and in O. MMA 23001.50 he is mentioned as one of the people responsible for providing (?) stone blocks along with the vizier Rekhmire ('List of the stones which are ⟨under⟩ the authority of … Benermerut'). The status of this high official is perhaps the reason for the extraordinary sense of urgency in the message (*bꜥ sp-sn sp-sn sp-sn*). Römer (pers. comm.) has identified two more examples of his name in this corpus: O. BM EA 47908 (vso., line 2), and O. Eg. Exp. 23001.51 (line 12; cf. Hayes 1960: 44 no. 17, but there misread; subsequently correctly identified by Römer). O. BM EA 47908 is particularly interesting in that it mentions both Ahmose (the addressee of A53) and 'his

lord, the Overseer of the House of Silver, Benermerut', in a letter also dealing with the management of personnel (line rto. x+3 includes the order 'Do not let [the workers?] be hindered', *m rdi isk* [...]).

(5) The syntax here is difficult. I interpret this as a participial statement, interpreting *m* as *in*. Alternatively *hзb* could perhaps in principle be the stative, which would yield a passive sense ('Benermerut has been sent about it'), but this does not suit the social context, given Benermerut's high status. In any case this would not be the only mistake in the text here, as there was clearly some confusion in the writing of the following signs: the scribe starting writing *hr≠s*, but left out the absolute stroke after 𓄿 and then seems to have changed his mind and inserted the masculine suffix ⌐ instead. I am grateful to Matthias Müller for the identification of the interjectory *bꜥ* (*Wb.* 1, 446.1–2).

(vso. 4) The traces of Djeseru are faint but certain. Römer (pers. comm.) notes that this would demonstrate construction activity at this site quite late (in the fourth decade of Thutmose IV) even if the precise nature of the work is not stated.

T3.A54 (pl. 41)

Excavation number: 21156/940S4L817

Description: Limestone, with eight lines of hieratic in black ink in an 18th Dynasty hand; complete on all sides.

Contents: A letter from a builder to his superior.

Translation:

(1) The builder Senna speaks to his lord,
(2) Senenmut. This is a letter to say
(3) that one has caused the directors to come
(4) in order to make the tents. Concern
(5) yourself with it.
(6) One (tent), look, it belongs to you;
(7) the other (tent) has been prepared for
(8) the Overseer of the South.

Notes:

(1) Römer (pers. comm.) reports that a builder Senna is well attested in the Deir el-Bahri ostraca from the building activities under Hatshepsut, including O. Eg. Exp. 23001.155 (line x+3), O. BM EA 51839 (line 4), and O. Chicago 13692 (line 1). The first gives the title 'builder' (*ḳd*), the second 'Overseer of Builders' (*imy-r ḳd.w*), while the third has no title, but deals with the delivery of 600 *mny*-jars of plaster, probably implying a builder. These sources may refer to a single individual. The activities of this individual under Hatshepsut in the aforementioned sources might indicate that A54 is among the earliest of the documents from the temple of Thutmose III, and Römer notes that the mention of Senenmut—if indeed this is the famous

one—further suggests a date before regnal year 20. Senenmut is admittedly not a unique name during this period, but the final line of the letter mentions another official of extremely high rank, the Overseer of the South, and so it seems likely that it is in fact the Steward Senenmut who is to be identified with the individual addressed here.

(3) The reading of the first group is difficult: 𓏭 is largely conjecture.

(4) The word *imзw* in most cases refers to tents or pavilions (*Wb.* 1, 81.1–7); it seems here to refer to temporary structures erected in connection with the visit of high-ranking officials to the work-site at Deir el-Bahri, because the message appears to have been sent from there (by Senna) to the temple of Thutmose III where it was found.

(5) The expression *ir sḥr* (*Wb.* IV, 260.5–16) seems to have the sense of ordering the addressee to direct his attention to the matter at hand. Römer (pers. comm.) notes that it is a relatively frequent expression in the Deir el-Bahri corpus of ostraca, mainly used as an imperative (followed by an object, either a suffix or a noun phrase introduced by an indirect genitive), but sometimes also following the imperative of *rdi*, as in this case.

(6) The syntax here is not entirely straightforward, and the following is based partly on comments by Römer. The initial group is clearly ⌐, and the scribe presumably omitted the following noun (*imз*, 'tent'?). For the expression of possession *n≠k imy*, see Satzinger (1986: 150–152), here with the dependent pronoun -*sw* as the antecedent.

(7) The expression *ḥr imз*, 'erect' or 'prepare' a tent, is relatively rare, with the *Wb.* (3, 146.15) listing only a single example from the love songs of P. Harris 500 (rto. 3.2–3; *ibꞋi r šmt ḥr ḥr⟨.t⟩ nз n imзw*, 'I wish to go and prepare the tents'), but as Mathieu (1996: 71) notes it also occurs in *The Pleasures of Fishing and Fowling* (Caminos 1956: 10, pl. 2, col. 2 line 3, translated as 'hut') and in the Hatshepsut Punt reliefs (*Urk.* IV, 325.12), where the Egyptian royal envoy is shown in front of a tent-like structure erected for him upon arrival (Naville 1898: pl. 69).

(8) The office of 'Overseer of the South' (*imy-r rsy*) was held by Min, Mayor of Thinis, at the time of Thutmose III (*Urk.* IV, 981.11).

T3.A55 (pl. 42)

Excavation number: 21523/910N8L218

Description: A limestone flake with faint traces of three lines of hieratic in black ink.

Contents: A message regarding offerings for a festival.

Translation:

(1) Now then, you should [prepare/provide?] the offerings

(2)   for the *w3g* festival [...]

(3)   the morning (?).

Notes:

(1) The verb is unclear but it certainly contains the sign ⟜.

    (3) After *dw3* there are some further signs but written with a different, broader reed pen—these are presumably unrelated to the preceding text. Perhaps they could be read 𓏤𓏤𓎱?

1.5   *Varia*

T3.A56 (pl. 43)

Excavation number: 15131/930–940N5L113

Description: A limestone flake with three columns of hieratic, largely complete except for a flake missing on the left hand edge.

Contents: Three recipes for mudbrick, all with varying amounts of clay, straw, sand, and something called *nms*-soil. Water is not mentioned but would obviously have used to bind the mixture together.

Translation:

	Column I	Column II	Column III
(1)	Clay: 1/3	Another (recipe):	Another (recipe):
(2)	*nms*-soil: 2/3	Clay: 1/2	*nms*-soil: 2/3
(3)	Straw: 1/3	*nms*-soil: 1/2	Sand: 1/3
(4)	Sand: 1/3	Straw: 1/2	Straw: 1/3
(5)		Sand: 1/4	[...]

Notes:

(I.1) The fraction here (and in I.3, I.4, III.3 and III.4) is not identical to the standard forms listed by Möller, but roughly similar to some of the Middle Kingdom writings of '1/3' (Möller no. 669), e.g. in the Kahun mathematical papyrus (P. UC 32160, I.4; II.4, 5; II.6, 7; IV.1; Griffith 1898: pl. VIII, no. IV.3; Collier and Quirke 2004: 84–89).

    (I.2) The precise meaning of *nms*-soil escapes me; perhaps a type of mixed earth?

    (II.1) The word *kt*, 'another' is used as a heading as is common in medical and religious literature.

    (III.5) There are illegible traces under line 4, which may have corresponded to a final ingredient, but they are not compatible with the expected *sin*, 'clay' (as in columns I and II).

T3.A57 (pl. 44)

Excavation number: 15619/950N6L114

Description: A sherd from the base of a slightly rounded jar with red slip surface ('Middle or New Kingdom'), with a single line of hieratic, and some ink blots.

Contents: Perhaps an administrative jotting mentioning scribes of Amun and Khonsu?

Translation:

(1)   The scribes (?) of Amun (?) and Khonsu (?) [...]

T3.A58 (pl. 44)

Excavation number: 8943/970S1L114

Description: Perhaps a body sherd from a marl clay jar, with only a few signs visible, distributed randomly across the surface.

Contents: The only clearly visible sign, in the middle, might be an identity mark. No translation is possible, but for these identity marks in general, and on this sign in particular, see Haring (2018: 15, 170–173).

T3.A59 (pl. 45)

Excavation number: 21140/980S6L717

Description: A limestone fragment with a single line of hieratic; complete.

Contents: A measurement of length.

Translation:

(1)   8 cubits, 5 palms, and 2 fingers.

Notes:

(1) The sign for *db*ꜥ is repeated twice: it cannot be 𓏤𓏤𓏤, based on the form of 𓏤 immediately before. In total the measurement given corresponds to c. 460 cm.

T3.A60 (pl. 45)

Excavation number: 21434/900N8L118

Description: A rather bulky and heavy (just over 2 kg) limestone piece with one line of hieratic in the middle of the surface; complete on all sides.

Contents: Orders to bake (?).

Translation:

(1)   The *bit*-bread: 4 times; *psn*-bread: 1 (time?).

Notes:

(1) The definite article would be rare in a regular account, as would the specification '4 times'. Combined with the unusual physical size of the ostracon—almost like a marker of sorts—it makes for a curious object. Could it be baking instructions, perhaps meant to be displayed somewhere? Or should the initial group be read 𓂝, 'giving', instead?

T3.A61 (pl. 46)

Excavation number: 21471/970N4L4018

Description: A small Nile clay pottery sherd from a beer jar, of the early- to mid-18th Dynasty, with four lines of signs in black ink. Some of the signs are recognisably hieratic but I cannot read the text. It is included here mainly to make it accessible to colleagues.

Contents: Unknown.

Translation: Not possible.

2   Dockets

Unless otherwise noted all dockets come from the rubbish dump to the north-east of the temple.

2.1   *Wine*

T3.D01 (pl. 46)

Excavation number: 15414/900N5L6613

Description: A sherd from a Phoenician amphora with the beginning of two lines of hieratic.

Translation:

(1)   Regnal year [...]

(2)   Wine [...]

T3.D02 (pl. 47)

Excavation number: 15424/900N5L6613

Description: A body sherd of a jar of marl clay, with the parts of three lines of hieratic. The last line is in a broader brush and looks like a different hand, and probably does not belong to the docket. Our ceramicist writes that it is 'probably dated to the Late Period', but I think this would be incompatible with the date of the regnal year in the opening formula, as well as the style of the hieratic.

Translation:

(1)   Regnal year 37. Wine of the [Western?] river (?) [...]

(2)   (by) the chief vintner Neferrenpet (?)

(3)   [...] divine offerings (?) [...]

Notes:

(1) Regnal year 37 has to refer to either Thutmose III or Amenhotep III; the latter is perhaps more likely in view of the similar label below (D05). The end of the line is difficult, and the restoration is simply a suggestion based on the many similar labels from Malqata and Amarna.

(2) The first sign in the name of the chief vintner is not clear, and my reading is perhaps speculative: Demarée suggests that this sign might also be 𓏭.

T3.D03 (pl. 47)

Excavation number: 15439/930–940N5L213

Description: A indeterminate pottery sherd with two lines of hieratic.

Translation:

(1)   [Regnal year ...] Wine of the temple of [...]

(2)   [...] the vintner [...]

Notes:

(1) The traces at the beginning are faint but certain.

(2) The final signs are difficult; presumably the sign after the house determinative of *kꜣmw* is the beginning of the name of the vintner.

T3.D04 (pl. 48)

Excavation number: 15449/910–920N5L413

Description: A small indeterminate pottery sherd, but probably from a wine jar, with a single line of hieratic.

Translation:

(1)   [Year] 2. Wine of [...]

T3.D05 (pl. 48)

Excavation number: 15622 + 20432/890N5L114

Description: A body sherd, probably of an oasis jar, with a wine jar label consisting of two lines of hieratic.

Translation:

(1)   [Year] 37. Wine of the estate of Amenhotep, l.p.h., on

(2)   the western [river], the chief vintner Hat.

Notes:

(1) The high year date can only refer to Thutmose III or Amenhotep III; if the vintner is the same as in the Malqata wine jar labels (see below) then it must be the latter pharaoh.

(2) The reading of the name is not quite certain: Demarée suggests as an alternative 𓀁𓏏, but I think 𓀁𓏏𓎡 is marginally more likely. Admittedly the name Hat is relatively common in the New Kingdom (Ranke 1935: 232.13), but a 'chief vintner Hat' is named in one of the Malqata wine jar labels from year 30 dockets, and this could be the same individual (Hayes 1951: fig. 20).

T3.D06 (pl. 49)

Excavation number: 15655/940N6L214

Description: A pottery sherd of an indeterminate nature, with two lines of hieratic on the outside.

Translation:

(1)   Year 35 (?).

(2)   [The vin]tner Amenmose of Amenhep (?).

Notes:

(1) The year number is difficult to decipher, but if 35 is correct then this could be either Thutmose III or Amenhotep III. Demarée suggests 55 as an alternative, which would have to refer to the latter king, but this would be the highest year date attested for him: a year 53 has so far been the highest (Hornung, Krauss and Warburton 2006: 202).

(2) If the two lines share the right hand margin then there would not have been space for 'chief vintner' (*ḥry kꜣmw*). Demarée plausibly interprets 'Amenhep (?)' as a locality rather than a filiation.

T3.D07 (pl. 49)

Excavation number: 15679/970N6L115

Description: Probably a body sherd of a Canaanite jar, with two lines of hieratic on the outside; several of the readings are due to Rob Demarée.

Translation:

(1)　Year [...]

(2)　Merywaset, the chief [vintner ...]

Notes:

(1) The traces are compatible with *rnpt*, but the reading is far from certain.

(2) One expects the end of the name of the institution from which the commodity (most likely wine) came here, so a royal name may be missing, followed by the epithet 'beloved of Thebes'. The most likely candidate is perhaps Thutmose IV, whose titulary included 'Strong Bull, Beloved of Thebes' (Beckerath 1999: 139). The traces at the end would fit the first word of the title *ḥry kꜣmw*.

T3.D08 (pl. 50)

Excavation number: 20047/890N5L114

Description: An indeterminate pottery sherd with two lines of hieratic.

Translation:

(1)　Year 20+ [...].

(2)　river [...]

Notes:

(2) Probably *itrw* rather than *irp* (suggestion by Démaree).

T3.D09 (pl. 50)

Excavation number: 20433/890N5L114

Description: Perhaps a body sherd of an oasis jar, although the section is unclear, which carries three lines of hieratic.

Translation:

(1)　Year 32.

(2)　Very good wine of Ma[...]

(3)　Chief vintner of the estate (?) [...]

Notes:

(1) Again a relatively high year date, perhaps also of Amenhotep III (or, conceivably, of Thutmose III). This is the only mention of 'very good' (*nfr nfr*) quality wine in the corpus.

(2) The traces at the end are largely illegible, but one expects a toponym.

(3) The group [glyph] at the end is probable, and is more likely to refer to the institution to which the vintner belonged, rather than being the first element of a (feminine) personal name.

T3.D10 (pl. 51)

Excavation number: 20458/890N5L214

Description: A pottery sherd ('probably of an imported fabric') with traces of two lines of hieratic.

Translation:

(1)　[... Year ...]

(2)　Wine of the estate [...]

(3)　Chief vintner [...]

T3.D11 (pl. 51)

Excavation number: 20879/890N6L116

Description: A body sherd, 'probably an imported jar (Canaanite)', with two lines of hieratic.

Translation:

(1)　[Year ... wine] of the estate of the Aten, l.p.h., for/of

(2)　[... by the] chief vintner Neferperet (?)

Notes:

(1) For the estate of the Aten, see the wine jar labels from Amarna published by Petrie (1894: pl. xxii nos. 18, 23, 27, 28, 29); the same estate was also responsible for the delivery of other commodities to Amarna (cf. pls. xxiii–xxiv), but is notably absent in the thousands of dockets from Malqata of the reign of Amenhotep III. The mention of this estate here is interesting in that it suggests that this particular docket post-dates the Amarna period, despite the lack of a year date and royal name, and so provides evidence of wine deliveries at the temple of Thutmose III in the mid- to late 18th Dynasty. This would at least not contradict the interpretation of high year dates in other dockets (see above) as belonging to Amenhotep III, rather than Thutmose III.

(2) The reading of the final element of the name is not quite certain, but he seems not to be otherwise attested among the 'chief vintners' of other 18th Dynasty dockets.

T3.D12 (pl. 52)

Excavation number: 21340/970N6L317

Description: A pottery sherd from an imported New Kingdom amphora, with two lines of hieratic.

Translation:

(1)　[Year ...] of the estate of Menmaatre, l.p.h. [...]

(2)　[...] pharaoh, forever.

Notes:

(1) The initial part of the docket is lost, so the date (and commodity) remains unknown, but the mention of an estate of Seti I obviously provides a *terminus ante quem non*, and thus represents the only docket that is demonstrably from the Nineteenth Dynasty in this corpus.

(2) This line presumably contained details of who was responsible for the manufacture (and/or delivery) of the commodity contained in the jar, identified by title, name and institutional affiliation (compare e.g. Hayes 1951: fig. 5 no. 34; fig. 6 nos. 47, 51; fig. 7 nos. 59 for examples with a similar structure).

T3.D13 (pl. 52)

Excavation number: 21519/900N8L118

Description: A pottery sherd from an imported 18th Dynasty amphora, with traces of one line of hieratic.

Translation:

(1)   Wine of the temple (ḥw.t) of [...]

2.2   *Fowl*

T3.D14 (pl. 53)

Excavation number: 20425/900N5L214

Description: A body sherd, probably of an imported jar, with one line of hieratic.

Translation:

(1)   [... meat of pond-fowl] of *ms.t*-birds: 60 (?)

Notes:

(1) The reading [... *ꜣpd mr*] *n mst* [...] and its interpretation as a docket for a jar of fowl was initially suggested to me by Démaree; cf. the similar examples from Malqata published by Hayes (1951: fig. 13), and the Deir el-Medina dockets listed by Valbelle (1985: 278). One expects a number to follow: '60' is just possible and would be in line with numbers from the Malqata dockets (which have an example with 70); as Hayes remarked most of these types of birds must therefore have been rather small. For the rather general term 'pond-fowl' see the discussion by Hayes (1951: 92), and for the specific *ms.t*-bird, see Grandet (1994: II, 98 n. 388; 'espèce indéterminée'); the restoration is based on D15 below.

T3.D15 (pl. 53)

Excavation number: 20482/890N5L214

Description: A pottery sherd ('probably from an imported jar'), with one line of hieratic.

Translation:

(1)   Good quality meat of pond-fowl of *ms.t*-birds

(2)   [for the] *sed*-festival [...]

Notes:

(1) For the (mis)writing of ⟨glyph⟩ as ⟨glyph⟩ see Hayes (1951: 92 n. 132, and fig. 13 no. 180). Like other commodities the quality of fowl meat could be indicated, as in this case, by the addition of *nfr* (or even in some cases *nfr nfr*, 'very good').

(2) The reading *ḥb-sd* is certain (cf. D23), despite the faintness of the traces, but whether this refers to Thutmose III or Amenhotep III is unknown. Cf. D21 and D23 below.

T3.D16 (pl. 53)

Excavation number: 21467/910N8SD18

Description: A marl clay pottery sherd from an 18th Dynasty amphora, with traces of two lines of hieratic.

Translation:

(1)   [...] of *ms.t*-birds: 60, for [...]

(2)   [...] l.p.h.

T3.D17 (pl. 3)

Excavation number: 15078/920N4L213

Description: An indeterminate pottery sherd with traces of three lines of hieratic; incomplete at the right and left hand edge, but perhaps nothing lost above in view of the empty space.

Contents: A jar label mentioning a specific festival.

Translation:

(1)   [...] of butchered pond-fowl for the sixth-day festival [...]

(2)   [...] the estate of Meryptah (?) of [...]

(3)   50.

Notes:

(1) The 'sixth-day festival' (*snwt*, from an abbreviation of the ordinal number *srs/sis-nwt*, 'sixth') occurs in offering lists of Thutmose III from Buto (Bedier 1994: 38, 43 n. 38) and Karnak (*Urk.* IV, 177), and is here attested also on an ostracon from his Temple of a Million Years; there are further mentions in some fragments from the daybook of the temple (Hagen, In preparation B). For a discussion of this recurrent monthly festival in a diachronic perspective, see Barta (1969) and Winter (1970), with references to a number of other New Kingdom sources. This festival was an important part of the temple year, and activities mentioned in relation to it in roughly contemporary sources include 'presenting great offerings to Re on the sixth-day festival in Heliopolis' in the Book of the Dead (BD 1, 17–18) and 'bringing the garland (*ms ꜥnḫ*) on the day of the sixth-day festival' in the *Daily Ritual of Amenhotep I* (= P. Chester Beatty 9, rto. 14.8–9; Gardiner 1935: I, 97; II, pl. 56); this latter source also contains the ritual instructions which include the presentation of water, beer, meat, wine, milk and various types of fruit, albeit not in quantities that would match the number '50' in line 3.

(2) The reading of this line is uncertain. One expects a provenance here, so I tentatively read [...] *pr mryw-ptḥ*, but I am not sure how to reconcile the traces at the beginning with any known formulae. The name is also difficult: one of the crucial signs is the *p* in *ptḥ*, which is faint, and there may or may not be a horizontal stroke above it (and so could be either *ḫr* or *p*). In view of this one of my reviewers suggests the alternative reading *pr-ḫry*, (*Wb.* 3, 389.1), so '[...] the cellar (?) of Mery [...]' or similar.

2.3 Date-Beer

T3.D18 (pl. 54)

Excavation number: 20551/1000S6L114

Description: A small body sherd from a jar of marl clay, with traces of two lines of hieratic on one side.

Contents: A jar label for date beer or date mash.

Translation:

(x+1) [...] date beer [...]

(x+2) [...]

Notes:

(1) In the Malqata dockets *srm.t* is always followed by *dbḥw*, which Hayes (1951: 90) translated as 'date-beer of offerings', indicating the central role of this social context for this commodity. The precise nature of *srm.t* is contested, and seems to vary depending on the context: it has been variously interpreted as some kind of date beer, date mash, or, in dried form, as a solid brick (Gardiner 1947: I, 15; II 234.563; Helck 1960–1970: 691–692; 1971: 23, 30, 32; Caminos 1954: 81; Wallert 1962: 29–32), or even as a sweet malt-grain by-product of beer brewing (Samuel 2000: 554–557).

2.4 Uncertain Commodities

T3.D19 (pl. 54)

Excavation number: 9244/910S2L110

Description: An indeterminate pottery sherd with traces of the beginning of one line of hieratic, probably a (wine?) jar label. The surface has partly fallen off in places, complicating the reading.

Translation:

(1) Regnal year 4 [...]

Notes:

(1) The signs after the year number are difficult to interpret. The first sign looks like a reed leaf which might mean that it is another wine label, but the determinative doesn't look quite right.

T3.D20 (pl. 54)

Excavation number: 15197/R1L113

Description: A pottery sherd from a Canaanite jar with traces of the beginning of one line of hieratic, probably a jar label.

Translation:

(1) Regnal year 2 [...]

T3.D21 (pl. 55)

Excavation number: 15571/930N6L114

Description: A small indeterminate pottery sherd with three lines of hieratic, where the surface is flaking off.

Translation:

(1) Year 33 [...

(2) [... for] the repetition of the *sed*-festival [...]

(3) [... made by ...] Thutmose.

Notes:

(x+1) The year number is clearly 30 + a single digit number. This second number is partly damaged but was most likely '3' as there is no trace of a fourth stroke; the reading '6' might be possible if it had been written with six separate strokes, but this would be unusual for a hieratic docket.

(x+2) The reading of *wḥm*, which I owe to Rob Demarée, is unclear but plausible; compare the Malqata dockets published by Hayes (1951: 83–84, with nos. 34, 130–131, 134, 136, 158, 159–161). At Malqata, wine, date-beer (? *srm.t*), fat, meat, fowl, and oil are all said to have been manufactured specifically for the *sed*-festivals of Amenhotep III. Thutmose III is known to have celebrated three *sed*-festivals (Hornung and Staehelin 1974: 31–32; 2006: 23–24; Troy 2006: 148–150); of these the first is mentioned in the famous Akhmenu or Festival Hall at Karnak (e.g. *Urk.* IV, 594.13), and the third in the inscription on the London obelisk from Heliopolis (*Urk.* IV, 590.15). The first may have been celebrated in his year 30 (but cf. Redford 1986: 185), according to the standard ideal, but when the next two took place is never explicitly stated. An inscription from Deir El-Bersha (*Urk.* IV, 597.12–13) opens with 'Year 33, 4th month of Shomu, day 12. Beginning of many millions of *sed*-festivals' (*ḥзt ḥḥ m ḥb.w-sd ʿšз wrt*), which has been interpreted to mean that this was when the second festival took place (Hornung and Staehelin 2006: 34). The current docket seems to confirm that this second *sed*-festival of Thutmose III took place in year 33, and that it was celebrated in his mortuary temple. This is of some interest because similar documentation from deliveries in connection with actual *sed*-festivals is otherwise rare, being in practice restricted to Amenhotep III's celebrations at Malqata in year 30, 34, and 37 of his reign (Hornung and Staehelin 2006: 33). Cf. D23 for another mention of a 'repetition' of a *sed*-festival.

T3.D22 (pl. 55)

Excavation number: 21495/910N8L118

Description: A marl clay pottery sherd from a New Kingdom amphora, with traces of two lines of hieratic.

Translation:

(1) [...]

(2) [... *nḥḥ*?]-oil, fresh and best quality, from the chief vintner [...]

Notes:

(2) The traces at the beginning might suit [*n*]*ḥḥ*, which is probably 'olive oil' (Krauss 1999). There are relatively few published jar labels for *nḥḥ*-oil (Pendlebury 1951: pl. xcv no.

268, 271–274; Hayes 1951: fig. 14 no. 200; cf. Bouvier 2003: 32), so comparanda for the formula is not easy to find. It is attested as 'fresh', like so many other oils and fats (e.g. *ꜥḏ*-fat and *bꜣḳ*-oil; Hayes 1951: figs. 10–11; fig. 13 nos. 183, 186, 191–193). I cannot cite any examples of *nḥḥ*-oil with the description 'best' (*tp*), but it is occasionally used to describe other oils, perhaps as a synonym for *nfr*, 'good' (compare Hayes 1951: fig. 13 no. 194 with Pendlebury 1951: pl. xcvi nos. 293–294, with *bꜣḳ*-oil as, respectively, *tp*, 'best' and *nfr nfr*, 'very good').

T3.D23 (pl. 78)

Excavation number: 15321/910–920N5L313

Description: A pottery sherd with two lines of hieratic.

Contents: A docket, probably for meat or fat.

Translation:

(1)   [...] for the repetition of the *sed*-festival, from the stock-yard of

(2)   [...] Hapy-aa (?)

Notes:

(1) I am grateful to Müller for assistance with the identification of this as a docket (and for the reading of line 2). The mention of a 'stock-yard' (*ꜣḥ.t*) suggests either meat or fat as the original commodity contained in the jar (cf. Hayes 1951: 92). There are relatively few dockets from the temple mentioning a *sed*-festival (D23 and D15), but the festival is depicted or alluded to in the temple decoration (Chapon 2018).

3   Literary Texts

3.1   *The Instruction of Amenemhat*

T3.L01 (pl. 56)

Excavation number: 9137 RM (Ricke Magazine)

Description: A body sherd from an Egyptian marl clay amphora, with the end of four lines of hieratic in black ink, with red verse-points in lines x+2, x+3, and x+4. On the right-hand edge there are extremely faint traces of one or more lines, probably intentionally erased in antiquity; these are illegible but contain both black and red ink.

Contents: *The Instruction of Amenemhat I* (§ 2c–3a)

Translation:

(x+1)   [...]

(x+2)   [... Do not approach them when you are alone.] Trust no [brother ....]

(x+3)   [... Make for yourself] no intimates—this is of no [avail ...]

(x+4)   [... You should sleep with ⟨your own heart⟩ watching] over you [...]

Notes:

(x+1) Only traces are left here (perhaps 𓂝?) but they are difficult to reconcile with the expected verse-lines of the text.

(x+4) The ink is faint but the scribe has clearly left out *ib≠k ḏs≠k* before the verse-point, as was also done on O. DeM 1021 (Adrom 2006: 21).

T3.L02 (pl. 57)

Excavation number: 15399/930N6L113

Description: A body sherd of medium Nile clay jar, with three broken lines of hieratic in a broad and unpractised hand.

Contents: *The Instruction of Amenemhat I* (§ 1d).

Translation:

(x+1)   [...]

(x+2)   [... Listen to what I tell] you, that [you] may be king [of the land ...]

(x+3)   [...]

Notes:

(x+1) The traces here are not easy to interpret—might they belong to § 1a?

T3.L03 (pls. 58–60)

Excavation number: 15537/930N4L714

Description: A body sherd of a marl clay jar, seemingly complete on all sides, with four lines of hieratic in a Ramesside literary hand, with red verse-points. To the left of the last line is a date in red ink.

Contents: *The Instruction of Amenemhat I* (§ 2a–3a)

Translation:

(x+1)   Concentrate against subjects who prove non-existent, in whose respect

(x+2)   no faith can be placed! Do not approach them when you are alone! Trust no brother!

(x+3)   Know no friend! Make for yourself no intimates—this is of no avail!

(x+4)   You should sleep with [your own heart watching over you]. **Month 2 of Shomu, day 6.**

Notes:

(x+1) There is a rather unusual omission of 𓏏 in *smdt*.

(x+2) The addition of 𓀀𓏤 before the verse-point is not attested in any other source for the text, and the copyist appears to have been confused by the similarity of the pronoun *ntk* and the construction *m tkn* ('Do not approach'). He clearly also had problems with Middle Egyptian negations, and has for good measure put in both *nn* and *m* here and in line 3 below, instead of the simple negative imperative *m* which most other sources have: this double negation is also attested on an ostracon from the Ramesseum (O. CRB 96/SE/32; Adrom 2006: 14). Finally, the scribe omitted a verse-point at the end of the line (before *m mḥ ib≠k* …).

(x+3) The negation is written *nn m*, as in the line above.

(x+4) As often with ostraca containing extracts of literary texts, the scribe has ended with the first line of the next stanza of the text. The final part of this line is partly illegible because of the faintness of the ink, but there does not appear to be quite enough space for the whole verse-line before the date on the left.

T3.L04 (pl. 57)

Excavation number: 15686/980N5L315

Description: A pottery sherd of indeterminate fabric, with traces of two lines of hieratic in black ink. The signs are large and elaborated, almost like cursive hieroglyphs.

Contents: *The Instruction of Amenemhat I* (§ 2a–d).

Translation:

(x+1)   [Focus yourself against subjects who are] non-existent, in whom one cannot [place any faith.]

(x+2)   [Do not approach them when you are alone. Do not trust] a brother, do not know a friend […]

Notes:

(x+1) The traces match the text of the end of § 2a and the beginning of § 2b, although the determinative of *tmt* appears to have been omitted, judging from the space available (compare Adrom 2006: 10–11).

T3.L05 (pl. 57)

Excavation number: 15718/1010N6L215

Description: A sherd from marl clay jar ('New Kingdom or Late Period') with traces of two lines of hieratic in black ink. The hand is characterised by relatively large signs (perhaps copied by a student?), but there is nothing to suggest a post-New Kingdom date, despite the uncertainty of the ceramic diagnostics.

Contents: *The Instruction of Amenemhat I* (§ 1b–d).

Translation:

(x+1)   [Beginning of the Teaching made by the majesty of the Dual King, Sehetepibre, the Son of Re, Amenem]hat, the justified, [when he spoke in a revelation to his son, the Lord of All.]

(x+2)   [He said: 'Rise as a god! Listen to what I tell you, that you may be king of] the land, and rule [the Banks …']

Notes:

(x+1) Despite the brevity of the extract the identification is plausible: the reading of the royal name '[Amenem]hat' can hardly be doubted, and combined with the traces on the second line the conclusion must be that this is from *The Instruction of Amenemhat I*.

T3.L06 (pl. 57)

Excavation number: 20478 + 20547/940N6L214

Description: A small body sherd of a sandy fabric jar with gritty touch, very similar in fabric to L07, with remains of three lines of hieratic in black ink.

Contents: *The Instruction of Amenemhat I* (§ 4b–d)

Translation:

(x+1)   […]

(x+2)   [It was someone who ate my food who caused trouble, someone to whom I had given my help was raising plots] with it […]

(x+3)   [someone clad in my fine linen] was looking at me [as if needy]

(x+4)   [someone anointed with my myrrh] was [pouring water in return.]

T3.L07 (pl. 61)

Excavation number: 20749/1010N6L215

Description: A small body sherd of a jar, similar to L06, with traces of two lines of hieratic.

Contents: *The Instruction of Amenemhat I* (§ 1b)

Translation:

(x+1)   […]

(x+2)   [Beginning of the Teaching made by] the Dual King Sehetep[ibre …]

Notes:

(x+1) There is only a long diagonal stroke left of this line, but this does not seem to belong to the same text.

(x+2) The traces of *ḥtp* at the end are certain. The identification of this as a copy of *The Instruction of Amenemhat I* rests solely on his name, but it is difficult to imagine a different context for it in an 18th Dynasty (or Ramesside?) manuscript like this.

T3.L08 (pl. 61)

Excavation number: 20771/1000N6L115

Description: A small body sherd, 'probably from a Levantine jar', with remains of the beginning of three lines of hieratic in black ink.

Contents: *The Instruction of Amenemhat I* (§ 1a–c)

Translation:

(1)   Beginning [of the Teaching made by the majesty of the Dual King, Sehetepibre,]

(2)   the Son of Re, [Amenemhat, the justified, when he spoke in a revelation]

(3)   to his son [the Lord of All …]

Notes:

(1) The traces are faint but combined with the other lines both the reading and the identification of the text is certain.

T3.L09 (pl. 61)

Excavation number: 20532/950N6L114

Description: A small pottery sherd from a fine marl clay jar, with parts of two lines of hieratic in black ink; quite similar in style and fabric to L06 and L07 above.

Contents: *The Instruction of Amenemhat I* (§ 1a–c)

Translation:

(x+1)   [... to his son, the Lord] of All [...]

(x+2)   [...], that you may rule [the land ...]

T3.L10 (pl. 62)

Excavation number: 21053/980N5L517

Description: A marl clay pottery sherd from the rim of a New Kingdom meat jar, with remains of three lines of hieratic in black ink, and a single red verse-point in line 3.

Contents: *The Instruction of Amenemhat I* (§ 6a–e)

Translation:

(1)   It was after supper, when darkness [had fallen, and I had spent a happy time.]

(2)   I was lying on my bed [since I was tired, and my heart had begun to follow sleep.]

(3)   [...]

Notes:

(3) The traces of a verse-point followed by 𓏏𓏭 suggests the start of § 6e.

3.2 *Kemit*

T3.L11 (pl. 63)

Excavation number: 9163/940S2L910

Description: A rim sherd of a New Kingdom beer jar, with two columns of hieratic in an archaic style. The hand is unpractised and irregular, giving the impression of a beginning student. The text is written in columns with black dividing lines.

Contents: *Kemit* (sections 3–4)

Translation:

(x+1)   [...] Lord of Thebes, like [this servant] wants

(x+2)   [...] its walls [...]

T3.L12 (pl. 63)

Excavation number: 9186/940S2L1510

Description: A pottery sherd with a single column of hieratic in an archaic style. The hand is unpractised and irregular, very similar to that of T3.L11 above. There are traces of a black dividing line immediately to the right of the column, but the vertical line to the left seems too far from the text to delineate the column width.

Contents: *Kemit* (section 1)

Translation:

(x+1)   [... a se]rvant speaks to his lord [...]

T3.L13 (pl. 64)

Excavation number: 15421/920N6L113

Description: A limestone fragment, perhaps from a stela or a relief. On the front there is a raised ridge, the only sign of original decoration; the surface is polished on all sides with the exception of the back. A slight trace of ink at the bottom shows that the object was already broken when it was inscribed. The narrowness of the fragment means that each side only carries a single column of text, all of which is in the usual "archaic" style of hieratic. The hand is relatively unpractised, and despite the shortness of the extract there is at least one mistake. On the back are only a few signs, perhaps pen trials using the signs 𓏥 and 𓂝.

Contents: *Kemit* (section 1).

Translation:

Side A

(1)   A servant speaks to his lord [...]

Side B

(2)   as he loves life [...]

Side C

(3)   [individual signs only]

Notes:

(2) The quail chick is virtually unrecognisable but can hardly be anything else. The student has mistakenly switched the sequence of signs in the writing of *ꜥnḫ*.

T3.L14 (pl. 63)

Excavation number: 20564/920N6L414

Description: A small hard rock pebble with naturally rounded edges carrying the faint remains of three columns in black ink on one side and a drawing (?) on the other. Complete but for a small piece broken away at the bottom. The script is the regular archaising style used for *Kemit*, but the use of hard stone (as opposed to a limestone flake or a pottery sherd) is unusual.

Contents: *Kemit* (section 1)

Translation:

(1)   It is a servant who speaks [to]

(2)   his lord (?) [...]

(3)   69 (?) [...]

Notes:

(2) There are only faint traces left of the second column, and my reading is tentative: only the top sign is vaguely recognisable.

(3) This column is also mostly illegible. The first sign might be either '60' or ☐, and the sign underneath could be '9'; in any case it is incompatible with the expected continuation of *Kemit*.

T3.L15 (pl. 65)

Excavation number: 20877/980N5L416

Description: A small pottery sherd, of indeterminate nature, with a single column of hieratic in an archaic style. The hand seems confident and experienced. There are traces of black dividing lines. The other side has a competent drawing of an uraeus in front of a sun-disc.

Contents: *Kemit* (section 1)

Translation:

(1)   [It is a servant] who speaks to [his lord …]

T3.L16 (pl. 65)

Excavation number: 20729/1010N6L215

Description: A pottery sherd with traces of a column of hieratic in an archaising style.

Contents: Probably *Kemit* (section 1) on one side—the identification is based partly on the script—and a drawing on the other (unidentified motif).

Translation:

(x+1)   [… servant?] there […]

3.3   *The Instruction of Khety*

T3.L17 (pl. 66)

Excavation number: 9321/940S5L211

Description: A small indeterminate pottery sherd with the remains of two lines of hieratic on the outside.

Contents: Probably *The Instruction of Khety* (§ 25b), although there is only a word or two preserved so it is impossible to be certain.

Translation:

(x+1)   […]

(x+2)   [… speak no secret matters;] the discreet man [makes himself a shield …]

T3.L18 (pls. 67–68)

Excavation number: 15685/1010N4L115

Description: A rim sherd from a hole-mouthed jar of marl B clay, probably New Kingdom in date, with three lines of hieratic in black ink, with red verse-points throughout and a date at the end.

Contents: *The Instruction of Khety* (§ 15.1–5).

Translation:

(1)   The weapon-maker is utterly despondent as he goes out into the desert; great is that which he has to give the donkeys,

(2)   more than (the worth of) the work thereof; great is that which he has to give to those who dwell in the marshes, who show him [the way];

(3)   [and when he finally reaches his house in the evening,] he is broken by the walking. **Month 2 of Shomu, day 20.**

Notes:

(3) Most copies of the text have *wdꜥ* (literally 'to cut') here, as opposed to the 18th Dynasty writing board Louvre 693 which has *mdd* ('to hit/press'), with the determinative ⸗⸗ (Aa23; cf. Jäger 2004: LVII). The phonetic signs are faint, but they seem to match the expected *wdꜥ*, with the exception of the determinative which is almost certainly the same as on the Louvre board.

T3.L19 (pl. 66)

Excavation number: 20873/980N5L316 + 980N5L416

Description: Two pottery sherds from the body of a marl clay jar that join, one of which is very faint, with the remains of four lines of hieratic in black ink, and several red verse-points.

Contents: *The Instruction of Khety* (§ 28.3–5); this is a difficult passage and the translation below follows Parkinson (1997: 280–281).

Translation:

(x+1)   [Speak no falsehood with your mouth …]

(x+2)   […] Do not take enjoyment [with the troublesome …]

(x+3)   [… If you are fed with three loaves of bread,] and 2 jars of beer have been drunk […]

(x+4)   [… If another is being fed,] do not wait around; beware [of going up to the table …]

Notes:

(x+1) Only a verse-point visible; the hieratic is completely washed away.

(x+4) This version has a clear negative imperative (*m sꜣw*) here, like P. Sallier II and O. DeM 1019, probably incorrectly: see Jäger (2004: 152).

T3.L20 (pls. 79–80)

Excavation number: 15500/900N5L214

Description: A body sherd of Nile clay of a vat ('it belongs to the same pot as 15545 but does not join'), with two extracts from literary classics: the first (A) is a single long line running across the entire sherd, whereas the second (B) consists only of the ends of four lines. There are also faint traces of red ink at the very top, in a larger hand, which are very difficult to read.

Contents: The first line, running across the sherd, is from *The Instruction of Khety* (§ 9.1–2), and the ends of the four other lines from *The Instruction of Amenemhat* (c.

§1d–3c, perhaps also §4c). I owe the identification of both to Matthias Müller (pers. comm.).

Translation:

A

(1)   [The potter is under the earth] during his whole life-time, he is one who wallows (?) in the dirt (?) ⟨more than⟩ pigs

B

(1)   [... listen] to what I say to you,
(2)   [... do not trust] a brother, do not
(3)   [...] and I raised the orphan
(4)   [... like] a needy one (?).

Notes:

(A1) These verse-lines are notoriously difficult to trans-late precisely, even if the general sentiment seems clear (Jäger 2004: 137, 171; and cf. the TLA commentary to the text).

(B1) The scribe has written [sḏ]m n ḏd.t{ḏd}≠i n≠k, i.e. repeating the verb ḏd by mistake. Judging by the amount of text lost between §1d and §2d (some 85–90%), the original lines would have been very long—at least twice the length of the line from *Khety* above—and would also have contained the beginning of the composi-tion.

(B4) One of my reviewers suggests that the traces might correspond to the end of §4c; perhaps one could read something like 𓇋𓏤𓈖𓄇𓏤, '[like] a needy one (?)', with determinatives omitted (as in *nḥm*, 'orphan', in the previ-ous line).

T3.L21 (pl. 89)

Excavation number: 21264/1020N2L117 + 21263/1020N2L117

Description: A New Kingdom marl clay pottery sherd, in two pieces, from a jar, with traces of two lines of hier-atic in black ink, in a literary hand.

Contents: *The Instruction of Khety* (§12.3).

Translation:

(x+1)   [... The gardener ... spends his morning watering] leeks (?), [his] evening [with the cabbage,]
(x+2)   [having spent midday looking] after his date trees [...]

Notes:

(x+1) The initial sign looks like ⌣, and is not easy to recon-cile with the preceding word which should have been *iwḥ*, 'to water' (𓈎 ▭𓏤𓈗𓀀𓂡), unless it is an elaborate ⌣. The distance between *iȝ*[*ḳ.t*], 'leeks' (if this is the correct restor-ation), and *mšrw*, 'evening' seems too long by ca. one group when compared to the other text sources (Jäger 2004: 140–141; Helck 1970: 1, 72), but this might be explained by an extra determinative.

(x+2) This verse-line is not well preserved in other sources apart from P. Sallier II, where it is quite cor-rupt. Most Ramesside copies wrongly have *ḫt≠f*, 'his belly' instead of *ḫt≠f*, 'his trees', and *bin*, 'evil' instead of *bnr*, 'dates' (except O. DeM 1535 which has *bnr*). As Helck (1970: 1, 74) suggested, P. Amherst preserves determinatives that suggest an original reading *bnr*, 'dates', in that manuscript, which is probably correct, and he also hypothesised, based on this, that the preceding words *m-sȝ ḥ.t≠f* in P. Sallier II and Anastasi VII should be emended to 𓅓𓊪𓏤𓆱▭𓊪𓆱𓀜, *m st ḫt bnri*, 'in the orchard'. Jäger (2004: 141) instead read *ir.n≠f ḥry-ib hrw m-sȝ ⟨ḫt⟩-bnr*, 'nachdem er den Mit-tag mit dem Obst zugebracht hat', which in view of this ostracon—in fact the only source that has *ḫt*, 'trees'—is probably correct.

3.4   *The Instruction of a Man for His Son*

T3.L22 (pl. 69)

Excavation number: 15682/1010N4L115

Description: A body sherd of a medium Nile clay jar, with three lines of hieratic in black ink, in a literary hand.

Contents: *The Instruction of a Man for his Son* (§Prolog-1.5).

Translation:

(x+1)   [... Do not turn away your heart from what I say to] you
(x+2)   [... Silence] is precise, [that which bends the arm ...]
(x+3)   [... The exhaustion of words leads to] violence [...]

Notes:

(x+1) The traces at the end of the line are not compatible with the beginning of the next verse-line. Perhaps we have here another example of the misplaced relative ending (𓍿𓏭) as on the copy on O. Turin 54016 (see Fischer-Elfert 1999: vol. II, §Prolog).

3.5   *The Hymn to the Nile*

T3.L23 (pl. 69)

Excavation number: 15711/1010N3L215

Description: A New Kingdom rim sherd of a hole-mouthed jar (meat jar) of Marl B clay, with traces of three lines of hieratic in black ink. The faint red traces above 𓊽 in the first line are probably just an ink blot, but there is cer-tainly a verse-point in line 2.

Contents: *The Hymn to the Nile* (§13.1–4).

Translation:

(1)   [...] When the flood strikes, [one] offers [to you, one slaughters cattle for you]
(2)   [one makes for you] great [offerings], [one] fattens [birds for you ...]
(3)   [...]

3.6 *Various Literary (?) Texts*

T3.L24 (pl. 70)

Excavation number: 9060/940N1L108

Description: A body sherd of a restricted bowl with red splash decoration inside, probably dated to the reign of Thutmose III, with two columns of cursive hieroglyphs in black ink on the exterior side.

Contents: The names of two gods, both written without determinatives.

Translation:

(1)   Montu

(2)   Atum

T3.L25 (pl. 70)

Excavation number: 9283/920S4L311

Description: A small indeterminate pottery sherd with a few hieratic signs on the outside; probably a practice piece as the hand seems more literary than administrative.

Contents: Cartouche with the name of Thutmose III

Translation:

(1)   Men[kheper]re

T3.L26 (pl. 70)

Excavation number: 9371/950S1L111

Description: A small body sherd, probably from an oasis jar, with a hieroglyphic inscription on the outside.

Contents: The name of Thutmose III, followed by the phrase *di ꜥnḫ*, and some illegible traces.

Translation:

(1)   Menkheperre

(2)   given life.

T3.L27 (pl. 70)

Excavation number: 9419/910N1L911

Description: A rim sherd of a New Kingdom restricted bowl of medium Nile clay, decorated with a red band outside and inside, with a cartouche and royal name in red ink.

Contents: Probably the name of Thutmose III.

Translation:

(1)   [Men]kheper[re]

T3.L28 (pl. 71)

Excavation number: 15436/930–940N5L213

Description: A New Kingdom pottery sherd from a jar, made from medium Nile clay (NB2), with a single line of text in a mixture of hieratic and hieroglyphs (for the royal name)

Contents: The name of a god (Khonsu), followed by the titulary of Thutmose III.

Translation:

(1)   [...] Khonsu, Menkheperre, Son of Re [...]

Notes:

(1) One might expect the Dual King title before the throne name of the king, especially in view of the use of the Son of Re title following, but the hieratic clearly has Khonsu.

T3.L29 (pl. 71)

Excavation number: 20473/890N5L214

Description: An indeterminate pottery sherd with two lines of hieratic in black ink.

Contents: The names of Thutmose II and III written in cartouches (without titles).

Translation:

(x+1)   Aakheper[en]re

(x+2)   Menkheperre

T3.L30 (pl. 71)

Excavation number: 15600/950N6L114

Description: A body sherd, perhaps from a marl clay jar, with four lines of hieratic on the outside, with red verse-points. The hand is a fine literary hand of the Ramesside Period. Part of the surface of the sherd has come off at the top, but the ink of the first line is superimposed on the secondary surface, demonstrating that this break took place prior to the text being copied. In other words it is unlikely that the sherd contained the full paragraph of the parallel text from the British Museum.

Contents: A model letter concerning the delivery of various commodities to a temple; paralleled in P. Chester Beatty V (= BM EA 10685), rto. 8.12–13.

Translation:

(x+1)   [... papyrus], (black) ink, reed pens (?)

(x+2)   black [copper], lead, red pigment

(x+3)   [yellow, blue, green mixed green, ꜣw?] red ochre, and

(x+4)   [everything which is demanded for the treasury of Amun-Re ...]

Notes:

(x+2) If the text listed exactly the same sequence of commodities as in P. Chester Beatty V then there would only be a single word (*ḥmt*, 'copper') lost at the beginning of the line; however, this is difficult to reconcile with the next line.

(x+3) It is clear that if the missing part of the right-hand side of the ostracon was small enough to only accommodate the one word missing in the line above, then there would simply not have been enough room for all of the commodities listed between 'red pigment' (*twr*) and 'red ochre' (*tmḥy*) in the papyrus. The traces at the beginning of the line do not match exactly the orthography of the papyrus, but they may conceivably correspond to the end of the word *knìt*, 'yellow pigment' in rto. 8.13 (*Wb.* 5, 52.10–16; Harris, 1961: 153–154), although the writing with the *tìw*-bird seems unattested. The final word before the verse-point is clearly *tmḥy*, 'red ochre' (*Wb.* 5, 369.4; Harris 1961: 154), and the writing in P. Chester Beatty V (▨𓄿𓂝𓍼) is probably corrupt, rather than *tḥn*, 'faience', as Gardiner had supposed. The word may have caused problems also for the copyist of the ostracon as there are traces of another sign (written by mistake) visible under the double reed leaves.

(x+4) Could the top of the tall curved sign visible be the *aleph* in *ꜣḫt*, 'things', as on P. Chester Beatty V, rto. 8.14?

T3.L31 (pl. 72)

Excavation number: 20041/930N6L114

Description: A body sherd of a medium Nile clay open vessel, with traces of perhaps three lines of hieratic. There are dots of red ink, at least one of which looks like a verse-point (line 2), but its position under the line is odd.

Contents: Perhaps a model letter?

Translation:

(x+1)   [...]
(x+2)   [...]
(x+3)   [...] your [...]

T3.L32 (pl. 72)

Excavation number: 20752/1010N6L215

Description: A small sherd from a marl clay jar with three lines of hieratic, in a literary hand.

Contents: Perhaps a model letter.

Translation:

(x+1)   [...] to you the [...]
(x+2)   [...] your companions [...]
(x+3)   [...]

Notes:

(x+2) At the end, above the line, there are traces of red ink, perhaps a verse-point which would indicate a model letter.

T3.L33 (pl. 73)

Excavation number: 21343/970N6L817

Description: A marl clay pottery sherd from a New Kingdom jar, with four lines of hieratic in a literary hand.

Contents: A ritual text related to offering, which Quack (pers. comm.) suggests is a direct parallel for the so-called *Litany of the Eye of Horus* in *The Opening of the Mouth Ritual* (cf. Otto 1960: I, 180–181; II, 153–155, Scene 69C). It is not identical to the manuscripts published by Otto, but with the exception of line (x+3) it corresponds to the text of some later sources (see Quack 2006:

117–119). The use of line (x+4) in headings to New Kingdom offering lists in both royal and private contexts (see Notes, below) raises questions about the social context of the ostracon—might it represent a local use of an extract of this central ritual text for a presentation of offerings in the temple?

Translation:

(x+1)   [... The *setem*-priest] calls out the requisites [of the offerings?]
(x+2)   [... Take] for yourself the Eye of Horus which is before you,
(x+3)   [... that you may be satisfied?] with your eye.
(x+4)   [... Take for yourself the Eye of] Horus, which you have requested in order that you be satisfied [with it ...]

Notes:

(x+1) This line is very faint but the traces are compatible with the expected 'the *setem*-priest calls out the requisites [of the offerings]' ([*stm*] ḥr nìs dbḥ.t [?-ḥtpw ...]).

(x+2) The formula 'Take for yourself the Eye of Horus' is of course ubiquitous in magical and religious texts, normally with the verbs *ìt*, *mn* or *šsp*; given the parallel with *The Opening of the Mouth Ritual* Scene 69C it is presumably *ìt* that is lost here. The final part of the line ('which is before you') is similar to the opening line of Scene 69B, where the *setem*-priest is presenting libations; a later copy (P. Carlsberg 395 + PSI Inv. I 100) has *rdì* [*m ḫnt≠k*], 'which is placed on your forehead' (Quack 2006: 118).

(x+3) This line does not seem to be identical to any known manuscript with *The Opening of the Mouth Ritual* (Quack, pers. comm.).

(x+4) The phrasing here is reminiscent of headings of offering lists, e.g. from the temple of Seti I at Abydos: '(Take for yourself the Eye of Horus,) which is offered to you in order that you be satisfied with it' (*dbḥ n≠k ḥtp≠k ḥr≠s*; Mariette 1869: pls. 28a, 33), and in TT 57 (Khaemhat, temp. Amenhotep III; Loret 1889: 117, col. 1). As Quack notes, it constitutes a play on words with the common expression *dbḥ.t ḥtp.w*, 'requisites of offerings', which is probably also used in line (x+1).

T3.L34 (pl. 72)

Excavation number: 15545/900N5L214

Description: A body sherd of a large vase of Nile clay (perhaps belonging to the same pot as L20, although they do not join), with several traces of hieratic.

Contents: The only legible signs, at the top, contain the first signs of the opening formula common with wisdom instructions and other literary texts.

Translation:

(1)   Beginning of

T3.L35 (pl. 74)

Excavation number: 21524/1020S4L118

Description: A small body sherd of a Phoenician jar, with faint traces of hieratic written with very large signs.

Contents: The ostracon has the initial signs of the opening formula commonly used for wisdom instructions and other literary texts

Translation:

(1)   Beginning of the wis[dom instruction ...?]

Notes:

(1) There are no traces of any further signs at the end, so the scribe simply stopped copying here, but the last signs might be read *sb*, for *sbꜣy.t*, 'wisdom instruction'. For similar examples with only the opening words having been copied, see Spiegelberg (1898: pl. 1, nos. 3 and 4) and Leblanc (2004: pl. 12A).

T3.L36 (pl. 75)

Excavation number: 15601/890N5L114

Description: A sherd from a marl clay jar with one line of hieratic on the outside; complete on all sides. The hand is strange and written with a relatively thin brush; perhaps the product of an unpractised individual (see below).

Contents: The beginning of a wisdom instruction.

Translation:

(1)   Beginning of the instruction

Notes:

(1) The scribe has only written the opening words of the common title for wisdom instructions (compare L34 and L35 above). The hand is peculiar, with some odd hieratic shapes: the sign ⟨ is missing the top stroke of the lion's head, the ⟨ is formed by lifting the pen in the middle, and the ★ was not written with the usual strokes. The impression is of a beginning student of hieratic.

T3.L37 (pl. 76)

Excavation number: 9269/920S5L311

Description: A pottery sherd of indeterminate nature (the section is unclear and edges abraded), perhaps from a Late Period jar, with traces of hieratic signs. Most are illegible to me, but the ostracon is included here in the hope that others may be able make sense of it. The three lines at the top may not belong to the same text as the ones below, and might even be written upside-down in relation to them.

Contents: Unknown; perhaps a literary text or a letter, but very uncertain.

Translation:

(x+1)   [...]

(x+2)   [...]

(x+3)   [...]

(x+4)   [...] the royal house (?), the gods (?) [...]

(x+5)   [...]

T3.L38 (pl. 77)

Excavation number: 9377/950S5L111

Description: A sherd from the shoulder of an Egyptian jar of medium Nile clay, with three lines of hieratic on the outside. The first line is entirely illegible, and the two last lines are too fragmentary to translate.

Contents: Unknown—style of script may suggest a literary fragment, or perhaps a letter (?).

T3.L39 (pl. 77)

Excavation number: 9497/R6L113

Description: A body sherd from a jar of medium Nile clay, with two lines of hieratic in a literary hand.

Contents: A narrative (?) featuring some *wꜥb*-priests from Karnak.

Translation:

(x+1)   [... Amun]-Re, King of the Gods, and Mut [...]

(x+2)   [...] the *wꜥb*-priests (?) of the temple of Amun-Re [...]

Notes:

(1) The Mut vulture is very elaborate, with a clearly visible white crown and flail.

T3.L40 (pl. 81)

Excavation number: 15583/930N6L114

Description: A small limestone sherd with traces of three lines of hieroglyphs.

Contents: Unknown—only a few words are preserved.

Translation:

(x+1)   [...] Amun [...]

(x+2)   [...] in [...]

(x+3)   [...] the city [...]

T3.L41 (pl. 82)

Excavation number: 15591/950N6L114

Description: An indeterminate pottery sherd with traces of three lines of hieratic on the outside and a drawing of an animal (?) on the inside; complete at the top and the right side.

Contents: Unknown, perhaps a wisdom text in view of the mention of 'the silent one' in line 3, but it is difficult to say much about it in the absence of a better preserved copy of the text.

Translation:

(x+1)   Beneficial is [...]

(x+2)   his shoulder [...]

(x+3)   the silent one. There is no pleasant one [...]

Notes:

(x+2) The word *rmn* can also be used to mean 'side' (so 'at his side', or similar), in which case the flesh determinative would be a simple scribal mistake.

T3.L42 (pl. 81)

Excavation number: 15669/1020N5L115

Description: A limestone flake with two lines of hieratic in an 18th Dynasty literary hand. Complete on all sides.

Contents: A date followed by the first line of a literary composition.

Translation:

(1)   Regnal year 34, Month 3 of Akhet, day 7.

(2)   The land brightened, and the sun rose.

Notes:

(1) The writing is clear and careful, yet the scribe has omitted the ⌒ in *rnpt-sp*. The regnal year could refer to either Thutmose III or Amenhotep III, but the date does not seem to coincide with any contemporary festivals; the closest candidate would be a festival of Amun of Elephantine established by Thutmose III (see Schott 1950: 968; *Urk.* IV, 824).

(2) The phraseology echoes other narrative texts, but despite its ring of familiarity I have been unable to identify it as being from a known literary text.

T3.L43 (pl. 83)

Excavation number: 15672/1020N4L115

Description: A pottery sherd from the flat base of a dish made of medium Nile clay, with a red slip both outside and inside, with two lines of hieratic on the outside; probably complete.

Contents: Perhaps a maxim or proverb: much of the reading is due to R. Demarée, who also suggested the interpretation, but the sense is rather elusive (partly due to problems of syntax) and the translation is little more than a guess at the meaning.

Translation:

(1)   Provoke an aggressive lady,

(2)   and a she-ass will have been begotten for you (?).

Notes:

(1) The imperative *imi* would of course yield the meaning 'give' or 'cause', but the context would seem to demand a more figurative meaning like 'provoke', a usage for which I can cite no parallels. Grammatically one might have expected a conditional construction (with a subjunctive *sdm=f*), or perhaps a habitual imperfective *sdm=f* instead. In any case the presence of the woman determinative at the end suggests that *ʿhꜣ* is a participle (*ḥnw.t ʿhꜣ⟨.t⟩*, 'a lady who is aggressive').

(2) Literally 'the she-ass', with the definite article, but this would make for awkward English. The phallus determinative of *wtt*, 'beget', has been wrongly placed at the end, after *n=k*.

T3.L44 (pl. 83)

Excavation number: 15673/1020N5L115

Description: A limestone flake with two lines of hieratic in a literary hand. Very faint ink, with much of the middle section erased. There are traces of red ink between the two lines, perhaps from a verse-point.

Contents: Unknown, but literary on the basis of the hieratic register.

Translation:

(1)   God's father [...]

(2)   [...] in the mouth (?) [...]

Notes:

(1) The title 'God's father' may imply both status and function, but is often used as essentially a ranking title. It is well attested in literary texts (Blumenthal 1987: 10–35), especially in wisdom poems like *The Instruction of Ptahhotep* or *The Instruction of Kairsu* (= *The Loyalist Instruction*), but the traces preserved here preclude an identification with either of those two compositions I think.

T3.L45 (pl. 84)

Excavation number: 15680/1010N4L115 + 21133/1020N2L116

Description: Two pieces of mixed Nile and marl clay pottery, probably from a canopic jar, found in debris some ten metres apart (outside the western side of the enclosure wall) during two different seasons.

Contents: A few hieroglyphs written in a single column with black dividing lines. The text was first traced in red ink and then overwritten in black ink.

Translation:

(1)   [...] an honoured one before Qebehsenuef.

Notes:

(1) As noted above, these two joining fragments are probably from a canopic jar. The text was first written in red and then black ink, superimposed on each other, which brings to mind some of the copies of *Kemit* published by Gasse (2005), but here it presumably relates to the decoration process of the canopic jar, and not scribal training. The use of red ink to lay out a drawing or decorative element, before going over the final design with black ink, is well known from both monumental contexts and on figurative ostraca (for the latter see Brunner-Traut 1979: 3).

T3.L46 (pl. 85)

Excavation number: 15683/1010N4L115

Description: An indeterminate type of pottery sherd with

the remains of four lines of hieratic in black ink, in a literary hand. There is a red verse-point at the beginning of line three.

Contents: Unknown.

Translation:

(x+1)   [...]

(x+2)   [...] words (?)

(x+3)   [...] There is no [...]

(x+4)   [...]

T3.L47 (pl. 86)

Excavation number: 15759/960S5L916

Description: A limestone flake, rather wide and heavy, with traces of five lines of hieratic in black ink. The surface is much rubbed, and the text is almost entirely erased, but the ductus is clearly Ramesside. There are palimpsest traces throughout. Despite attempts to bring out the text by D-Stretch and Photoshop I have been unable to provide a legible facsimile.

Contents: A hymn.

Translation:

(1)   Giving praise to Re [...]

(2)   [...]

(3)   [...]

(4)   [...]

(5)   [...]

Notes:

(1) Only the first word is preserved, but this provides the genre-label *dw3*, 'praise' or 'hymn'. The name of the deity is faint, but Re seems relatively certain.

T3.L48 (pl. 87)

Excavation number: 15765/980N5L416

Description: A pottery sherd, perhaps from a New Kingdom amphora, with the ends of three lines of hieratic in black ink. There are verse-lines at the end of each line, and a date, all in red ink.

Contents: A magico-religious text?

Translation:

(x+1)   [... protection?] behind you in life.

(x+2)   [...] towards the sky, that the gods will be satisfied.

(x+3)   [...] against him; you are him, **and vice-versa. Month 2 of Shomu, day 12.**

Notes:

(x+1) There are no traces of the subject here, but the phrase *h3k m ʿnḫ* (and similar) in other texts is often associated with concepts of safety and protection, see e.g. PT 715A (Faulkner 1969: 62, and cf. the TLA edition with plausible restorations), the Speos Artemidos inscription of Seti I (KRI I, 41.8–9), *The Blessing of Ptah* (in 5 copies temp. Ramesses II and III; KRI II 270.13), or the later

Osorkon inscription from Bubastis (Naville 1892: pl. XVII no. 13).

(x+2) The final signs of *ḥtp* look more like an aleph, but are presumably to be read ⸗.

(x+3) The red stroke appears to be ⸗, added as a correction. The two signs in red at the end before the date (⸗) are clear, but I owe the interpretation *ts-pḥr*, 'vice-versa' (*Wb.* 5, 404.1–4; cf. Westendorf 1955) to Matthias Müller (pers. comm.).

T3.L49 (pl. 85)

Excavation number: 20090/890N5L114

Description: A body sherd of marl clay, with a single line of hieroglyphs in black ink.

Contents: A title and name.

Translation:

(1)   The *wʿb*-priest Khaemwaset.

Notes:

(1) The use of hieroglyphs makes this ostracon distinct from the name-stones described under administrative ostraca above. The ⸗ was initially forgotten, and was inserted below the line in hieratic (but with the full and not the abbreviated form).

T3.L50 (pl. 88)

Excavation number: 15702/1010N5L215

Description: A body sherd, probably from a New Kingdom Canaanite amphora, with traces of three lines of hieratic black ink, with a verse-point in red in line 2.

Contents: Unknown literary text.

Translation:

(x+1)   [...]

(x+2)   [...] the heart. You (?) shall not pass [...]

(x+3)   [...]

Notes:

(x+2) The reading of the pronoun is not certain (it could also be ⸗, but this makes little grammatical sense).

T3.L51 (pl. 88)

Excavation number: 20912/1000N4L1016

Description: A body sherd, probably of an oasis jar, with a light red/orange slip (Phoenician torpedo amphora?), with a handful of hieratic signs in black ink.

Contents: The signs ∧ and × are repeated several times, as if writing *sw3*, 'pass by'. Combined with the seemingly unpractised hand this suggests a trial piece by a scribal student.

T3.L52 (pl. 88)

Excavation number: 20801/990N6L116

Description: A small pottery sherd of indeterminate

nature, with two fragmentary lines of hieratic in a literary hand.

Contents: Unknown literary text; the classification of genre is mainly based on the literary style of the hand.

Translation:

(x+1)   [... ho]tep (?)[...]

(x+2)   [...] the living (?) Horus [...]

T3.L53 (pl. 89)

Excavation number: 20840/1020N1L116

Description: A body sherd of an imported jar, probably a Phoenician amphora, with remains of three lines of hieratic in black, as well as a verse-point and a date in red ink, all in a literary hand.

Contents: Probably an unidentified literary text, but reminiscent of *The Instruction of Khety* in line x+2.

Translation:

(x+1)   [...] flies (?) [...]

(x+2)   [...] any profession (?) [...]

(x+3)   [...] **day 26.**

Notes:

(x+1) The reading ⬚⬚⬚ *ḥmy.wt*, 'flies', seems certain, despite the missing determinative.

(x+2) The phrase ⬚⬚⬚[...] sounds like *Khety* (§ 3.4, *wr -sw grt r iꜣ.t nb.t*, 'It is greater than any profession'), but the word in the line above is difficult to reconcile with the expected text passages preceding § 3.4, because 'flies' could only refer to a much later part of *Khety,* namely § 8.3.

(x+3) Of the date, only the day is preserved; the red dot underneath seems like a misplaced verse-point.

T3.L54 (pl. 89)

Excavation number: 21134/1020N2L116

Description: A marl clay pottery sherd from a New Kingdom amphora with the beginning of a (final) line of hieratic in black ink, in a literary hand.

Contents: A divine name.

Translation:

(x+1)   Hapy [...]

Notes:

(x+1) In principle this could also be a copy of *The Hymn to the Nile*. In that case it would have to be from the end of the text because the name stands at the beginning of the line—this means that any lines above would have been extremely short, only one or two words long, if it had contained the opening lines. It might fit § 14.6–7, however, but in the absence of more text on the ostracon this cannot be proven.

T3.L55 (pl. 90)

Excavation number: 21078/980N6L517

Description: A pottery sherd from an imported Late Period amphora, with remains of one line of hieratic in black ink, in a rather cursive hand.

Contents: Unknown, but sounds literary; the late date is noteworthy.

Translation:

(1)   [...] he hides behind (?) 13 ½

Notes:

(1) The signs following to the left are Demotic for '13 ½', as opposed to the hieratic of the preceding text. The implications are not clear, but the presence of the fraction shows that this is not a numbered excerpt of a text, such as is occasionally found on ostraca. Despite the literary sounding phrase, there is also the possibility that it might refer to the contents of the jar (e.g. 13 ½ units of 'He-hides-behind', perhaps as the name of plant living in shade?), but the absence of a determinative is vexing. Perhaps others will be able to make sense of it. I am grateful to my reviewers for the reading of the numeral '13', and to Kim Ryholt for the reading of the fraction, as well as a discussion about the possible implications.

4   Figured Ostraca

T3.F01 (pl. 91)

Excavation number: 15053/900N2L813

Description: A limestone flake with a very smooth curved surface on one side. This has a few hieroglyphic signs (perhaps a writing of Amun), in a broad and seemingly unpractised hand. Underneath is a drawing in red and black ink, with fine lines and exquisite details.

Contents: The drawing appears to be of a pectoral, of which the middle and the left-hand side is still visible. After a band decorated with geometrical shapes follows a winged scarab, holding a *shen*-ring. Underneath this are more decorated bands, and then a rectangular plaque showing a seated figure of Amun, wearing the feathered crown, facing two offering tables.

T3.F02 (pl. 90)

Excavation number: 7568/1000N5L315

Description: A small limestone flake with a single unfinished drawing in black ink.

Contents: The drawing is of a human head, perhaps a king if the ink traces above the forehead was a ureaus.

T3.F03 (pl. 92)

Excavation number: 8268/1010N5L215

Description: A pottery sherd, probably from an imported jar, with a drawing in black ink on the outside.

Contents: The drawing is of a standing or walking human figure with a stick, similar to the hieroglyph 𓀞.

T3.F04 (pl. 92)

Excavation number: 8398/920S2L210

Description: A pottery sherd from the base of a shallow dish with an incised figure of an ibis.

Contents: The incision, made before the firing of the pot, shows an ibis standing on its legs at ground level, with a small round shape in front. The latter might perhaps be a ◠ but there is no sign of ◟◟ on the other side, nor is the ibis perched on a standard as one would have expected for the writing *ḏḥwty*.

T3.F05 (pl. 92)

Excavation number: 8400/940N2L510

Description: A body sherd of a jar of marl B clay, with various lines in black ink crossing each other, on both sides.

Contents: The lines as preserved yield no recognisable shape as far as I can establish—could it conceivably be a crude architectural drawing?

T3.F06 (pl. 93)

Excavation number: 8991/930N6L114

Description: A sherd from a marl clay jar, of either New Kingdom or Late Period date, with several curved lines in black ink crossing each other.

Contents: I do not recognise the motif; perhaps somebody else might.

T3.F07 (pl. 93)

Excavation number: 8993/900N5L214

Description: A pottery sherd with a fragment of a basic sketch in black ink.

Contents: Perhaps a kilted human figure with hands raised in adoration, in front of something that might be an offering table with two loaves (or two cuts of beef?) on top.

T3.F08 (pl. 93)

Excavation number: 9267/920S4L212

Description: A body sherd of an Egyptian marl or Mycenaean imported jar with orange slip and a black line, of an odd shape, with some lines on the inside in black ink which partly follows the shape of the sherd. The outside has a single line which runs alongside one of the edges.

Contents: Unknown.

T3.F09 (pl. 94)

Excavation number: 9343/920S3L211

Description: A body sherd of indeterminate fabric, with a drawing in black and red on the outside.

Contents: On the left are two partially preserved branches in red with black leaves. To the right are three hieroglyphs: 𓊬, 𓏲 and traces of a third unidentified sign.

T3.F10 (pl. 94)

Excavation number: 9370/TVIICL111 (found in grid 960/S4)

Description: A body sherd of a medium Nile clay jar, with a drawing in black on the outside.

Contents: A drawing of a sphinx (body of a lion, with wings).

T3.F11 (pl. 94)

Excavation number: 15004/950S6L112

Description: A body sherd of Nile B2 clay jar, New Kingdom in date, with a small drawing in black on the outside.

Contents: Unclear—perhaps an animal?

T3.F12 (pl. 94)

Excavation number: 15021/940S4L212

Description: A body sherd of Nile clay ('perhaps of a Middle Kingdom beer jar'), with a drawing in black ink (maybe Coptic motif?).

Contents: The drawing is of a naked human figure, with what looks like a fig leaf covering the genitals.

T3.F13 (pl. 95)

Excavation number: 15433/950N5L613

Description: A limestone flake with a drawing in black ink, and some hieratic signs underneath.

Contents: The incomplete nature of the ostracon means it is difficult to be sure what is depicted. On the upper left hand side is an object or figure, which stands on the edge of what could be a table (or a shaft?). The straight vertical and horizontal lines may be an attempt to lay out borders for the scene, or they could represent architectural elements. The layout of the hieratic suggests some connection with the drawing, but too little is preserved to make much sense of the text. The transcription of the first line might be 𓏭𓎶𓇼𓃀 ('in weight'?), the second has only a single sign, perhaps 𓃢.

T3.F14 (pl. 95)

Excavation number: 15460/900N5L313

Description: A small pottery sherd from a New Kingdom jar with a basic sketch in black ink.

Contents: The figure is a small animal in a reclining position, perhaps a jackal or antelope.

T3.F15 (pl. 95)

Excavation number: 15588/990S6L114

Description: A body sherd of a New Kingdom jar of medium Nile clay, with a drawing of two figures in black ink.

Contents: The figure on the right is a cobra wearing a feather crown incorporating a *wꜣs*-sceptre and sun disc; behind this is a humanoid figure, perhaps Amun or a king, wearing the double feather crown and holding a staff or sceptre.

T3.F16 (pl. 96)

Excavation number: 15630/920N6L214 + 20440 + 20441/890 N5L214

Description: A body sherd of a Middle Kingdom beer jar, of coarse Nile clay, with a drawing in black ink.

Contents: The drawing depicts a shrine in which one or two divine figures are represented, along with what seems to be an offering stand. To the right of this is the beginning of an offering formula in hieroglyphs ('An offering which the king gives [...]').

T3.F17 (pl. 96)

Excavation number: 15663/920N6L414

Description: A body sherd from an amphora with several figures drawn in black ink on both sides.

Contents: The outside has a single drawing of Sobek in crocodile form with a crown; the back has several semi-hieratic signs, including four attempts at rendering the same crocodile form as on the other side, albeit in a simplified form (one of which includes the crown).

T3.F18 (pl. 97)

Excavation number: 15671/970N6L115

Description: A body sherd of a medium Nile clay jar ('Middle or New Kingdom') with several lines in black ink on the outside.

Contents: The ostracon is too fragmentary for me to identify the motif, but perhaps others will be able to recognise it (might it belong with F15?). One of my reviewers proposes that if turned clockwise it might be the bottom of a sparrow, but I confess I do not quite see it—readers may judge for themselves.

T3.F19 (pl. 97)

Excavation number: 20449/910N5L114

Description: A body sherd, probably from a New Kingdom Canaanite amphora, with a drawing (?) in black ink on the outside, and some traces of hieratic (?).

Contents: The drawing is perhaps a human figure with a kilt, with something in his hand; the hieratic is illegible.

T3.F20 (pl. 97)

Excavation number: 20754/1010N6L215

Description: An indeterminate pottery sherd with a drawing in black ink on the outside, drawn partly across three lines of hieratic.

Contents: The drawing is largely lost except for a few lines. A handful of hieratic signs are still visible, with the third and final line perhaps to be read ⟨hieratic signs⟩, suggesting a text written in Late Egyptian.

T3.F21 (pl. 65)

Excavation number: 20877/980N5L416 (= L15)

Description: A pottery sherd with a drawing in black ink on the inside.

Contents: A ureaus in front of a sun disc (with *Kemit* on the other side of the sherd: see L15 above).

Fragments without a Separate Entry in the Catalogue

A number of minor fragments were found which have not been given a full entry in the catalogue (Table 4). A small and arbitrary selection of such fragments is depicted on pls. 99–100, in order to give an impression of the state of preservation of these objects. In the following table all fragments included on these plates are indicated by an asterisk (*) after the inventory number.

TABLE 4   A list of minor fragments which have not been given a full catalogue entry, with short descriptions and brief characterisations of their contents

Reg. no.	Material	Recto	Verso	Notes
7457/950N6L114	Limestone	Single sign in red (rectangle with lines across)	Empty	Shaped with smooth surface, with a groove (not writing board)
7521/920N6L414*	Limestone	One sign group (illegible)	Empty	Perhaps corner fragment of a limestone writing board
7566/910N6L115	Hard stone	A single line of hieratic with a few illegible signs	Empty	
8163/940S5L115*	Pottery	A single line	Empty	Bottom of a dish; writing on the underside; nothing lost in front but perhaps traces of a line above; only the words *nꜣ n* […] visible
8964/920N6L414*	Pottery	A single line	Empty	Perhaps ▨ 𓂧𓏏𓏤 [*th*]*ꜣw Jn-ḥr*[…], 'Onuris transgresses'?
8973/940N2L210*	Pottery	A few fragmentary signs in a column with black dividing lines	Empty	Perhaps 𓉐 (probably not *Kemit* despite script and layout)
8978/1000S6L114*	Pottery	A few illegible hieratic signs next to a fragmentary drawing in black ink	Empty	
9077/950N1L208	Pottery	Fragment of a drawing in black ink	Empty	
9081/950N1L208*	Limestone	Small fragment with a few illegible signs	Empty	Probably administrative; perhaps ▨ in the second line
9098/940S1L409	Pottery	A handful of faint and illegible hieratic signs	Empty	
9103/940N1L109	Pottery	Traces of black ink, perhaps of a drawing	Empty	
9106/940S1L409	Pottery	Very faint lines of a drawing	Empty	
9107/910S4L109*	Pottery	Faint traces of two lines	Empty	The last line has ▨
9108/940N2L110*	Pottery	Faint traces of two lines	Empty	The first may have ▨, the second perhaps ▨
9113/910S4L209	Pottery	A handful of faint signs, possibly hieratic	Empty	
9114/940S2L410*	Pottery	Two signs, perhaps cursive hieroglyphs	Empty	
9120/940S2L510	Pottery	A couple of signs	Empty	Quite similar to no. 9114 above
9139 (RM)*	Pottery	Traces of a single line below the rim of the sherd	Empty	Perhaps ▨
9140 (RM)*	Pottery	Illegible traces of signs on the outside	Traces of three lines	Second line on the inside has ▨
9151/940S1L409	Pottery	Traces of two lines	Beginning of two lines	The first line on the outside has ▨; the first on the inside may have ▨
9185/940S2L1510	Pottery	Traces of two illegible lines of hieratic	Empty	
9187/940S2L1510	Pottery	Traces of two illegible lines of hieratic	Empty	
9216/1000N6L115*	Pottery	Traces of two lines of hieratic	Empty	The first line has ▨, the second perhaps ▨
9271/920S4L111	Pottery	Very faint traces of five or six lines, in at least two columns, but illegible	Empty	The first column ends in numbers, so probably an account
9339/920S4L111	Pottery	Very faint traces of three lines	Empty	All three end in numbers, perhaps '185, […]9, and […]10'. Rim fragment very similar to 9271 above
9378/950S5L111	Pottery	Faint traces of a geometric pattern (?)	Empty	

© FREDRIK HAGEN, 2021 | DOI:10.1163/9789004447561_004

TABLE 4   A list of minor fragments which have not been given a full catalogue entry (*cont.*)

Reg. no.	Material	Recto	Verso	Notes
9379/950S5L111*	Pottery	Traces of a few signs	Empty	Drawn in broad strokes, perhaps cursive hieroglyphs (?); one group may be [glyph]
9380/950S5L111	Pottery	Faint traces of perhaps five hieratic signs, all illegible	Empty	
9381/950S5L111*	Pottery	Traces of ink, perhaps a few hieratic signs but illegible	Empty	
9382/950S5L111	Pottery	Faint ink traces	Faint ink traces, perhaps hieroglyphs?	
9384/930S4L1011	Pottery	Faint traces of illegible signs	Empty	One sign might be a crudely drawn [glyph]
9420/940S5L312	Pottery	Faint traces of a single line of hieratic	Empty	The beginning may have [glyphs]
9444/970S6L112	Pottery	Illegible traces of perhaps two lines	Empty	
9449/970S6L112*	Pottery	Traces of two illegible lines of hieratic	Empty	First line maybe [glyphs]; second line perhaps has [glyphs]
9462/950S6L112	Pottery	Faint illegible traces	Empty	
9491/920N3L613*	Pottery	Traces of a single word, perhaps a name?	Empty	The beginning has [glyphs]
15013/950S6L112*	Pottery	A few signs of two lines	Empty	First line may have [glyphs], the second looks like the end of a line, perhaps with [glyphs]
15038/960S6L112	Pottery	Very abraded surface with two lines of hieratic	Empty	First line seems to have [glyphs]
15049/R4/5L213	Pottery	Faint remains of perhaps three lines of hieratic	Empty	Final line has [glyphs]
15061/1010N3L115*	Pottery	Fragments of signs from a single line	Empty	Difficult despite the clear ink
15121/930–940N5SD13*	Limestone	Two faint lines of hieratic, probably bread account	Empty	The second line has [glyphs], 'ten great *psn*-bread'
15129/930–940N5L113	Pottery	A few numbers only	Empty	'35', '80'
15191/910S4L209	Pottery	Faint ink traces (hieratic?)	Empty	
15193/R6L313*	Pottery	Traces of two lines of hieratic	Empty	Probably literary: the first seems to have [glyphs]; the second line has [glyphs]
15195/R6L113	Pottery	Traces of end of two lines—perhaps numbers	Empty	
15196/R6L113	Pottery	Two lines from top of a jar	Empty	Very faint, but first line has [glyphs]
15244/950N5L113	Pottery	Faint traces of the beginning of four lines	Empty	
15350/950N5L213	Pottery	A few traces of ink on this small sherd	Empty	Fragment of an illustrated ostracon
15375/R4/5L1414	Limestone	This lower right-hand corner of a rectangular limestone writing tablet (surface on one side polished smooth) has a few ink traces	Empty (coarse surface)	Cursive hieroglyphs written in columns(?), only [glyph] visible
15377/950N5L213	Pottery	Fragment with traces of a few signs	Empty	
15415/900N5L6613	Pottery	Very faint traces of ink	Empty	
15431/900N4L713	Pottery	Faint traces of signs with no discernible layout	Empty	Perhaps pen trials or disassociated numbers?
15448/920N4L113	Pottery	Faint traces of some signs	Empty	
15463/960N6L113	Pottery	Illegible traces of a few signs	Empty	
15467/960N6L113*	Pottery	Traces of two lines in a literary hand	Empty	Second line has [glyphs]
15488/SD14	Pottery	Traces of three lines	Empty	First line has [glyphs]
15512/900N5L214*	Pottery	Traces of two lines	Empty	First line has something that looks like [glyphs]
15565/980S6L114	Pottery	Traces of two lines in a literary hand	Illegible traces of one line	
15689/1010N4L215	Pottery	Traces of one line	Empty	Perhaps [glyphs] (cf. *Sinuhe* B261, but with so little preserved it is not possible to identify the composition)
15697/1010N5L215	Pottery (rim sherd)	Traces of one line	Empty	

TABLE 4   A list of minor fragments which have not been given a full catalogue entry (*cont.*)

Reg. no.	Material	Recto	Verso	Notes
15710/950N6L115	Pottery	Traces of two lines	Empty	Second line has [hieroglyphs]
20030/990S6L114	Pottery	Very faint traces of one (?) line	Empty	Remains of a verse-point visible so probably literary
20048/950N6L114*	Pottery (rim sherd)	Parts of one line in a literary hand	Empty	[hieroglyphs]
20049/890N5L114	Pottery	Illegible traces of one line of hieratic	Empty	
20050/890N5L114	Pottery	Faint traces of ink	Empty	Perhaps a drawing rather than hieratic
20052/890N5L114	Pottery	Faint traces of one or two signs of hieratic	Empty	Perhaps [hieroglyph]
20053/950N6L114*	Pottery (handle of amphora)	Traces of a few hieroglyphic signs with a border around, possibly a cartouche	Empty	The top three signs are [hieroglyphs]; could it be [Amen]hotep?
20054/890N5L114	Pottery	Traces of two lines in rather large hand	Empty	Line two may have [hieroglyphs]
20095/890N5L114	Pottery	Illegible traces of two lines	Empty	
20411/890N5L214	Pottery	A few traces of a drawing in black ink	Empty	
20423/900N5L214	Pottery	A single stroke from a hieratic sign	Empty	Possibly the opening stroke of a cartouche
20424/900N5L214	Pottery	Part of a drawing	Empty	
20434/890N5L114	Pottery	Traces of some illegible hieratic (?) signs	Empty	
20439/890N5L214	Pottery	Traces of black ink	Empty	Perhaps part of a drawing rather than hieratic
20446/890N5L214	Pottery	Faint traces of a stylised scarab	Empty	Almost pencil-like appearance
20474/890N5L214	Pottery	A sherd with five or more illegible lines of hieratic in black ink	Empty	The lines are distributed across the sherd with no obvious connection between them, one may have the beginning of a docket: [hieroglyphs]
20531/940N6L214	Pottery	Three hieratic signs from the beginning of a line, probably the name of the temple	Empty	Restore [hieroglyphs]?
20533/920N6L414	Pottery	A few strokes in black ink	Empty	Probably a fragment of a drawing
20581/1010N4L115	Pottery	A few lines of black ink	Empty	Fragment of a drawing
20589/1010N4L115	Pottery	A single hieratic sign	Empty	Perhaps [hieroglyph]?
20591/1010N4L115	Pottery	Faint traces of a single sign	Empty	
20592/1010N4L115	Pottery	Faint traces of ink	Empty	
20596/970N6L115	Pottery	Faint traces of ink	Empty	
20605/1010N5L215	Pottery	Faint traces of a drawing	Empty	
20613/910S5L310	Pottery	Ink traces	Empty	
20651/950N6L114	Pottery	Illegible traces of two lines of hieratic	Empty	Probably administrative hand
20695/920S4L115	Pottery	Traces of a cartouche with royal name, very similar hand to L07 (with *Amenemhat*)	Empty	Perhaps [hieroglyphs]
20702/970N5L315	Pottery	Traces of two lines of hieratic, perhaps literary hand, almost invisible under normal light	Empty	First line has [hieroglyphs] the second illegible; compare perhaps *Neferti* (§ 9b), but the traces at the end do not match (cannot be [hieroglyph] rather than [hieroglyph]) so probably not a copy of that text.
20706/900N6L415	Pottery (rim of offering dish)	A red border around the edge of the dish	Faint traces of ink	Writing illegible, but clay stamped with cartouche, probably Thutmose III
20716/1000N5L415	Pottery	Three lines of hieratic, perhaps a letter	Empty	First line has [hieroglyphs], the second [hieroglyphs], the third only [hieroglyphs]
20731/1020N3L115	Pottery	Beginning of five lines of hieratic, extremely faint	Empty	First line has [hieroglyphs], second [hieroglyphs]
20858/970S3L116	Pottery	Traces of beginning of four lines, all illegible	Empty	
20956/890N6L116	Pottery	A few faint traces, perhaps of a drawing	Empty	
20973/890NL6116	Pottery (in 3 pieces)	A single large hieroglyph (practice piece?)	Empty	A simple [hieroglyph]
20918/890N6L116	Pottery	Traces of two lines of hieratic, at different ends (no relation to each other)	Empty	The second line (on the left) has [hieroglyphs]
20809/990N5L216	Pottery	Three signs in a literary hand	Empty	Perhaps [hieroglyphs]

TABLE 4   A list of minor fragments which have not been given a full catalogue entry (*cont.*)

Reg. no.	Material	Recto	Verso	Notes
20800/990N5L216	Pottery	Perhaps two lines of hieratic, rather large signs	Empty	Second line has ▨▭▨ (traces of a determinative might suit *šꜥ.t*, 'letter')
20878/980N5L416	Pottery	A small fragment of a drawing	Empty	Motif unidentified
21024/940N4L716	Pottery	A single line, very thin brush	Empty	Perhaps ▨ ⌐▨
21061/960S5L512	Pottery	Traces of two lines of hieratic	Empty	Largely illegible traces in an administrative hand; second line may have ⌐▨
21064/980N5L517	Pottery	Two hieratic signs	Empty	Perhaps from a docket, but only ▨⊙ preserved, and no traces above this where a date might be expected.
21065/980N5L517	Pottery	Trace of ends of two lines	Emtpy	First line has '[…] 12'
21086/980N6L116	Pottery (rim sherd)	Five lines with only numbers preserved	Empty	Reads '1, 1.5, 2, 2, 3'; illegible traces of writing to the right, presumably different commodities
21269/ 940S4L117	Pottery	Traces of three hieratic signs	Empty	Only the middle sign is clear (▨)
16167/900N8L118	Limestone	Illegible traces of one line of hieratic	Empty	
21295/980N6L817	Pottery	Illegible traces of one or two signs only	Empty	
21308/940S4L1617	Pottery	Illegible traces of one line of hieratic	Empty	
21425/900N5L214	Pottery	Faint traces of four lines of hieratic	Empty	Administrative hand
21438/910N8SD18	Pottery	Faint traces of one line of hieratic	Empty	Perhaps ▨ ▨ (Nakhtamun?)
21470/910N8SD18	Pottery	Empty	Traces of two or three lines; very faint	Unusually only the inside is inscribed; the first line may have ▨ ⌐▨
21524/1020S4L118	Pottery	Only a handful of signs on two lines	Empty	Perhaps a cursively written ⌐ repeated twice
21525/1020S4L118	Pottery	Illegible traces of one or two signs	Empty	

CHAPTER 4

Concordance List of Excavation Numbers and Sigla

7568	T3.F02	15321	T3.D23	15675	T3.A34		
7727	T3.A45	15399	T3.L02	15677	T3.A44		
7894	T3.A26	15414	T3.D01	15679	T3.D07		
7984	T3.A37	15421	T3.L13	15682	T3.L22		
8268	T3.F03	15424	T3.D02	15683	T3.L46		
8398	T3.F04	15433	T3.F13	15685	T3.L18		
8400	T3.F05	15436	T3.L28	15686	T3.L04		
8943	T3.A58	15439	T3.D03	15702	T3.L50		
8991	T3.F06	15449	T3.D04	15711	T3.L23		
8993	T3.F07	15452	T3.A07	15718	T3.L05		
9035	T3.A39	15460	T3.F14	15759	T3.L47		
9060	T3.L24	15462	T3.A08	15765	T3.L48		
9079	T3.A27	15466	T3.A09	15855	T3.A53		
9080	T3.A49	15486	T3.A50	9036 + 9138	T3.A48		
9083	T3.A40	15498	T3.A31	9138 + 9036	T3.A48		
9096	T3.A01	15500	T3.L20	20041	T3.L31		
9137	T3.L01	15503	T3.A10	20047	T3.D08		
9163	T3.L11	15510	T3.A11	20090	T3.L49		
9164	T3.A02	15537	T3.L03	20425	T3.D14		
9186	T3.L12	15545	T3.L34	20433	T3.D09		
9244	T3.D19	15546	T3.A12	20449	T3.F19		
9245	T3.A03	15571	T3.D21	20458	T3.D10		
9267	T3.F08	15583	T3.L40	20473	T3.L29		
9269	T3.L37	15588	T3.F15	20482	T3.D15		
9270	T3.A41	15591	T3.L41	20532	T3.L09		
9283	T3.L25	15600	T3.L30	20551	T3.D18		
9321	T3.L17	15601	T3.L36	20564	T3.L14		
9343	T3.F09	15602	T3.A13	20698	T3.A35		
9369	T3.A04	15619	T3.A57	20729	T3.L16		
9370	T3.F10	15627	T3.A14	20749	T3.L07		
9371	T3.L26	15628	T3.A32	20752	T3.L32		
9377	T3.L38	15633	T3.A33	20754	T3.F20		
9419	T3.L27	15639	T3.A15	20771	T3.L08		
9497	T3.L39	15654	T3.A16	20801	T3.L52		
15004	T3.F11	15655	T3.D06	20840	T3.L53		
15012	T3.A05	15657	T3.A24	20852	T3.A19		
15021	T3.F12	15658	T3.A25	20873	T3.L19		
15053	T3.F01	15661	T3.A17	20877	T3.L15		
15075	T3.A23	15663	T3.F17	20877	T3.F21		
15078	T3.D17	15668	T3.A42	20879	T3.D11		
15090	T3.A06	15669	T3.L42	20912	T3.L51		
15131	T3.A56	15670	T3.A43	20922	T3.A51		
15188	T3.A28	15671	T3.F18	20923	T3.A52		
15197	T3.D20	15672	T3.L43	20968	T3.A36		
15215	T3.A29	15673	T3.L44	21053	T3.L10		
15217	T3.A30	15674	T3.A18	21078	T3.L55		

21134	T3.L54	21471	T3.A61	20478 + 20547	T3.L06
21140	T3.A59	21472	T3.A22	20547 + 20478	T3.L06
21156	T3.A54	21495	T3.D22	21263 + 21264	T3.L21
21160	T3.A20	21519	T3.D13	21264 + 21263	T3.L21
21268	T3.A21	21523	T3.A55	15630 + 20440 + 20441	
21340	T3.D12	21524	T3.L35		T3.F16
21343	T3.L33	21530	T3.A38	20440 + 15630 + 20441	
21414	T3.A46	15622 + 20432	T3.D05		T3.F16
21433	T3.A47	20432 + 15622	T3.D05	20441 + 15630 + 20440	
21434	T3.A60	15680 + 21133	T3.L45		T3.F16
21467	T3.D16	21133 + 15680	T3.L45		

CHAPTER 5

Concordance List of Sigla and Excavation Numbers

T3.A01	9096	T3.A47	21433	T3.F07	8993
T3.A02	9164	T3.A48	9036 + 9138	T3.F08	9267
T3.A03	9245	T3.A48	9138 + 9036	T3.F09	9343
T3.A04	9369	T3.A49	9080	T3.F10	9370
T3.A05	15012	T3.A50	15486	T3.F11	15004
T3.A06	15090	T3.A51	20922	T3.F12	15021
T3.A07	15452	T3.A52	20923	T3.F13	15433
T3.A08	15462	T3.A53	15855	T3.F14	15460
T3.A09	15466	T3.A54	21156	T3.F15	15588
T3.A10	15503	T3.A55	21523	T3.F16	15630 + 20440 + 20441
T3.A11	15510	T3.A56	15131	T3.F16	20440 + 15630 + 20441
T3.A12	15546	T3.A57	15619	T3.F16	20441 + 15630 + 20440
T3.A13	15602	T3.A58	8943	T3.F17	15663
T3.A14	15627	T3.A59	21140	T3.F18	15671
T3.A15	15639	T3.A60	21434	T3.F19	20449
T3.A16	15654	T3.A61	21471	T3.F20	20754
T3.A17	15661	T3.D01	15414	T3.F21	20877
T3.A18	15674	T3.D02	15424	T3.L01	9137
T3.A19	20852	T3.D03	15439	T3.L02	15399
T3.A20	21160	T3.D04	15449	T3.L03	15537
T3.A21	21268	T3.D05	15622 + 20432	T3.L04	15686
T3.A22	21472	T3.D05	20432 + 15622	T3.L05	15718
T3.A23	15075	T3.D06	15655	T3.L06	20478 + 20547
T3.A24	15657	T3.D07	15679	T3.L06	20547 + 20478
T3.A25	15658	T3.D08	20047	T3.L07	20749
T3.A26	7894	T3.D09	20433	T3.L08	20771
T3.A27	9079	T3.D10	20458	T3.L09	20532
T3.A28	15188	T3.D11	20879	T3.L10	21053
T3.A29	15215	T3.D12	21340	T3.L11	9163
T3.A30	15217	T3.D13	21519	T3.L12	9186
T3.A31	15498	T3.D14	20425	T3.L13	15421
T3.A32	15628	T3.D15	20482	T3.L14	20564
T3.A33	15633	T3.D16	21467	T3.L15	20877
T3.A34	15675	T3.D17	15078	T3.L16	20729
T3.A35	20698	T3.D18	20551	T3.L17	9321
T3.A36	20968	T3.D19	9244	T3.L18	15685
T3.A37	7984	T3.D20	15197	T3.L19	20873
T3.A38	21530	T3.D21	15571	T3.L20	15500
T3.A39	9035	T3.D22	21495	T3.L21	21263 + 21264
T3.A40	9083	T3.D23	15321	T3.L21	21264 + 21263
T3.A41	9270	T3.F01	15053	T3.L22	15682
T3.A42	15668	T3.F02	7568	T3.L23	15711
T3.A43	15670	T3.F03	8268	T3.L24	9060
T3.A44	15677	T3.F04	8398	T3.L25	9283
T3.A45	7727	T3.F05	8400	T3.L26	9371
T3.A46	21414	T3.F06	8991	T3.L27	9419

T3.L28	15436	T3.L38	9377	T3.L47	15759
T3.L29	20473	T3.L39	9497	T3.L48	15765
T3.L30	15600	T3.L40	15583	T3.L49	20090
T3.L31	20041	T3.L41	15591	T3.L50	15702
T3.L32	20752	T3.L42	15669	T3.L51	20912
T3.L33	21343	T3.L43	15672	T3.L52	20801
T3.L34	15545	T3.L44	15673	T3.L53	20840
T3.L35	21524	T3.L45	15680 + 21133	T3.L54	21134
T3.L36	15601	T3.L45	21133 + 15680	T3.L55	21078
T3.L37	9269	T3.L46	15683		

CHAPTER 6

Concordance List of Find Coordinates, Sigla, and Excavation Numbers

1000N3L316	T3.A19	20852	900N5L214	T3.A12	15546
1000N4L1016	T3.L51	20912	900N5L214	T3.A32	15628
1000N5L315	T3.F02	7568	900N5L214	T3.D14	20425
1000N6L115	T3.L08	20771	900N5L313	T3.F14	15460
1000S6L114	T3.D18	20551	900N5L6613	T3.D01	15414
1010N3L215	T3.L23	15711	900N5L6613	T3.D02	15424
1010N4L115	T3.L22	15682	900N8L118	T3.A60	21434
1010N4L115	T3.L46	15683	900N8L118	T3.D13	21519
1010N4L115	T3.L18	15685	900S2L810	T3.A03	9245
1010N4L115+1020N2L116	T3.L45	15680+21133	900S4L108	T3.A40	9083
1010N5L215	T3.F03	8268	910–920N5L313	T3.D23	15321
1010N5L215	T3.L50	15702	910–920N5L413	T3.D04	15449
1010N5L215	T3.A35	20698	910–920N5L413	T3.A07	15452
1010N6L215	T3.L05	15718	910N1L611	T3.A28	15188
1010N6L215	T3.L16	20729	910N1L911	T3.L27	9419
1010N6L215	T3.L07	20749	910N2L1014	T3.A13	15602
1010N6L215	T3.L32	20752	910N2L1114	T3.A15	15639
1010N6L215	T3.F20	20754	910N5L114	T3.A33	15633
1010S4L118	T3.A22	21472	910N5L114	T3.F19	20449
1020N1L116	T3.L53	20840	910N5L214	T3.A50	15486
1020N2L116	T3.L54	21134	910N6L215	T3.A42	15668
1020N2L117+1020N2L117	T3.L21	21263+21264	910N6L215	T3.A43	15670
1020N4L115	T3.L43	15672	910N8L118	T3.D22	21495
1020N4L115	T3.A44	15677	910N8L218	T3.A55	21523
1020N5L115	T3.L42	15669	910N8SD18	T3.D16	21467
1020N5L115	T3.L44	15673	910N8SD18-1	T3.A38	21530
1020N6L118	T3.A46	21414	910S2L110	T3.D19	9244
1020S4L118	T3.L35	21524	920N1L413	T3.A47	21433
840S3L717	T3.A53	15855	920N2L314	T3.A14	15627
890N5L114	T3.L36	15601	920N4L213	T3.D17	15078
890N5L114	T3.D08	20047	920N6L113	T3.L13	15421
890N5L114	T3.L49	20090	920N6L214+890N5L214	T3.F16	15630+20440+20441
890N5L114	T3.D09	20433	920N6L414	T3.A16	15654
890N5L114	T3.D05	15622+20432	920N6L414	T3.A24	15657
890N5L214	T3.D10	20458	920N6L414	T3.A25	15658
890N5L214	T3.L29	20473	920N6L414	T3.A17	15661
890N5L214	T3.D15	20482	920N6L414	T3.F17	15663
890N6L116	T3.D11	20879	920N6L414	T3.L14	20564
890N6L116	T3.A36	20968	920S2L210	T3.F04	8398
900N2L813	T3.F01	15053	920S3L111	T3.A41	9270
900N5L114	T3.A10	15503	920S3L211	T3.F09	9343
900N5L214	T3.F07	8993	920S4L212	T3.F08	9267
900N5L214	T3.A31	15498	920S4L311	T3.L25	9283
900N5L214	T3.L20	15500	930–940N5L113	T3.A23	15075
900N5L214	T3.A11	15510	930–940N5L113	T3.A06	15090
900N5L214	T3.L34	15545	930–940N5L113	T3.A56	15131

© FREDRIK HAGEN, 2021 | DOI:10.1163/9789004447561_007

930–940N5L113	T3.A29	15215	980N6L116	T3.A26	7894
930–940N5L213	T3.L28	15436	980N6L116	T3.A51	20922
930–940N5L213	T3.D03	15439	980N6L116	T3.A52	20923
930N4L714	T3.L03	15537	980N6L517	T3.L55	21078
930N6L113	T3.L02	15399	980S6L717	T3.A59	21140
930N6L114	T3.F06	8991	990N4L1517	T3.A37	7984
930N6L114	T3.D21	15571	990N6L116	T3.L52	20801
930N6L114	T3.L40	15583	990S6L114	T3.F15	15588
930N6L114	T3.L31	20041	R1L113	T3.D20	15197
940N1L108	T3.L24	9060	R4/5L613	T3.A30	15217
940N1L109	T3.A01	9096	R6L113	T3.L39	9497
940N2L510	T3.F05	8400	Ricke Magazine	T3.A39	9035
940N6L214	T3.D06	15655	Ricke Magazine	T3.L01	9137
940N6L214	T3.L06	20478+20547	Ricke Magazine	T3.A48	9036+9138
940S2L1510	T3.L12	9186	S5L3	T3.L37	9269
940S2L910	T3.L11	9163	TVIICL111	T3.A04	9369
940S2L910	T3.A02	9164	TVIICL111	T3.F10	9370
940S4L212	T3.F12	15021			
940S4L817	T3.A54	21156			
940S5L211	T3.L17	9321			
950N1L208	T3.A27	9079			
950N1L208	T3.A49	9080			
950N5L613	T3.F13	15433			
950N6L114	T3.L41	15591			
950N6L114	T3.L30	15600			
950N6L114	T3.A57	15619			
950N6L114	T3.L09	20532			
950S1L111	T3.L26	9371			
950S5L111	T3.L38	9377			
950S6L112	T3.F11	15004			
950S6L112	T3.A05	15012			
960N5L116	T3.A45	7727			
960N6L113	T3.A08	15462			
960N6L113	T3.A09	15466			
960S5L916	T3.L47	15759			
970N4L4018	T3.A61	21471			
970N6L115	T3.F18	15671			
970N6L115	T3.A18	15674			
970N6L115	T3.D07	15679			
970N6L317	T3.D12	21340			
970N6L817	T3.L33	21343			
970S1L114	T3.A58	8943			
980N4L317	T3.A21	21268			
980N5L117	T3.A20	21160			
980N5L315	T3.A34	15675			
980N5L315	T3.L04	15686			
980N5L316	T3.L19	20873			
980N5L416	T3.L48	15765			
980N5L416	T3.L15	20877			
980N5L416	T3.F21	20877			
980N5L517	T3.L10	21053			

Bibliography

Adrom, F. 2006. *Die Lehre des Amenemhet* (Bibliotheca Aegyptiaca 19). Turnhout: Brepols.

Ali, M.S. 1997. 'Der Papyrus Kairo CG 58078—Ein Teil von Papyrus Boulaq 11?' *Lingua Aegyptia* 5, 1–12.

Ali, M.S. 2000. 'Der Papyrus Kairo CG 58074 und der Bauplan auf der Rückseite', in Z. Hawass (ed.), *Egyptology at the Dawn of the Twenty-first Century*. Cairo: American University in Cairo Press, vol. 3, 122–126.

Bailleul-Lesuer, R.F. 2016. *The Exploitation of Live Avian Resources in Pharaonic Egypt: A Socio-Economic Study*. PhD Dissertation, University of Chicago.

Barbotin, C. 2013. 'Les ostraca hiératiques de l'école du Ramesseum', *Memnonia* 24, 73–79.

Barta, W. 1969. 'Zur Bedeutung des *snwt*-Feste', *ZÄS* 95, 73–80.

Beckerath, J. von. 1999. *Handbuch der Ägyptischen Königsnamen* (2nd rev. edition; Münchner Ägyptologische Studien 49). Mainz: Philipp von Zabern.

Bedier, S. 1994. 'Ein Stiftungsdekret Thutmosis' III aus Buto', in M. Minas and J. Zeidler (eds.), *Aspekte spätägyptischer Kultur: Festschrift für Erich Winter zum 65. Geburtstag* (Aegyptiaca Treverensia 7). Mainz: Philipp von Zabern, 35–50.

Blumenthal, E. 1987. 'Die "Gottesvater" des Alten und Mittleren Reiches', *ZÄS* 114, 10–35.

Borchardt, L. 1899. 'Der Zweite Papyrusfund von Kahun und die zeitliche Festlegung des mittleren Reiches der ägyptischen Geschichte', *ZÄS* 37, 89–103.

Borchardt, L. 1903. 'Besoldungsverhältnisse von Priestern im mittleren Reich', *ZÄS* 40, 113–117.

Bouvier, G. 1999–2002. *Catalogue des étiquettes de jarres hiératiques inédites de l'Institut d'Égyptologie de Strasbourg*, 4 vols. (DFIFAO 35, 36, 37, 40). Cairo: Institut français d'archéologie orientale.

Bouvier, G. 2003. *Les étiquettes de jarres hiératiques de l'Institut d'Égyptologie de Strasbourg* (DFIFAO 43). Cairo: Institut français d'archéologie orientale.

Brovarski, E. 1976. 'Senenu, High Priest of Amun at Deir el-Bahri', *JEA* 62, 57–73.

Brunner, H. 1957. *Altägyptische Erziehung* (2nd rev. edition). Wiesbaden: Harrassowitz.

Brunner-Traut, E. 1979. *Egyptian Artists' Sketches: Figured Ostraca from the Gayer-Anderson Collection in the Fitzwilliam Museum, Cambridge*. Istanbul: Nederlands Historisch-Archeologische Instituut te Istanbul.

Bryan, B.M. 2006. 'Administration in the reign of Thutmose III', in E.H. Cline and D. O'Connor (eds.), *Thutmose III: A New Biography*. Ann Arbor: University of Michigan Press, 69–122.

Burkard, G. 2018. *Dra' Abu el-Naga II: Hieratische Ostraka und Namensteine aus Dra' Abu el-Naga* (Archäologische Veröffentlichungen des Deutschen Archäologischen Instituts 129). Wiesbaden: Harrassowitz.

Caminos, R.A. 1954. *Late-Egyptian Miscellanies* (Brown Egyptological Studies 1). Oxford: Oxford University Press.

Caminos, R.A. 1956. *Literary Fragments in the Hieratic Script*. Oxford: Oxford University Press.

Caminos, R.A. 1963. 'Papyrus Berlin 10463', *JEA* 49, 29–37.

Chapon, L. 2018. 'Some Reliefs Representing the King in the *Heb Sed* Robe Discovered in the *Henket-Ankh*', *Études et Travaux* 31, 123–143.

Collier, M. and S. Quirke. 2004. *The UCL Lahun Papyri: Religious, Literary, Legal, Mathematical and Medical* (British Archaeological Reports International Series 1209). Oxford: Archaeopress.

Collier, M. and S. Quirke. 2006. *The UCL Lahun Papyri: Accounts* (British Archaeological Reports International Series 1471). Oxford: Archaeopress.

Daressy, G. 1901. *Catalogue général des antiquités égyptiennes du Musée du Caire. Nos. 25001–25385. Ostraca*. Cairo: Institut français d'archéologie orientale.

Daressy, G. 1926. 'Le voyage d'inspection de M. Grébaut en 1889', *ASAE* 26, 1–22.

Davies, Norman de Garies. 1922–1923. *The Tomb of Puyemrê at Thebes* (Publications of the Metropolitan Museum of Art Egyptian Expedition, Robb de Peyster Tytus Memorial Volumes 2–3), 2 vols. New York: Metropolitan Museum of Art.

Davies, Norman de Garies. 1943. *The Tomb of Rekh-mi-re at Thebes* (Publications of the Metropolitan Museum of Art Egyptian Expedition 11), 2 vols. New York: Metropolitan Museum of Art.

Davies, Norman de Garies. 1948. *Seven Private Tombs at Kurnah* (Mond Excavations at Thebes II, edited by A.H. Gardiner). London: Egypt Exploration Society.

Davies, Norman de Garies and M.F. Laming Macadam. 1957. *A Corpus of Inscribed Egyptian Funerary Cones, Part I: Plates*. Oxford: Oxford University Press for the Griffith Institute.

Demarée, R.J. 2002. *Ramesside Ostraca*. London: British Museum Press.

Dorn, A. 2011. *Arbeiterhütten im Tal der Könige: Ein Beitrag zur Sozialgeschichte aufgrund von neuem Quellenmaterial aus der Mitte der 20. Dynastie (ca. 1150 v. Chr.)* (Aegyptiaca Helvetica 23). Basel: Schwabe Verlag.

El-Hegazi, S. and Y. Koenig. 1993–1994. 'Noveaux ostraca hiératiques trouvés au Ramesseum', *Memnonia* 4–5, 55–58.

Faulkner, R.O. 1969. *The Ancient Egyptian Pyramid Texts*. Oxford: Clarendon Press.

Fischer-Elfert, H.W. 1999. *Die Lehre eines Mannes für seinen Sohn: eine Etappe auf dem "Gottesweg" des loyalen und solidar-*

ischen Beamten des Mittleren Reiches, 2 vols (Ägyptologische Abhandlungen 60). Wiesbaden: Harrassowitz.

Fischer-Elfert, H.W. 2016. 'Aus dem Inhalt einer *ꜥfḏ.t*-Bücherkiste (Pap. Berlin P. hier. 15779)', in S.L. Lippert, M. Schentuleit and M.A. Stadler (eds), *Sapientia Felicitas: Festschrift für Günter Vittmann*. (CENiM 14). Montpellier: Université Paul-Valéry, 149–169.

Gardiner, A.H. 1916. *Notes on the Story of Sinuhe*. Paris: Honoré Champion.

Gardiner, A.H. 1935. *Hieratic Papyri in the British Museum. Third series. The Chester Beatty gift*. London: The British Museum.

Gardiner, A.H. 1937. *Late-Egyptian Miscellanies* (Bibliotheca Aegyptiaca 7). Brussels: Fondation Égyptologique Reine Élisabeth.

Gardiner, A.H. 1947. *Ancient Egyptian Onomastica*, 2 vols. Oxford: Oxford University Press.

Gardiner, A.H. 1948. *Papyrus Wilbour II: Commentary*. Oxford: Oxford University Press.

Gasse, A. 1986. *Catalogue des ostraca figurés de Deir el Médineh, nos. 3100–3372* (Documents de fouilles publiés par les membres d'Institut français d'archéologie orientale 23). Cairo: Institut français d'archéologie orientale.

Gasse, A. 1992. 'Les ostraca hiératiques littéraires de Deir el-Médineh: Nouvelles orientations de la publication', in R.J. Demarée and A. Egberts (eds.), *Village Voices: Proceedings of the Symposium "Texts from Deir el-Medina and their Interpretation", Leiden, May 31–June 1, 1991* (Centre of Non-Western Studies Publications 13). Leiden: Leiden University, 51–70.

Gasse, A. 2005. *Catalogue des ostraca hiératiques littéraires de Deir el-Médina, nos. 1775–1873* (Documents de fouilles d'Institut français d'archéologie orientale 43). Cairo: Institut français d'archéologie orientale.

Germer, R. 1985. *Flora des pharaonischen Ägypten* (Deutsches archäologisches Institut Abteilung Kairo Sonderschrift 14). Cairo: Deutsches archäologisches Institut Abteilung Kairo.

Glanville, S.R.K. 1931. 'Records of a Royal Dockyard of the Time of Tuthmosis III: Papyrus British Museum 10056 (part I)', *ZÄS* 66, 105–121.

Glanville, S.R.K. 1933. 'Records of a Royal Dockyard of the Time of Tuthmosis III: Papyrus British Museum 10056 (part II)', *ZÄS* 68, 7–40.

Görg, M. 1980. 'Lexikalisches zum Papyrus Berlin 10463', *JEA* 66, 160–161.

Golenischeff, W. 1913. *Les papyrus hiératiques nos. 1115, 1116A et 1116B de l'Ermitage imperial à St. Pétersbourg*. St. Petersburg: Manufacture des papiers d'État.

Grandet, P. 1994. *Le Papyrus Harris*, 2 vols. Cairo: Institut français d'archéologie orientale.

Grandet, P. 2000. *Catalogue des ostraca hiératiques non littéraires de Deîr el-Médînéh*, vol. VIII, *nos. 706–830* (Documents de fouilles publiés par les membres d'Institut fran-

çais d'archéologie orientale 39). Cairo: Institut français d'archéologie orientale.

Grandet, P. 2003. *Catalogue des ostraca hiératiques non littéraires de Deîr el-Médînéh*, vol. IX, *nos. 831–1000* (Documents de fouilles publiés par les membres d'Institut français d'archéologie orientale 41). Cairo: Institut français d'archéologie orientale.

Grandet, P. 2006. *Catalogue des ostraca hiératiques non littéraires de Deîr el-Médînéh*, vol. X, *nos. 10001–10123* (Documents de fouilles publiés par les membres d'Institut français d'archéologie orientale 46). Cairo: Institut français d'archéologie orientale.

Grandet, P. 2010. *Catalogue des ostraca hiératiques non littéraires de Deîr el-Médînéh*, vol. XI, *nos. 10124–10275* (Documents de fouilles publiés par les membres d'Institut français d'archéologie orientale 48). Cairo: Institut français d'archéologie orientale.

Grandet, P. 2017. *Catalogue des ostraca hiératiques non littéraires de Deîr el-Médînéh*, vol. XII, *nos. 10276–10405* (Documents de fouilles publiés par les membres d'Institut français d'archéologie orientale 50). Cairo: Institut français d'archéologie orientale.

Griffith, F.Ll. 1898. *Hieratic Papyri from Kahun and Gurob*, vol. II: *Plates*. London: B. Quaritch.

Guksch, H. 1995. *Die Gräber des Nacht-Min und des Men-cheper-Ra-seneb: Theben Nr. 87 und 79* (Archäologische Veröffentlichungen 34). Mainz: Philipp von Zabern.

Hagen, F. 2011. *New Kingdom Ostraca from the Fitzwilliam Museum, Cambridge* (Culture and History of the Ancient Near East 46). Leiden: Brill.

Hagen, F. 2012. *An Ancient Egyptian Literary Text in Context: The Instruction of Ptahhotep* (Orientalia Lovaniensia Analecta 218). Leuven: Peeters.

Hagen, F. 2018. (with a contribution by Daniel Soliman). 'Archives in Ancient Egypt, 2500–1000 BC', in A. Bausi, C. Brockmann, M. Friedrich, S. Kienitz (eds.), *Manuscripts and Archives* (Studies in Manuscript Cultures 10). Berlin: De Gruyter, 71–170.

Hagen, F. 2019. 'Libraries in Ancient Egypt, 1600–800 BC', in K. Ryholt and G. Barjamovic (eds.), *Libraries Before Alexandria: Ancient Near Eastern Traditions*. Oxford: Oxford University Press, 244–318.

Hagen, F. 2020. 'New Copies of Old Classics: Early Manuscripts of *Khakheperreseneb* and *The Instruction of a Man for his Son*', *JEA* 105.

Hagen, F. In preparation A. 'Graffiti from Henket-ankh, the mortuary temple of Thutmose III'.

Hagen, F. In preparation B. *Papyri from the Temple of Millions of Years of Thutmose III*.

Hannig, R. 2003. *Ägyptisches Wörterbuch I: Altes Reich und Erste Zwischenzeit*. Mainz: Philipp von Zabern.

Haring, B.J.J. 1997. *Divine Households: Administrative and Economic Aspects of the New Kingdom Royal Memorial Temples in Western Thebes* (Egyptologische Uitgaven 12). Leiden: Nederlands Instituut voor het Nabije Oosten.

Haring, B.J.J. 2018. *From Single Sign to Pseudo-Script: An Ancient Egyptian System of Workmen's Identity Marks* (Culture and History of the Ancient Near East 93). Leiden: Brill.

Haring, B.J.J. 2020. 'The Survival of Pharaonic Ostraca: Coincidence or Meaningful Patterns?', in C. Caputo and J. Lougovaya (eds.), *Using Ostraca in the Ancient World: New Discoveries and Methodologies* (Materiale Textkulturen 32). Berlin: De Gruyter, 89–108.

Haring, B.J.J., O.E. Kaper, and R. van Walsem (eds). 2014. *The Workman's Progress: Studies in the Village of Deir al-Medina and Other Documents from Western Thebes in Honour of Rob Demarée* (Egyptologische Uitgaven 28). Leuven: Peeters.

Harris, J.R. 1961. *Lexicographical studies in ancient Egyptian minerals* (Deutsche Akademie der Wissenschaften zu Berlin, Institut für Orientforschung, Veröffentlichung 54). Berlin: Akademie Verlag.

Hayes, W.C. 1942. *Ostraka and Name-Stones from the Tomb of Sen-Mut (No. 71) at Thebes*. New York: Metropolitan Museum of Art.

Hayes, W.C. 1951. 'Inscriptions from the Palace of Amenhotep III' (in four parts), *Journal of Near Eastern Studies* 10, 35–56, 82–112, 156–183, 231–242.

Hayes, W.C. 1960. 'A Selecton of Tuthmoside Ostraca from Der el-Bahri', *Journal of Egyptian Archaeology* 46, 29–52.

Helck, W. 1958. *Zur Verwaltung des mittleren und des neuen Reiches*. Leiden: Brill.

Helck, W. 1960–1970. *Materialien zur Wirtschaftsgeschichte des Neuen Reiches* 7 vols. Wiesbaden: Akademie der Wissenschaften und der Literatur in Mainz.

Helck, W. 1971. *Das Bier im Alten Ägypten*. Berlin: Gesellschaft für die Geschichte und Bibliographie des Brauwesens.

Helck, W. 1974. *Altägyptische Aktenkunde des 3. und 2. Jahrtausends v. Chr.* (Münchner Ägyptologische Studien 31). Munich: Deutscher Kunstverlag.

Helck, W. 1982. 'Phyle', in *LÄ*, 1044.

Hoch, J.E. 1994. *Semitic Words in Egyptian Texts of the New Kingdom and Third Intermediate Period*. Princeton NJ, Princeton University Press.

Hornung, E. and E. Staehelin. 1974. *Studien zum Sedfest* (Aegyptiaca Helvetica 1). Basel: Ägyptologisches Seminar der Universität Basel.

Hornung, E. and E. Staehelin. 2006. *Neue Studien zum Sedfest* (Aegyptiaca Helvetica 20). Basel: Schwabe Verlag.

Hornung, E., R. Krauss, and D. Warburton (eds). 2006. *Ancient Egyptian Chronology* (Handbook of Oriental Studies, Section One: The Near and Middle East 83). Leiden: Brill.

Jäger, S. 2004. *Altägyptische Berufstypologien* (Lingua Aegyptia Studia Monographica 4). Göttingen: Seminar für Ägyptologie und Koptologie.

Janssen, Jac. J. 1975. *Commodity Prices from the Ramesside Period*. Leiden: Brill.

Jéquier, G. 1911. 'Essai sur la nomenclature des parties de bateaux', *BIFAO* 9, 37–82

Jurjens, J. 2019. 'The Teaching of Khety Twice—A New Reading of oBM EA 65597 as a school exercise', *JEA* 105, 127–134.

Kahl, J. 1999. *Siut—Theben. Zur Weltschätzung von Traditionen im alten Ägypten* (Probleme der ägyptologie 13). Leiden: Brill.

Kaper, O.E. 2010. 'A Kemyt Ostracon from Amheida, Dakleh Oasis', *BIFAO* 110, 115–126.

Kees, H. 1953. *Das Priestertum im ägyptischen Staat vom Neuen Reich bis zur Spätzeit* (PdÄ 1). Leiden: Brill.

Kees, H. 1958. *Das Priestertum im ägyptischen Staat vom Neuen Reich bis zur Spätzeit: Indices und Nachträge* (PdÄ 1). Leiden: Brill.

Kitchen, K. 1991. 'Building the Ramesseum', *CRIPEL* 13, 85–93.

Koenig, Y. 1979. *Catalogue des étiquettes de jarres hiératiques de Deir el-Médineh*, vol. 1, *nos. 6000–6241* (Documents de fouilles de l'Institut français d'archéologie orientale 21). Cairo: Institut français d'archéologie orientale.

Koenig, Y. 1980. *Catalogue des étiquettes de jarres hiératiques de Deir el-Médineh*, vol. 2, *nos. 6242–6497* (Documents de fouilles de l'Institut français d'archéologie orientale 21). Cairo: Institut français d'archéologie orientale.

Koenig, Y. 1992. 'Les textes hiératiques du Ramesseum', *Memnonia* 3, 49–58.

Krauss, R. 'nḥ(ḥ)-Öl = Olivenöl', *MDAIK* 55, 293–298.

Lacau, P. 1926. *Stèles du Nouvel Empire* I (Catalogue générale des antiquités égyptiennes du Musée du Caire Nos. 34001–34186). Cairo: Institut français d'archéologie orientale.

Lacovara, P. 1997. *The New Kingdom Royal City* (Studies in Egyptology). London: Kegan Paul.

Laskowski, P. 'Monumental Architecture and the Royal Building Program of Thutmose III', in E.H. Cline and D. O'Connor (eds.), *Thutmose III: A New Biography*. Ann Arbor: University of Michigan Press, 183–237.

Leahy, M.A. 1985. 'The Hieratic Labels, 1979–1982', in B.J. Kemp (ed.), *Amarna Reports* II. London: Egypt Exploration Society, 65–109.

Leblanc, C. 2004. 'L'école du temple (ât-sebait) et le per-ankh (maison de vie). Á propos de récentes découvertes effectuées dans le contexte du Ramesseum', *Memnonia* 15, 93–101.

Legrain, G. 1906. 'Notes d'inspection XXXVII: Sur le temple Manakhpirri-henq-ankh', *Annales du Service des Antiquités de l'Égypte* 7, 183–187.

Loret, V. 1889. 'La Tombe de Khâ-m-hâ', in G. Maspero, U. Bouriant, V. Loret and H. Dulac (eds.), *Mémoires publiés par les membres de la Mission Archéologique Française au Caire*, I, 113–132.

McDowell, A.G. 1996. 'Student Exercises from Deir el-Medina: The Dates', in P. Der Manuelian (ed.), *Studies in Honor of William Kelly Simpson*, vol. 2. Boston: Museum of Fine Arts, 601–608.

McDowell, A.G. 2000. 'Teachers and Students at Deir el-Medina', in R. Demarée, A. Egberts (eds.), *Deir el-Medina in the Third Millennium AD: A tribute to Jac. J. Janssen* (Egyptologische Uitgaven 14). Leiden: Nederlands Instituut voor het Nabije Oosten, 217–233.

McGovern, P.E. 1997. 'Wine of Egypt's Golden Age: An Archaeochemical Perspective', *JEA* 83 (1997), 69–108.

Martin, G.T. 2005. *Stelae from Egypt and Nubia in the Fitzwilliam Museum, Cambridge, c. 3000 BC–AD 1150*. Cambridge: Cambridge University Press.

Mariette, A. 1869. *Abydos: description des fouilles exécutées sur l'emplacement de cette ville*, vol. 1. Paris: Librairie A. Franck.

Mathieu, B. 1996. *La poésie amoureuse de l'Égypte ancienne: recherches sur un genre littéraire au Nouvel Empire* (Bibliothèque d'études 115). Cairo: Institut français d'archéologie orientale.

Meeks, D. 1977. *Année Lexicographique*, vol. I. Paris: privately published.

Möller, G. 1927. *Hieratische Paläographie* (2nd rev. edition), vols. I–III. Leipzig: J.C. Hinrichs'sche Buchhandlung.

Müller, M. 2014. 'Ostraka aus dem Totentempel des Merenptah in Theben', in J. Toivari-Viitala, T. Vartiainen, and S. Uvanto (eds.), *Deir el-Medina Studies: Helsinki June 24–26, 2009 Proceedings* (The Finnish Egyptological Society Occasional Publications 2). Vantaa: Multiprint, 144–153.

Müller, M. Forthcoming. 'Hieratische Ostraka und Gefässaufschriften' in: Horst Jaritz (ed.), *Untersuchungen im Totentempel des Merenptah in Theben VI: Tierknochen und Kleinfunde* (Beiträge zur Bauforschung und Altertumskunde). Gladbeck: PeWe-Verlag.

Naville, E. 1892. *The Festival-Hall of Osorkon II in the Great Temple of Bubastis*. London: Egypt Exploration Fund.

Naville, E. 1898. *The Temple of Deir el-Bahri*, vol. II (Egypt Exploration Fund Memoir 16). London: Egypt Exploration Fund.

Nelson, H.H. 1934. *Medinet Habu III: The Calendar, the "Slaughterhouse", and minor records of Rameses III* (Oriental Institute Publications 23). Chicago: University of Chicago Press.

Otto, E. 1960. *Das Ägyptische Mundöffnungsritual*, 2 vols. (Ägyptologische Abhandlungen 3). Wiesbaden: Harrassowitz.

Pantalacci, L. and J. Lesur. 2012. 'Élevage et consommation de viande à Balat (oasis de Dakhla). Fin de l'Ancien Empire-Première Période intermédiaire', *BIFAO* 112, 291–316.

Parkinson, R.B. 1997. *The Tale of Sinuhe and Other Ancient Egyptian Poems 1940–1640 BC*. Oxford: Oxford University Press.

Parkinson, R.B. 2009. *Reading Ancient Egyptian Poetry*. Chichester: Wiley-Blackwell.

Parkinson, R.B. 2019. 'Libraries in Ancient Egypt, c. 2600–1600 BCE', in K. Ryholt and G. Barjamovic (eds.), *Libraries Before Alexandria: Ancient Near Eastern Traditions*. Oxford: Oxford University Press, 115–167.

Peet, T.E. 1935–1938. 'The Unit Value of *š'ty* in Papyrus Boulaq 11', in *Mélanges Maspero*, vol. I (MIFAO 66/1). Cairo: Institut français d'archéologie orientale.

Pendlebury, J.D.S. 1951. *The City of Akhenaten III: The Central City and the Official Quarters* (Egypt Exploration Society Excavation Memoirs 44), 2 vols. London: Egypt Exploration Society.

Peterson, B.E.J. 1973. *Zeichnungen aus einer Totenstadt: Bildostraka aus Theben-West, ihre Fundplätze, Themata und Zweckbereiche mitsamt einem Katalog der Gayer-Anderson Sammlung in Stockholm* (Bulletin of the Museum of Mediterranean and Near Eastern Antiquities Stockholm 7–8). Stockholm: Medelhavsmuseet.

Petrie, W.M.F. 1894. *Tell el-Amarna*. London: Methuen & Co.

Pommerening, T. 2005. *Die altägyptischen Hohlmasse* (Studien zur altägyptischen Kultur Beihefte 10). Hamburg: Helmut Buske Verlag.

Posener-Kriéger, P. 1976. *Les archives du temple funéraire de Néferirkarê-Kakaï*, 2 vols. (Bibliothèque d'étude 65). Cairo: Institut français d'archéologie orientale.

Pouls Wegner, M.-A. 2009. 'The Construction Accounts from the "Portal Temple" of Ramesses II in North Abydos', in W.K. Simpson and J. Wegner (eds.), *Archaism and Innovation: Studies in the Culture of Middle Kingdom Egypt*. New Haven: Department of Near Eastern Languages and Civilizations, Yale University: University of Pennsylvania Museum of Archaeology and anthropology, 557–574.

Quack, J.F. 2002. 'Dienstanweisung des Oberlehrers aus dem Buch vom Tempel', in H. Beinlich (ed.), *5. Ägyptologische Tempeltagung. Würzburg, 23.–26. September 1999* (Ägypten und Altes Testament 33). Wiesbaden: Harrassowitz, 159–171.

Quack, J.F. 2003. 'Aus einer spätzeitlichen literarischen Sammelhandschrift (Papyrus Berlin 23045)', *ZÄS* 130, 182–185.

Quack, J.F. 2005. 'Überlieferungsstruktur des Buches vom Tempel', in S. Lippert and M. Schentuleit (eds.), *Tebtynis und Soknopaiu Nesos: Leben im römerzeitlichen Fajum: Akten des Internationalen Symposions vom 11. bis 13. Dezember 2003 in Sommerhausen bei Würzburg*. Wiesbaden: Harrassowitz, 105–115.

Quack, J.F. 2006. 'Fragmente des Mundöffnungsritual aus Tebtunis', in K. Ryholt (ed.), *The Carlsberg Papyri 7: Hieratic Texts from the Collection*. Copenhagen: Museum Tusculanum Press, 69–150.

Quack, J.F. 2016. 'Translating the Realities of Cult', in I. Rutherford (ed.), *Greco-Egyptian Interactions: Literature, Translation, and Culture, 500 BCE–300 CE*. Oxford: Oxford University Press, 267–286.

Quagebeur, J. 1971. 'Documents concerning a Cult of Arsinoe Philadelphos at Memphis', *JNES* 30, 239–270.

Ranke., H. 1935. *Die ägyptischen Personennamen*, vol. 1. Glückstadt: J.J. Augustin.

Redford, D.B. 1986. *Pharaonic King-Lists, Annals and Day-Books*. Mississauga: Benben.

Ricke, H. 1939. *Der Totentempel Thutmoses' III*. (Beiträge zur ägyptischen Bauforschung und Altertumskunde 3). Glückstadt: J.J. Augustin.

Römer, M. 2014. 'Miszellen zu den Ostraka der 18. Dynastie aus Deir el-Bahri und dem Asasif', in B.J.J. Haring, O.E. Kaper and R. van Walsem (eds.), *The Workman's Progress: Studies in the Village of Deir el-Medina and Other Documents from Western Thebes in Honour of Rob Demarée* (EU 28). Leuven: Peeters, 211–216.

Römer, M. 2017a. 'Bauarbeiten der 18. Dynastie in Deir el-Bahri: Bausteine. Arbeiten im Steinbruch und Schiffstransporte. Andere Transportmittel', *GM* 252, 119–133.

Römer, M. 2017b. 'Die *mr.t*-Leute: Was sich aus den Ostraka der frühen 18. Dynastie von Deir el-Bahri ergibt', *GM* 251, 79–93.

Sadek, A.I. 1980. *The amethyst mining inscriptions of Wadi el-Huli*, vol. 1: *Texts*. Warminster: Aris & Phillips.

Samuel, D. 2000. 'Brewing and baking', in P.T. Nicholson and I. Shaw (eds.), *Ancient Egyptian Materials and Technology*. Cambridge: Cambridge University Press, 537–576.

Satzinger, H. 1986. 'Syntax der Präpositionsadjektive', *ZÄS* 113, 141–153.

Sauneron, S. 2000. *The Priests of Ancient Egypt* [translated by David Lorton]. Ithaca: Cornell University Press.

Schott, S. 1950. *Altägyptische Festdaten*. Mainz: Verlag der Akademie der Wissenschaften und der Literatur.

Schwechler, C. 2020. *Les noms des pains en Égypte ancienne: Étude lexicologique* (Studien zur altägyptischen Kultur Beihefte 22). Hamburg: Helmut Buske Verlag.

Seco Álvarez, M. 2015a. 'The Henket-ankh Temple of Thutmosis III in Luxor West Bank: Five Years of Intervention', in A. Jiménez-Serrano and C. von Pilgrim (eds.), *From the Delta to the Cataract: Studies Dedicated to Mohamed el-Bialy*. Leiden: Brill, 240–253.

Seco Álvarez, M. 2015b. 'Latest news about the work in the Temple of Millions of Years of the pharaoh Thutmose III in Qurna', in M.S. Álvarez and A.J. Miñarro (eds.), *The Temples of Millions of Years in Thebes*. Granada: Editorial Universidad de Granada.

Seco Álvarez, M. and J.M. Babón. 2015. 'A Ramesside Building in the Temple of Millions of Years of Thutmose III in Luxor', *SAK* 44, 383–391.

Seco Álvarez, M. and A.G. Campuzano. 2015. 'Thutmosis III Temple of Millions of Years and the Mud Brick Marks: Conservation and first conclusions', in J. Budka, F. Kammerzell, and S. Rzepka (eds.), *Non-Textual Marking Systems in Ancient Egypt (and Elsewhere)* (Lingua Aegyptia Studia Monographica 16). Hamburg: Widmaier Verlag, 59–67.

Shalaby, N. 2012. 'A Headless Block Statuette of the XXVIth Dynasty (CGC 941)', *BIFAO* 112, 371–380.

Spalinger, A. 1985. 'Notes on the Day Summary Accounts of P. Bulaq 18 and the Intradepartmental Transfers', *SAK* 12, 179–242.

Spalinger, A. 1987. 'The grain system of Dynasty 18', *SAK* 14, 283–311.

Spencer, N. 2010. 'Priests and Temples: Pharaonic', in A. Lloyd (ed.), *A Companion to Ancient Egypt*. Chichester: Wiley-Blackwell, 255–273.

Spiegelberg, W. 1898. *Hieratic Ostraca and Papyri found by J.E. Quibell in the Ramesseum, 1895–1896* (British School of Archaeology in Egypt, Egyptian Research Account, Extra Volume). London: B. Quaritch.

Tallet, P. 2003. 'Les circuits économiques selon les étiquettes de jarres de Deir el-Médineh', in A. Guillemette (ed.), *Deir el-Médineh et la Vallée des Rois: la vie en Egypte au temps des pharaons du Nouvel Empire. Actes du colloque organisé par le Musée du Louvre, les 3 et 4 mai 2002*. Paris: Khéops/Musée du Louvre, 253–278.

Thomson, J.K. 1998. 'A First Acolyte of Amun', *JEA* 84, 215–220.

Troy, L. 2006. 'Religion and Cult during the Time of Thutmose III', in E.H. Cline and D. O'Connor (eds.), *Thutmose III: A New Biography*. Ann Arbor: University of Michigan Press, 123–182.

Valbelle, D. 1985. *Les ouvriers de la tombe: Deir el-Medinéh à l'époque Ramesside* (Bibliothèque d'étude 96). Cairo: Institut français d'archéologie orientale.

Vandier d'Abbadie, J. 1936–1959. *Catalogue des ostraca figurés de Deir el Médineh* (Documents de Fouilles publiés par les membres d'Institut français d'archéologie orientale 2.1–3). Cairo: Institut français d'archéologie orientale.

Verhoeven, U. 1984. *Grillen, kochen, backen im Alltag und im Ritual Altägyptens: ein lexikographischer Beitrag* (Rites Égyptiens 4). Brussels: Fondation Égyptologique Reine Élisabeth.

Verhoeven, U. 2013. 'Literatur im Grab—der Sonderfall Assiut', in G. Moers, K. Widmaier, A. Giewekemeyer, A. Lümers, and R. Ernst (eds), *Dating Egyptian Literary Texts* (Lingua Aegyptia Studia Monographica 11). Hamburg: Widmaier Verlag, 139–158.

Verhoeven, U. 2015. 'Iterationen im altägyptischen Schreiberalltag', in E. Cancik-Kirschbaum and A. Traninger (eds), *Wissen in Bewegung: Institution—Iteration—Transfer* (Episteme in Bewegung 1). Wiesbaden: Harrasowitz.

Vittmann, G. 1983. 'Eine genealogische Inschrift der Spätzeit im Tempel von Luxor', *SAK* 10, 325–332.

Wallert, I. 1962. *Die Palmen im Alten Ägypten* (Münchner Ägyptologische Studien 1). Berlin: Verlag Bruno Hessling.

Weigall, A.E.P. 1906. 'A Report on the Excavation of the Funeral Temple of Thoutmosis III at Gurneh', *Annales du Service des Antiquités de l'Égypte* 7, 121–141.

Weigall, A.E.P. 1908. 'Plan of the mortuary temple of Thoutmose III', *Annales du Service des Antiquités de l'Égypte* 8, 286.

Westendorf, W. 1955. 'Der Rezitationsvermerk *ts-pḥr*', in O. Firchow (ed.), *Ägyptologische Studien* (Institut für Orientforschung Veröffentlichung 29). Berlin: Akademie-Verlag,
383–402.

Wilson, P. 1997. *A Ptolemaic Lexikon: A Lexicographic Study of the
Texts in the Temple of Edfu* (Orientalia Lovaniensia Analecta
78). Leuven: Peeters.

Winter, E. 1970. 'Nochmals zum *snwt*-Fest', *ZÄS* 96, 151–152.

Wreszinski, W. 1908. 'Ein V. Prophet des Amon?', *Orientalistische
Literaturzeitung* 10, 471.

Indices of Egyptian Words

For reasons of space the references are given in the shortened format of sigla + line number (abbreviated to one or two digits only), so that e.g. 'A01.2' refers to 'O. T3.A01, line x+2'.

Place-Names

Wꜣst Thebes (L11.1)
Nꞽwt Thebes? (L40.3)

Ḏsrw Deir el-Bahri (A26.3; A49.1; A53.1 + vso. 4)

Names of Gods

Ꞽmn Amun (A57.1; L40.1)
Ꞽmn-Rꜥ Amun-Re (L39.1–2)
Ꞽtn Aten (D11.1; L42.2—of the sun disc)
Mwt Mut (L39.1)
Mntw Montu (L24.1)
Rꜥ Re (Lo8.2; L28.1; L47.1?)

Ḥꜥpy Hapy (L23.1; L54.1)
Ḥrw Horus (L33.2, 4)
Ḫnsw Khonsu (A57.1; L28.1)
Ḳbḥ-snw-f Qebehsenuef (L45.1)
Tm Atum (L24.2)

Royal Names

ꜥꜣ-ḫpr-n-rꜥ Thutmose II (L29.1)
Ꞽmn-m-ḥꜣt Amenemhat I (Lo5.1)
Ꞽmn-ḥtp Amenhotep I (?) (Do5.1)

Mn-mꜣꜥt-rꜥ Seti I (D12.1)
Mn-ḫpr-rꜥ Thutmose III (A53.vso.3; L25.1; L26.1; L27.1; L28.1, 29.2)
Sḥtp-ꞽb-rꜥ Amenemhat I (Lo5.1; Lo7.2; Lo8.1)

Titles

ꞽmy-r pr overseer of the house / steward (A39.1)
ꞽmy-r rsy overseer of the South (A54.8)
ꞽmy-st-ꜥ priest / ritual assistant (Ao4.2–3; A14.4)
ꞽn-mw water carrier (A40.1)
ꞽri-ꜥꜣ door-keeper (A17.4)
ꞽt-nṯr god's father (L44.1)
ꜥḥꜣ.w weapon-maker (L18.1)
wꜥb wab-priest (A11.3; A14.3, 6; A31.1.1–3, 11.1–2; A43, *passim*; A45.2–4; L39.2; L49.1)
bs (gold-)applier? (A43.1.9, 11, 13)
nb lord (A54.1; L11.1; L12.1; L13.A; L14.2)
nby goldsmith (A43.1.2, 9, 11, 13, 18, 20; vso. 3, 9)
ḥm-nṯr tpy high priest (A19.2–3)

ḥnw.t lady (L43.1)
ḥry sꜣw chief guardian? (A34.1)
ḥry kꜣmw chief vintner (Do2.2; Do5.2; Do7.2; Do9.3; D10.3; D11.2; D22.2)
ḥrp.w directors (A54.3)
ḥr.ti-nṯr stone mason (A23.1; A27.1; A53.1, 2, 6; vso. 1, 2, 4)
sr.w officials (A44.1)
sš scribe (T3.A3o.1; A37.1; A38.1; A40.2; A53.1; A57.1?)
sš nsw royal scribe (A39.1–2)
sḏm.w(-ꜥš?) workers (A47.1)
ḳd.w builder (A54.1)
kꜣmw vintner (Do3.2; Do6.2)

Personal Names

Ꞽꜥḥ-ms Ahmose (A43.1.9—a *wꜥb*-priest; A53.2—a stone mason)
Ꞽmn-m-ꞽpt Amenemope (A31.3—a *wꜥb*-priest)
Ꞽmn-m-ḥꜣt Amenemhat (A43.1.15—a *wꜥb*-priest, A43.1.19—a *wꜥb*-priest, A43.11.7—a *wꜥb*-priest, A43.11.12 (?)—probably a *wꜥb*-priest, A43.vso.1 (?)—a *wꜥb*-priest)
Ꞽmn-m-ḥb Amenemheb (A43.1.16—a *wꜥb*-priest, A43.vso.7—a *wꜥb*-priest)
Ꞽmn-ms Amenmose (A43.1.3—a *wꜥb*-priest, A43.11.11—a *wꜥb*-priest; Do6.2—a vintner)
Ꞽmn-ḥp (?) Amenhep (?) (Do6.2—or a locality)
Ꞽmn-ḥtp Amenhotep (A14.4—an *ꞽmy-st-ꜥ* priest; A27.2—a stone mason; A43.1.11—a *wꜥb*-priest; A43.1.18—a *wꜥb*-priest; A43.11.8—a *wꜥb*-priest; A43.11.9—a *wꜥb*-priest; A43.vso.8—a *wꜥb*-priest; A53.1—a scribe)

Ꞽny Iny (A43.11.2—a *wꜥb*-priest)
Ꞽnpw Inpu (A12.3)
ꜥbdy Abdy (A43.1.18—a goldsmith?)
Wꜥb Wab (A12.3)
Wbn Weben (A43.1.6—a *wꜥb*-priest)
Wḥm-ḏd Wehemdjed (A32.1)
Wsr-ḥꜣt Userhat (A53.7—a stone mason)
Bnr-mrwt Benermerut (A53.4—probably Overseer of the House of Gold and Silver, Overseer of All Works of the King)
Pꜣy⟨ꞽt⟩ꞽmn (?) Pay⟨it⟩amun (?) (A37.1)
Pꜣ-wꜣḥ-ḏꜣy (?) Pawahdjay (?) (A43.1.14—goldsmith and applier?)
Pꜣ-ḥw-mw Pahemu (A12.1)
Pr-s (?) Peres (?) (A11.2)
Mꜥy May (A42.1.2—son of Nebimose)

Mꜥḥw   Mahu (A12.4; A28.1)

Mnw-nḫt   Minnakht (A31.1.2)

Mn-ḫpr-rꜥ   Menkheperre (A43.1.5—a wꜥb-priest, A43.1.14—a wꜥb-priest)

Mry   Mery (A14.8—a wꜥb-priest; A43.1.8 (?)—a wꜥb-priest; A45.3—a wꜥb-priest)

Mryw   Meryu (A45.5—a wꜥb-priest)

Mry-ptḥ (?)   Meryptah (?) (D17.2)

Mrw   Meru (A43.vso.6—a wꜥb-priest)

Mr-wꜣst   Merywaset (D07.2—a chief vintner)

Mr-mꜣꜥt   Merymaat (A26.1)

Mnḫt   Menkhet (A43.1.11—a goldsmith and applier?)

Nꜣnꜣswy   Nanasuy (A26.2)

Nb-imn   Nebamun (A16.II, 2; A43.1.2—a goldsmith, A43.vso.9—a wꜥb-priest)

Nbi-ms   Nebimose (A42.I.2)

Nb-mrwt-f   Nebmerutef (A43.vso.2—a wꜥb-priest, A43.vso.10—a wꜥb-priest)

Nb-n-tꜣ   Nebenta (A43.1.11—a wꜥb-priest)

Nb-nḫt   Nebnakht (A11.4)

Nfr-prt   Neferperet (D11.2—a chief vintner)

Nfr-rnpt   Neferrenpet (A40.2—a scribe; D02.2—a chief vintner)

Nhm-rdi   Nehemredy (A42.I.1)

Nsw   Nesu (A43.1.10)

Hꜣwiꜣm (?)   Hauiam (?) (A33.1)

Hꜣy   Hay (A42.II.2—son of Seneb?)

Ḥꜣt   Hat (D05.2—a chief vintner)

Ḥꜣti   Hati (A29.1)

Ḥꜣtiꜣy   Hatiay (A45.4—a wꜥb-priest)

Ḥkꜣ-nfr   Hekanefer (A31.I.1—a wꜥb-priest; A43.I.17—a wꜥb-priest)

Ḫꜥiꜣ (?)   Khaia (? or Khaamun) (A30.1—a scribe)

Ḫꜥ-imn (?)   Khaamun (? or Khaia?) (A30.1—a scribe)

Ḫꜥ-m-wꜣst   Khaemwaset (L49.1—a wꜥb-priest)

Ḫnm-ms   Khnummose (A46.1)

Ḫryḥb (?)   Kheryheb (?) (A16.II.5)

S   Si (A38.1—a scribe)

Sꜣ-pꜣ-ir   Sapair (A43.II.10—a wꜥb-priest, A43.vso.11—a wꜥb-priest)

Sꜣfy (?)   Safy (?) (A43.I.20—a goldsmith)

Sꜣhkk (?)   Sahekek (?) (A43.I.9—a goldsmith and applier?)

Sbꜣ   Seba (A43.I.7—a wꜥb-priest)

Snn   Senna (A43.II.1 (?)—perhaps a wꜥb-priest; A54.1—a builder)

Snb   Seneb (A43.vso.5—a wꜥb-priest; A42.II.2 (?)—father of Hay?)

Sn-n-mwt   Senenmut (A54.2—probably the famous chief steward under Hatshepsut)

Sn-dḥwty   Sendjehuty (A50.1, A50.vso.3)

Ḳn-imn   Kenamun (A36.1)

Kꜣ   Ka (A43.vso.3—a goldsmith)

Kꜣ-m-wꜣst   Kaemwaset (A42.II, 1)

Tḫy (?)   Tekhy (?) (A41.4)

Dḥwty-ms   Thutmose (D21.3)

Incomplete Personal Names

[...]-m-ḥꜣt   [Amen?]emhat (A43.II.12—a wꜥb-priest)

[...]-nḫt   [...]nakht (?) (A46.2)

[...]mšꜣḳmw   [...]emshakemu (A35.1)

Imn-m-[...]   Amenem[hat?] (A43.vso.1)

Imn-[tꜣw] (?)   Amen[tjau] (?) (A43.vso.4—a wꜥb-priest)

Ptḥ-m-[...]   Ptahem[...] (A41.1)

Mntw-[...]   Montu[...] (A41.3)

Mr-[...]   Mer[mer?] (A14.3—a wꜥb-priest)

Nḫ-[...]   Neh[sheri?] (A43.I.13—a wꜥb-priest)

Ḫꜥ[...]   Kha[...] (A39.2—a royal scribe)

Ḫnsw-[...]   Khonsu[...] (A41.2)

Snim-[...]   Seniem[...] (A43.I.4)

Tn-[...]   Tjen[en?] (A14.6)

General Index of Egyptian Words

ꜣbd   month (A06.3; A17.1; A26.3; L03.4; L18.3; L42.1; L48.3)

ꜣpd   bird (A11.2; A14.4; A15.2, 3)

ꜣpd mr   pond fowl (D15.1)

ꜣḫ   to be beneficial (L41.1)

ꜣḫt   the season of Akhet (A17,1; A25.1; A26.3; L42.1)

ꜣḫt   horizon (A53.4; L38.1)

ꜣs   to hurry (A51.3)

iꜣrw (?)   reeds (?) (A05.2)

iꜣwt   profession, office (L53.2)

iꜣmw   tents (A54.4)

iw   to come, to be delivered (A05.1–4; A15.4; A18.4)

iwꜥ   a type of building-work (A24.II.2, 3, 5)

iwtn   ground level (A24.II.8)

ib   heart (L01.2; L03.1, 2; L50.2)

imꜣḫ   revered one (L45.1)

imnty   western (D05.2)

in(i)   to bring (A26.3)

inb   wall (L11.2)

ir(i)   to make (A48.2; A52.4; A53.2; A54.4, 5)

iry   companion (L32.2)

irp   wine (A14.3; A22.1; D01.2; D02.1; D03.1; D04.1; D05.1; D09.2; D10.2; D13.1)

ir.t   eye (L33.2, 3)

itrw   river (D02.1; D08.2)

ꜥ   hand, authority (A17.4)

ꜥꜣ   large (A07.1; A13.2; A18.vso.3; A18.2; A24.II.6; L23.2)

ꜥꜣ(.t)   donkey (L18.1; L43.2)

ꜥnḫ   life, to live (L13.B; L26.2; L20.A.1; L48.1; D05.1; D11.1; D12.1; D16.2)

ꜥr   reed pen(?) (L30.1)

ꜥrḳ.y   last day (A24.I.1)

ꜥḥꜣ   to fight, be aggressive (?) (L43.1)

ꜥḥꜥ   to wait, to stand (A51.4; L19.4)

ꜥḥꜥ.w   property (A04.2)

ꜥḥꜥ.w   lifetime (L20.A.1)

ꜥš   coniferous wood (A17.2, vso. 2)

ꜥšꜣ   a type of duck (A12.2, 3)

ꜥḳ.w   rations (A21.1)

ꜥḳ.w   intimates (L01.3; L03.3)

ꜥd   balk (A17.vso.3)

wꜣḥ   to place (A24.II.9; F20.3)

wꜣg   wꜣg-festival (A13.1; A55.2)

wꜣt   road, approach (?) (A24.II.6)

wꜣd   fresh (D21.2)

Index of Festivals Mentioned in the Ostraca

Plates

∵

PLATE 1

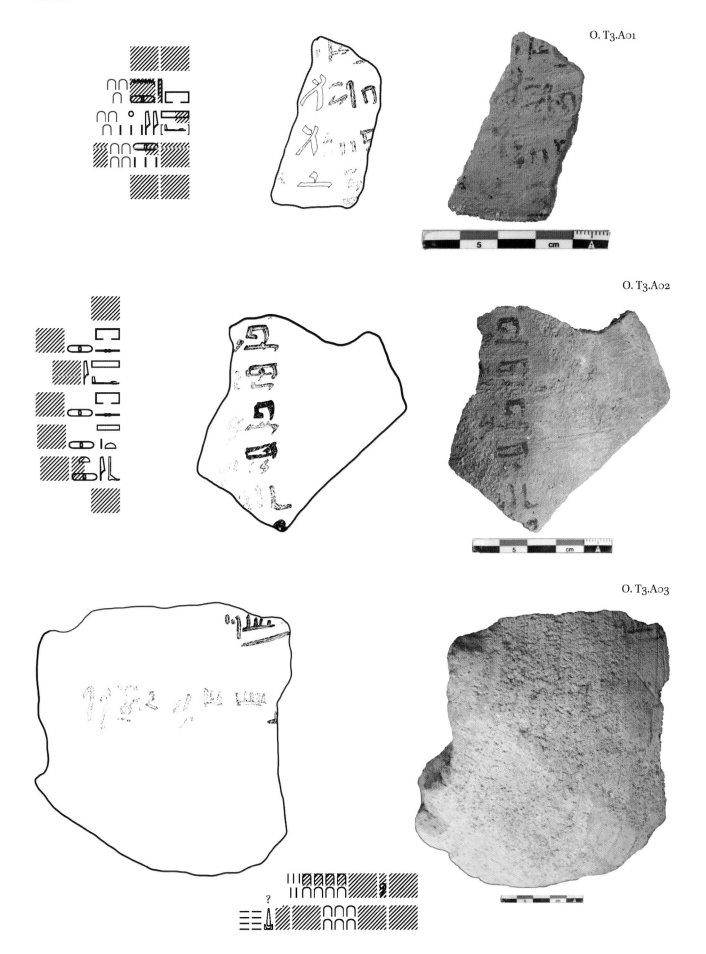

O. T3.A01

O. T3.A02

O. T3.A03

PLATE 2

PLATE 3

O. T3.A05

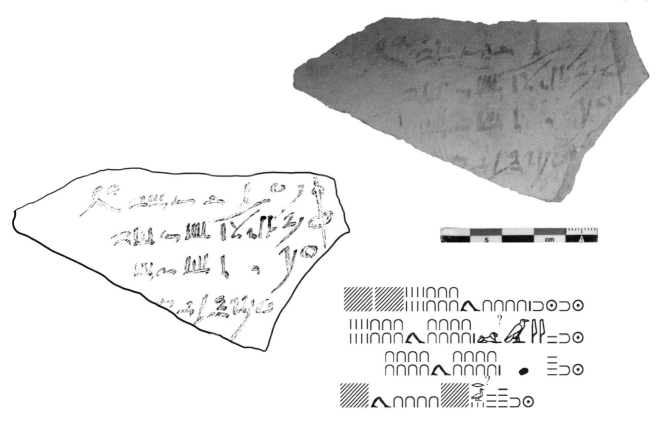

O. T3.D17

PLATE 4

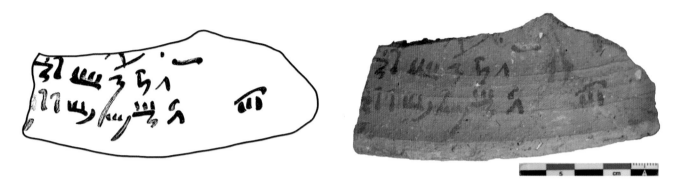

PLATE 5

O. T3.A08

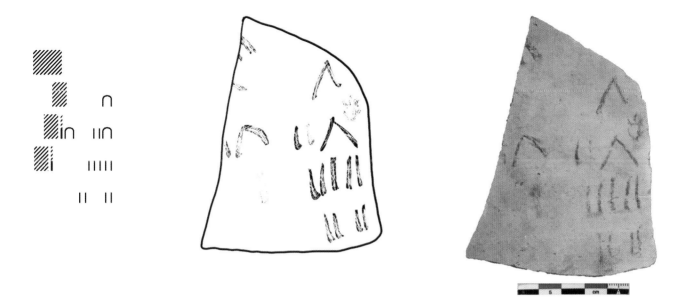

O. T3.A09

PLATE 6

O. T3.A10

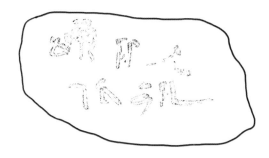

O. T3.A11

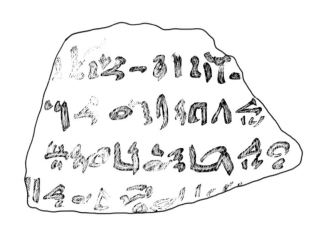

PLATE 7

O. T3.A12

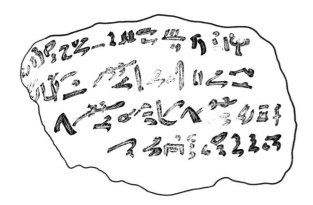 

O. T3.A15

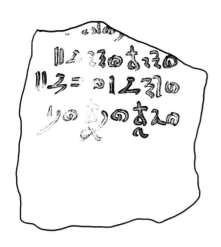 

PLATE 8

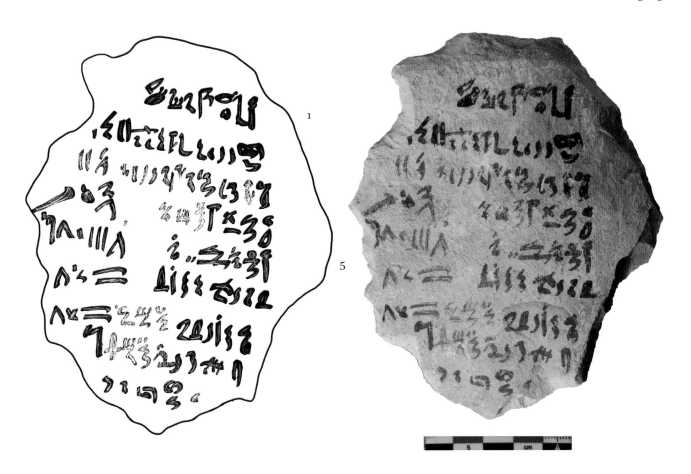

PLATE 9

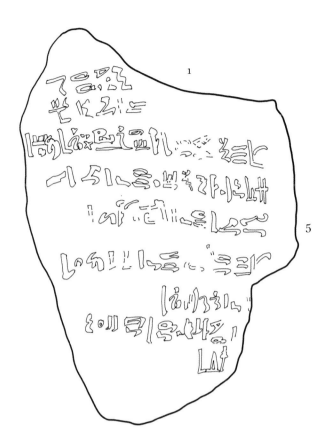

PLATE 10

O. T3.A16 (rto.)

O. T3.A16 (vso.)

PLATE 11

1

5

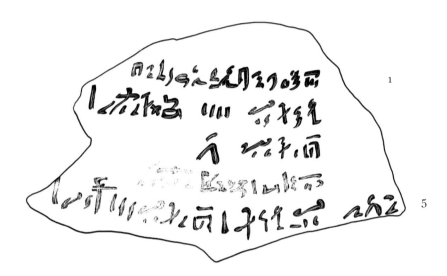

1

5

PLATE 12

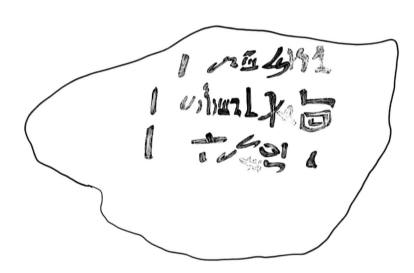

PLATE 13

O. T3.A18

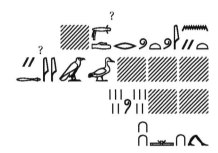

O. T3.A19

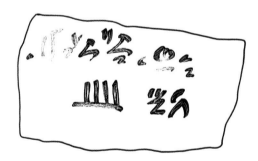

PLATE 14

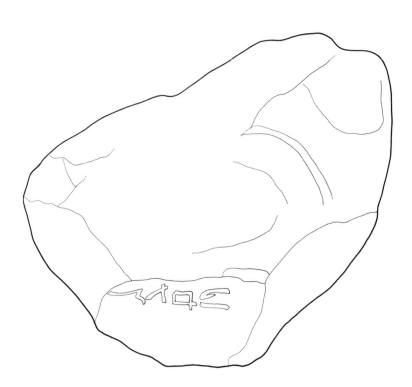

PLATE 15

O. T3.A21

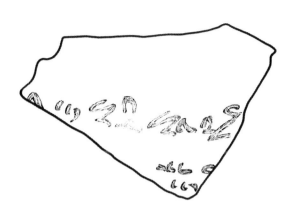

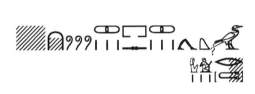

O. T3.A22

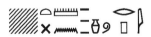

PLATE 16

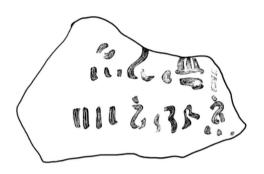

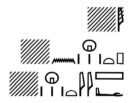

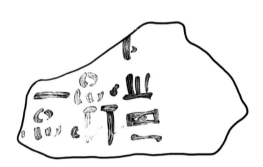

PLATE 17

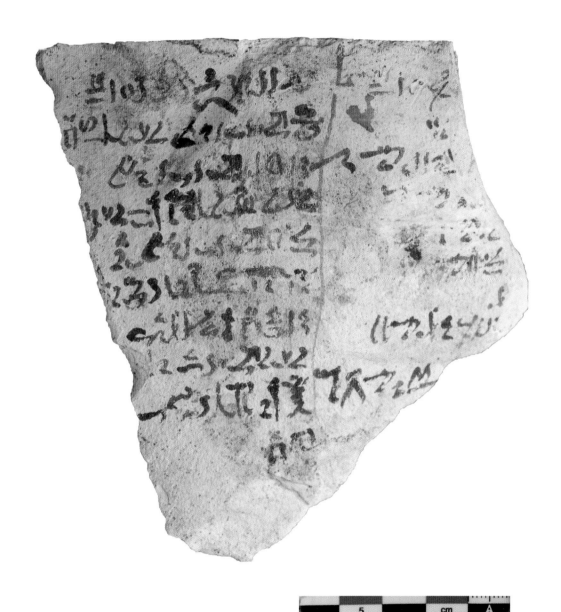

PLATE 18

Col. II   Col. I

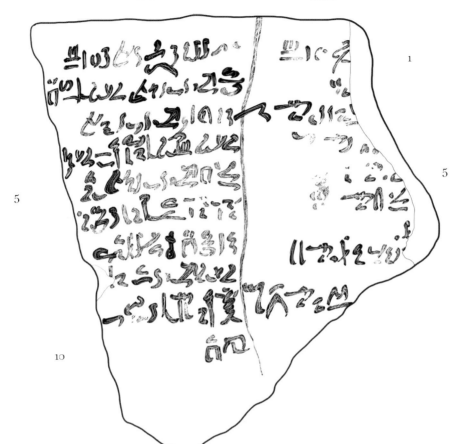

Col. II   Col. I

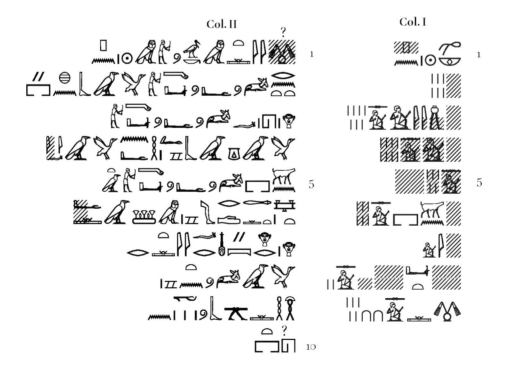

PLATE 19

PLATE 20

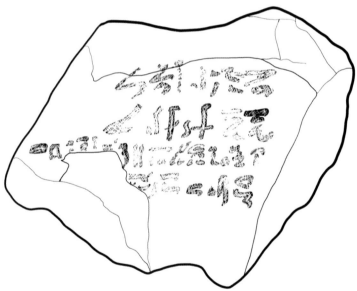

PLATE 21

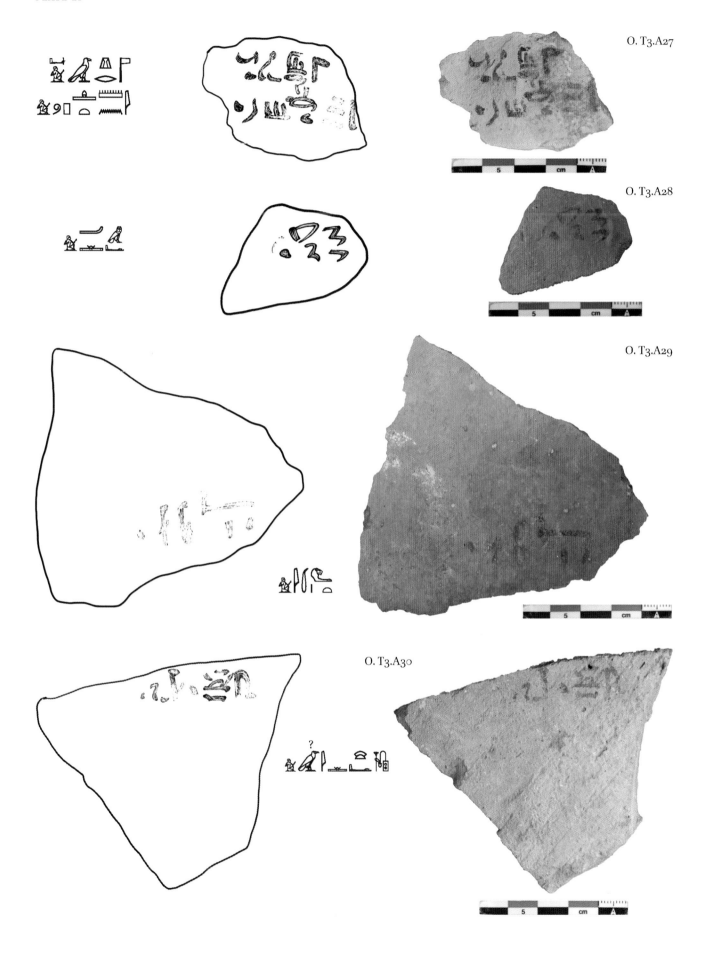

O. T3.A27

O. T3.A28

O. T3.A29

O. T3.A30

PLATE 22

Col. I

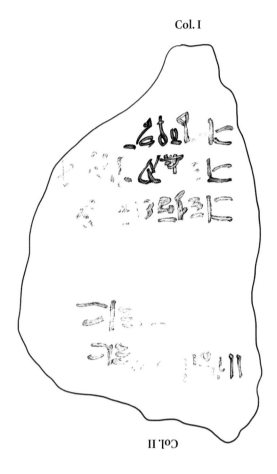

Col. II

Col. I

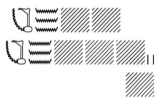

Col. II

PLATE 23

O. T3.A32

O. T3.A33

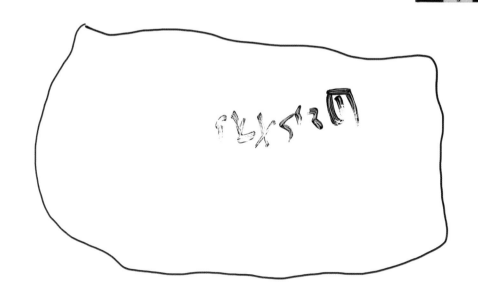

PLATE 24

O. T3.A34

O. T3.A35

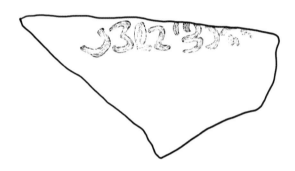 

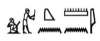

O. T3.A36

 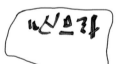 

PLATE 25

O. T3.A37

O. T3.A38

PLATE 26

O. T3.A39

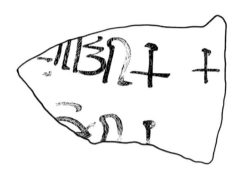

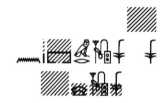

O. T3.A40

PLATE 27

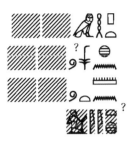

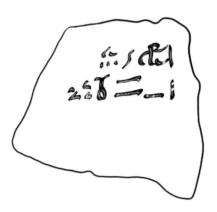

PLATE 28

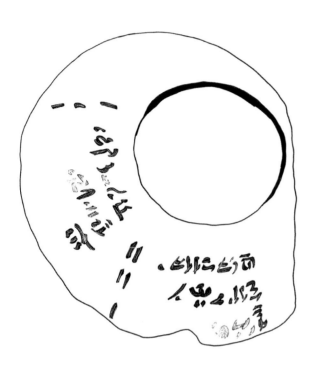

Col. II

Col. I

PLATE 29

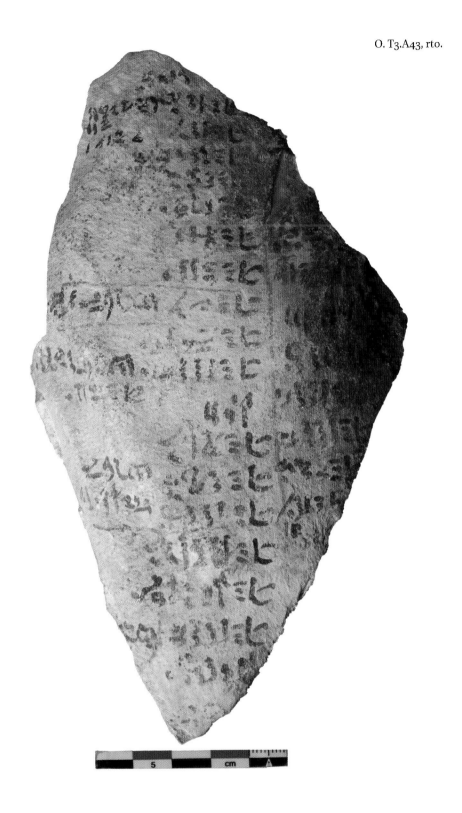

PLATE 30

Col. I

Col. II

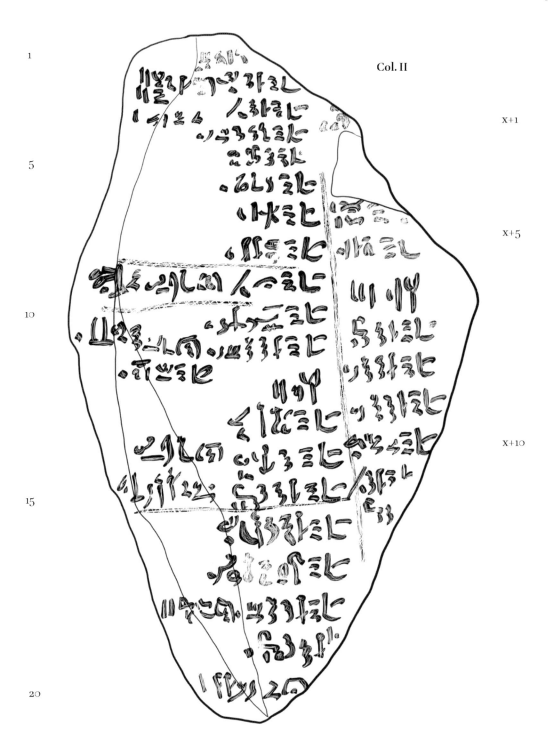

1

5

x+1

10

x+5

15

x+10

20

PLATE 31

Col. I

Col. II

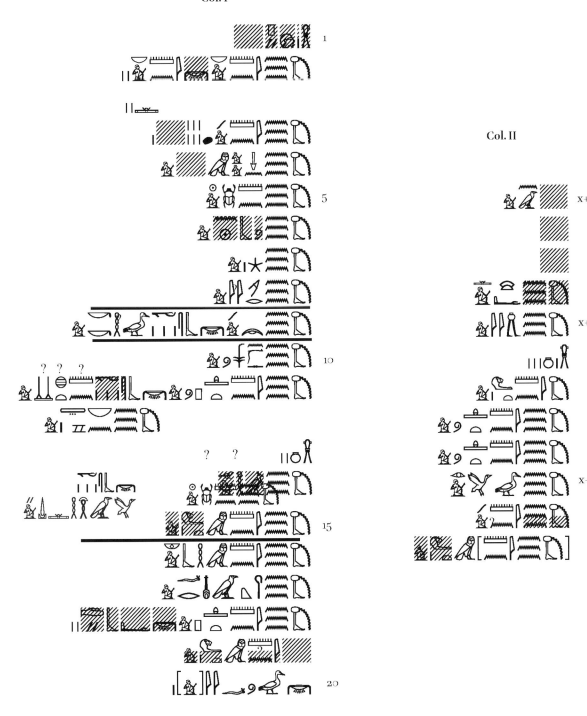

PLATE 32

PLATE 33

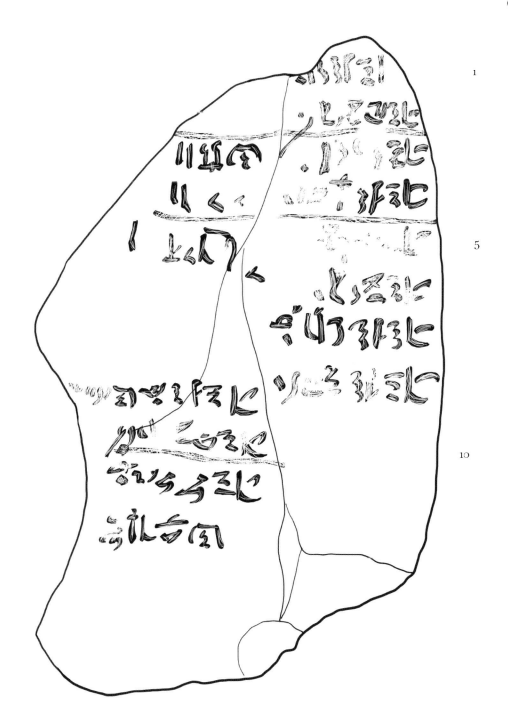

1

5

10

PLATE 34

1

5

10

PLATE 35

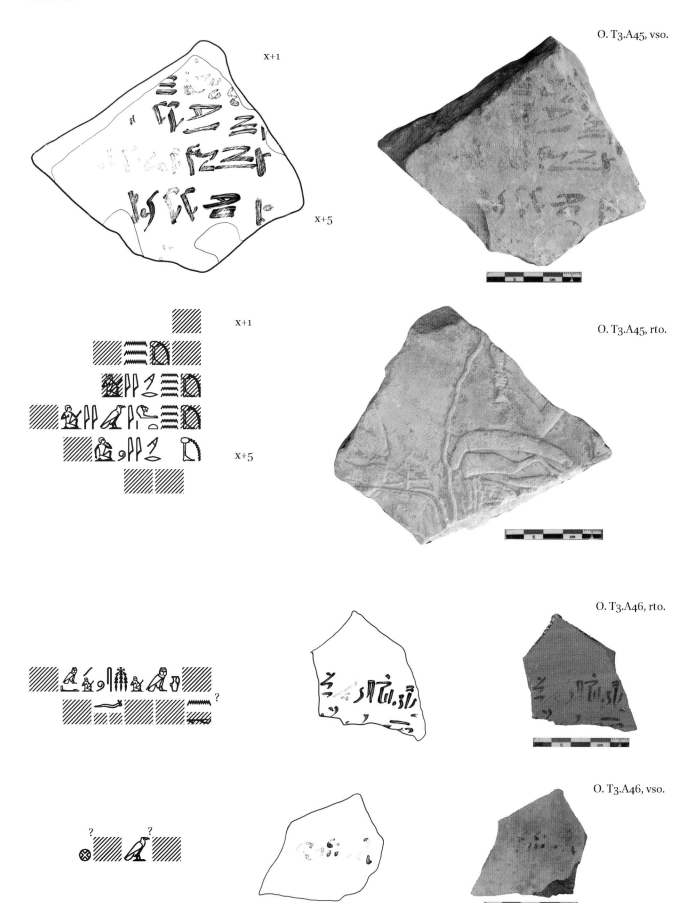

x+1

x+5

O. T3.A45, vso.

x+1

x+5

O. T3.A45, rto.

O. T3.A46, rto.

?

O. T3.A46, vso.

?   ?

PLATE 36

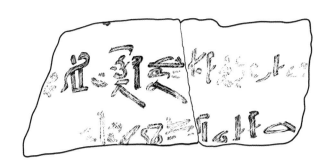

PLATE 37

O. T3.A49

O. T3.A50, rto.

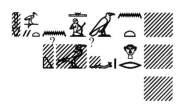

O. T3.A50, vso.

PLATE 38

O. T3.A51

O. T3.A52

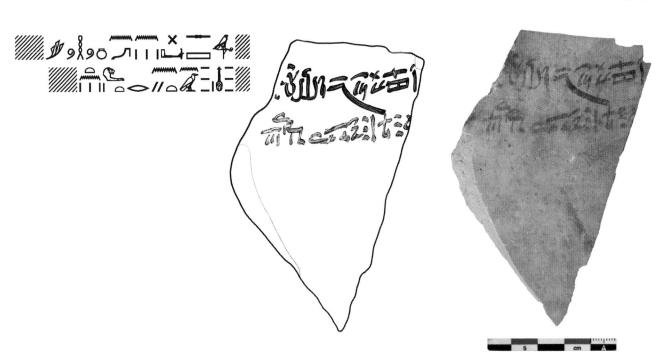

PLATE 39

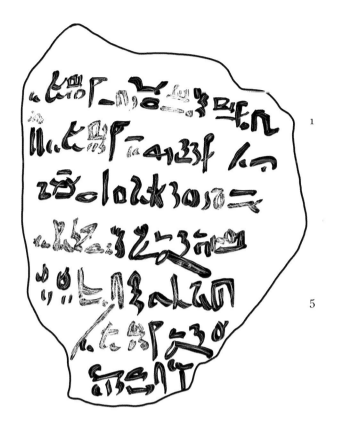

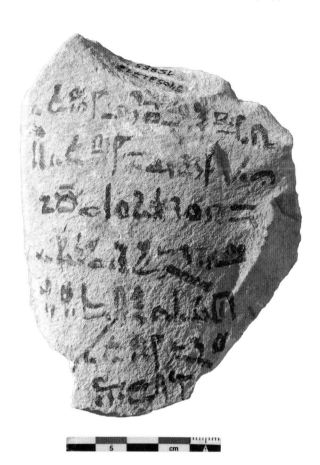

1

5

1

5

PLATE 40

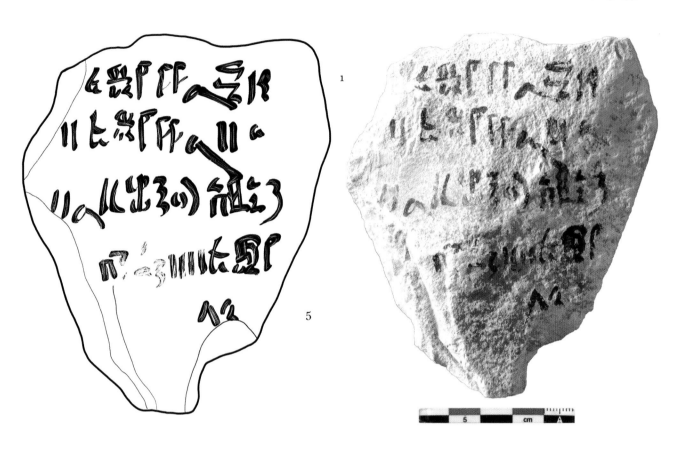

1

5

1

5

PLATE 41

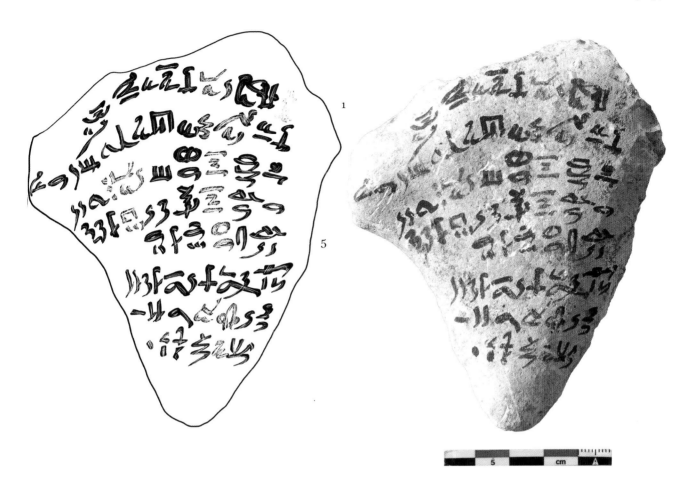

1

5

1

5

PLATE 42

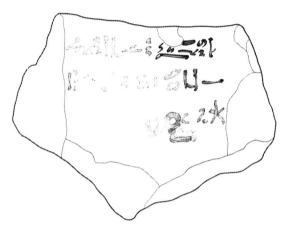

PLATE 43

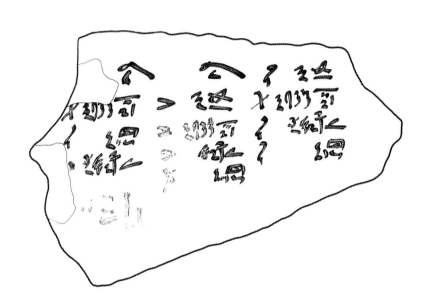

Col. III   Col. II   Col. I

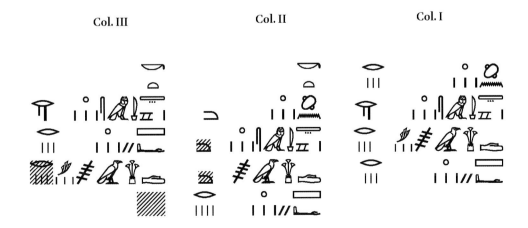

PLATE 44

O. T3.A57

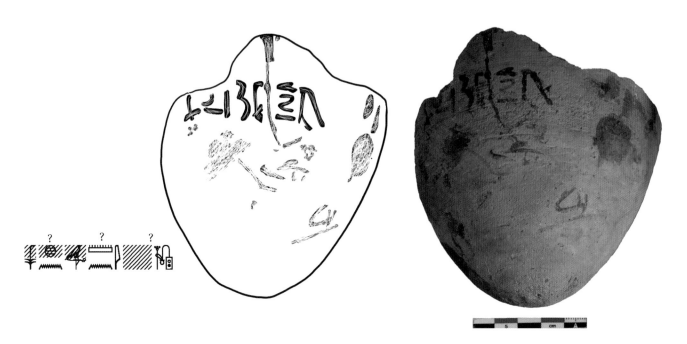

O. T3.A58

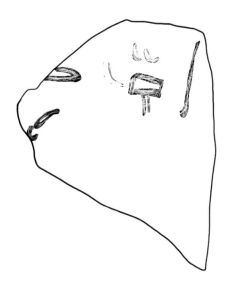

PLATE 45

O. T3.A59

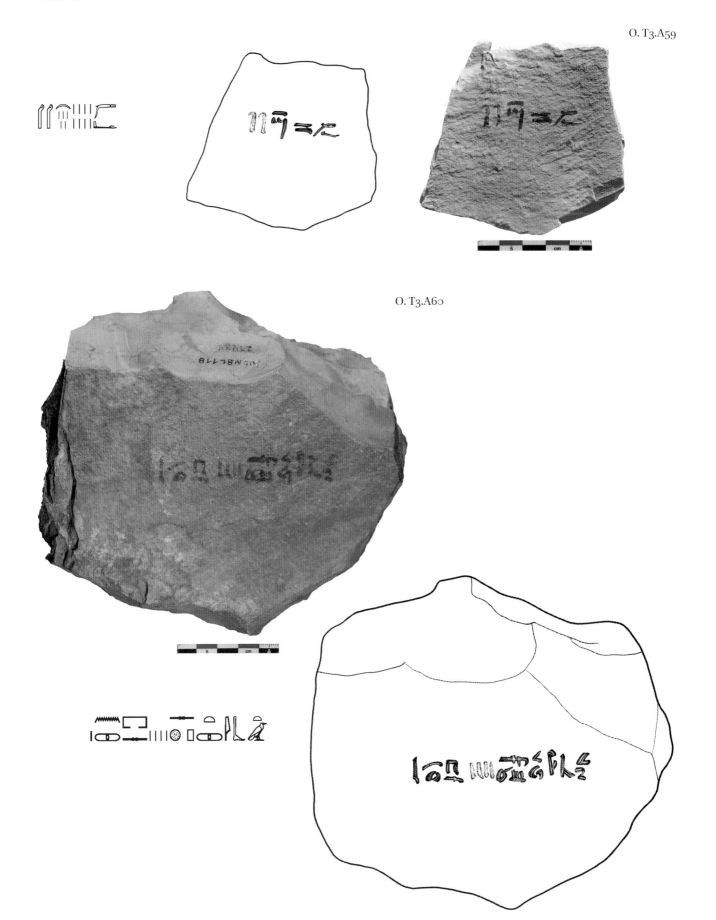

O. T3.A60

PLATE 46

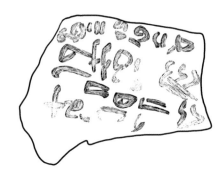

PLATE 47

PLATE 48

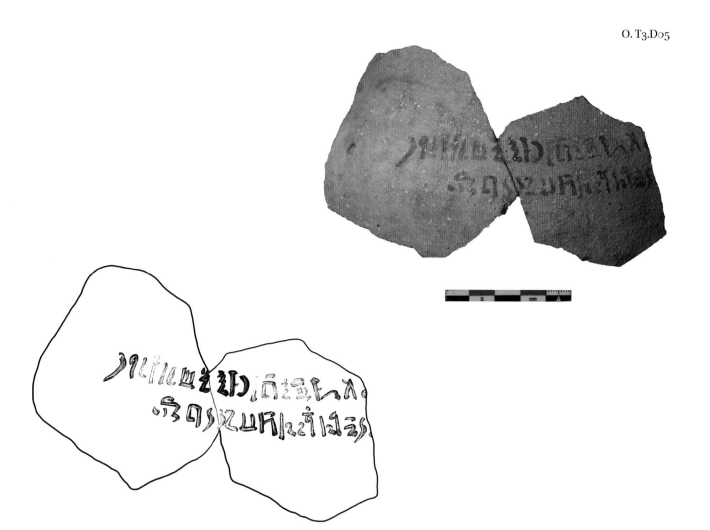

PLATE 49

PLATE 50

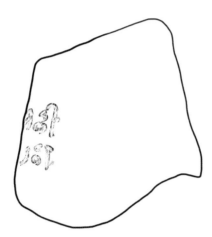

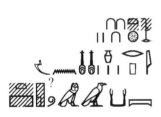

PLATE 51

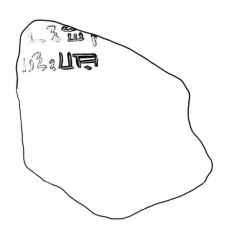

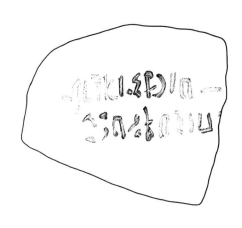

PLATE 52

O. T3.D12

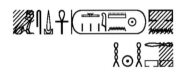

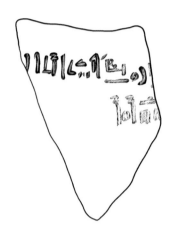

O. T3.D13

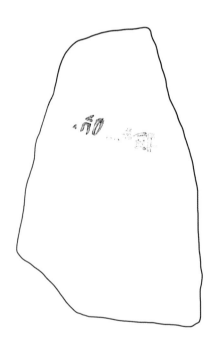

PLATE 53

O. T3.D14

?

O. T3.D15

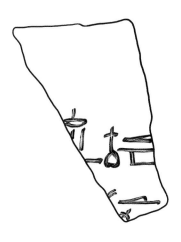

O. T3.D16

PLATE 54

O. T3.D18

O. T3.D19

O. T3.D20

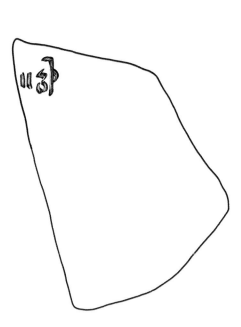

PLATE 55

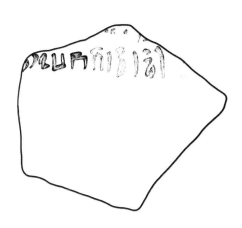

PLATE 56

PLATE 57

O. T3.Lo2

O. T3.Lo4

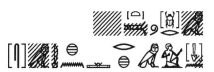  

O. T3.Lo5

O. T3.Lo6

PLATE 58

PLATE 60

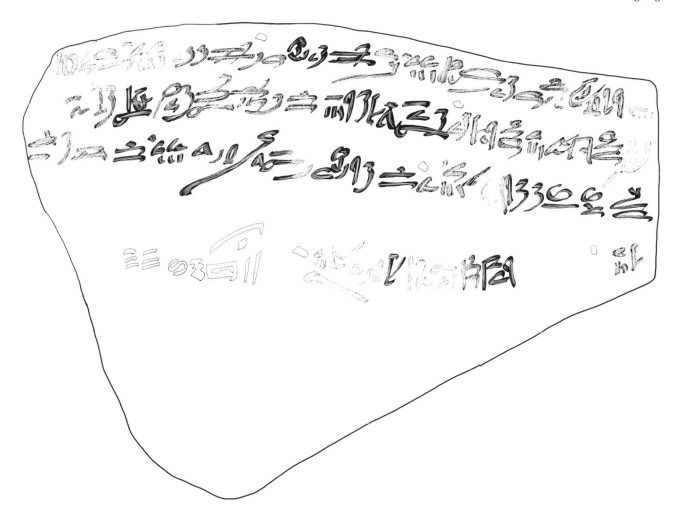

PLATE 61

O. T3.L07

O. T3.L08

O. T3.L09

PLATE 62

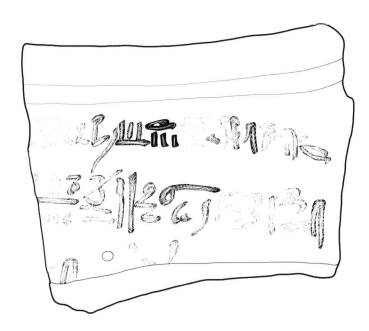

PLATE 63

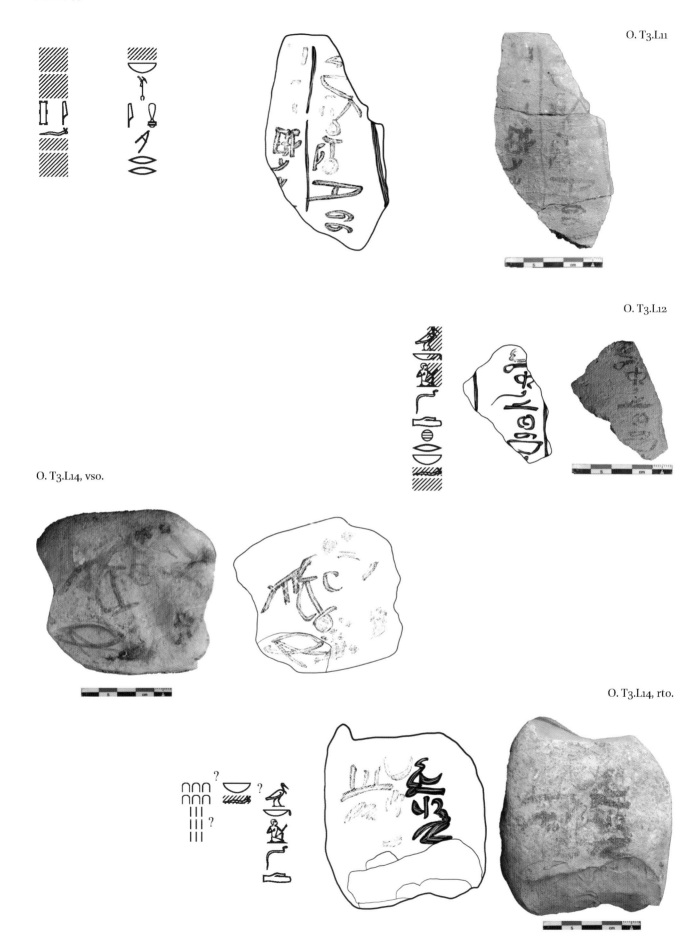

O. T3.L11

O. T3.L12

O. T3.L14, vso.

O. T3.L14, rto.

PLATE 64

O. T3.L13

(C) (B) (A)

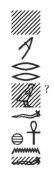

PLATE 65

O. T3.L15, rto.

O. T3.L15, vso.
(= T3.F21)

O. T3.L16, vso.

O. T3.L16, rto. (right) and vso. (left)

   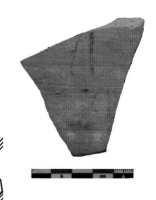

PLATE 66

O. T3.L17

O. T3.L19

PLATE 67

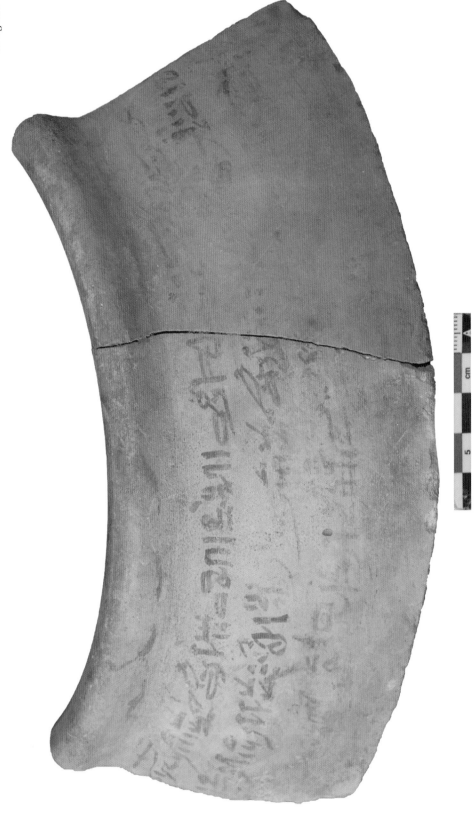

PLATE 68

O. T₃.L₈

O. T₃.L₃

PLATE 69

O. T3.L22

O. T3.L23

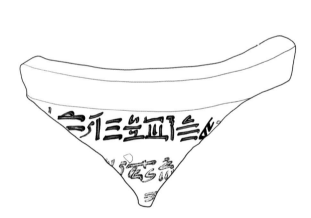

PLATE 70

O. T3.L24

O. T3.L25

O. T3.L26

O. T3.L27

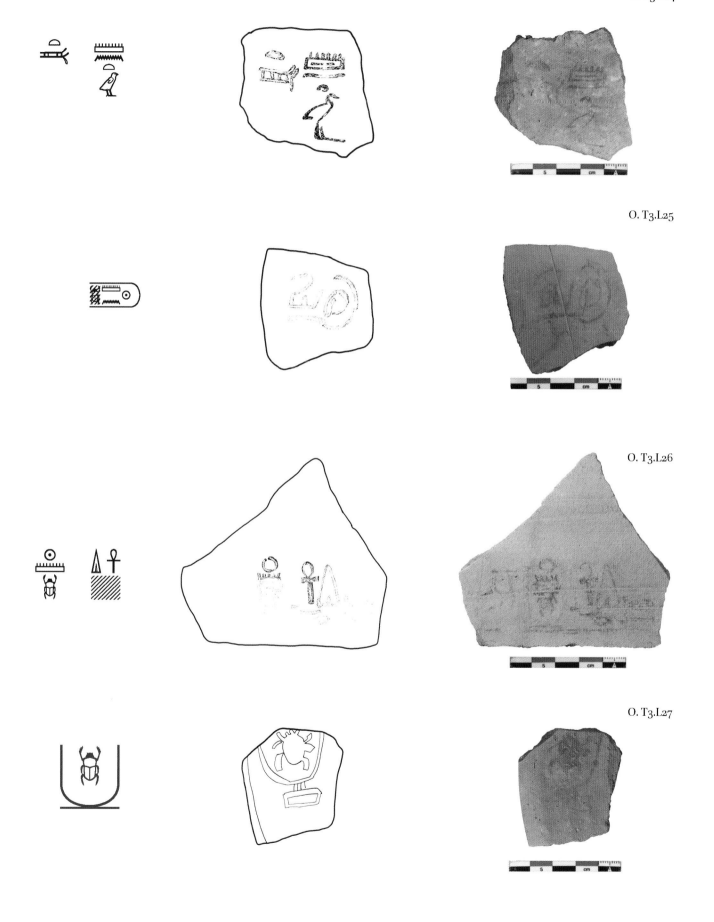

PLATE 71

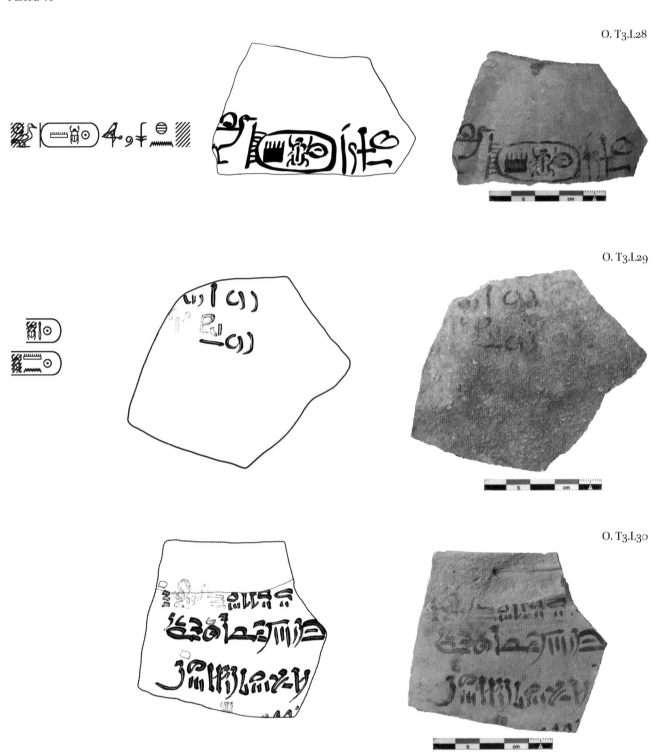

PLATE 72

O. T3.L31

O. T3.L32

O. T3.L34

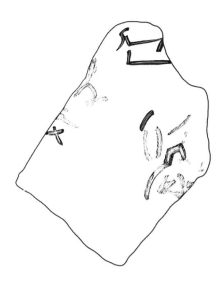 

PLATE 73

PLATE 74

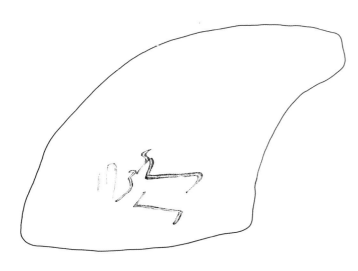

PLATE 75

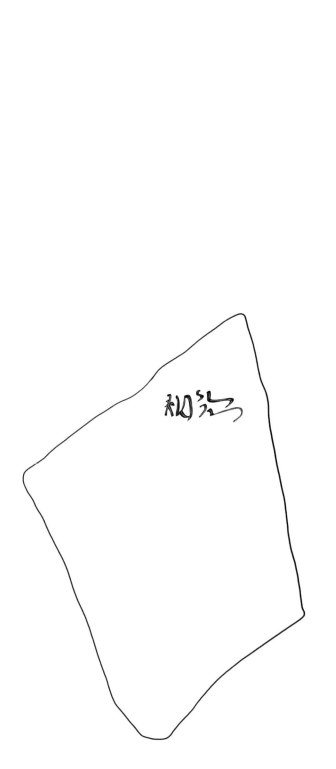

PLATE 76

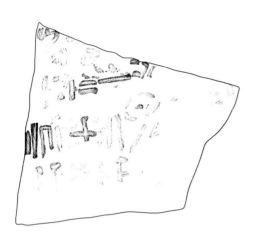

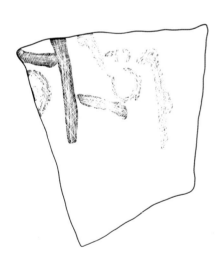

PLATE 77

O. T3.L38

O. T3.L39

PLATE 78

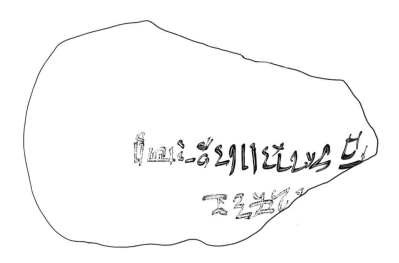

PLATE 79

PLATE 80

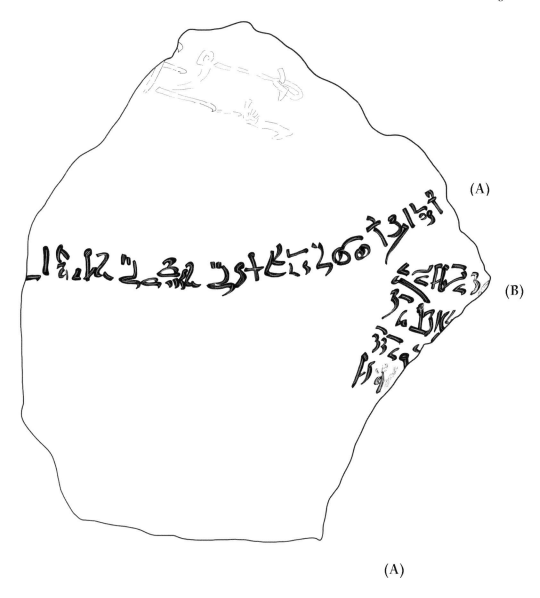

(A)

(B)

(A)

(B)

PLATE 81

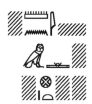

PLATE 82

O. T3.L41, rto.

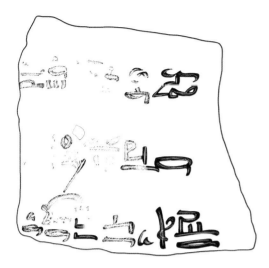

O. T3.L41, vso.

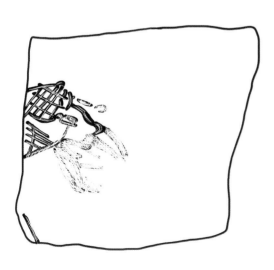

PLATE 83

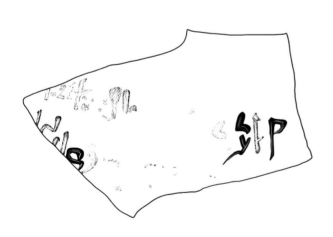

PLATE 84

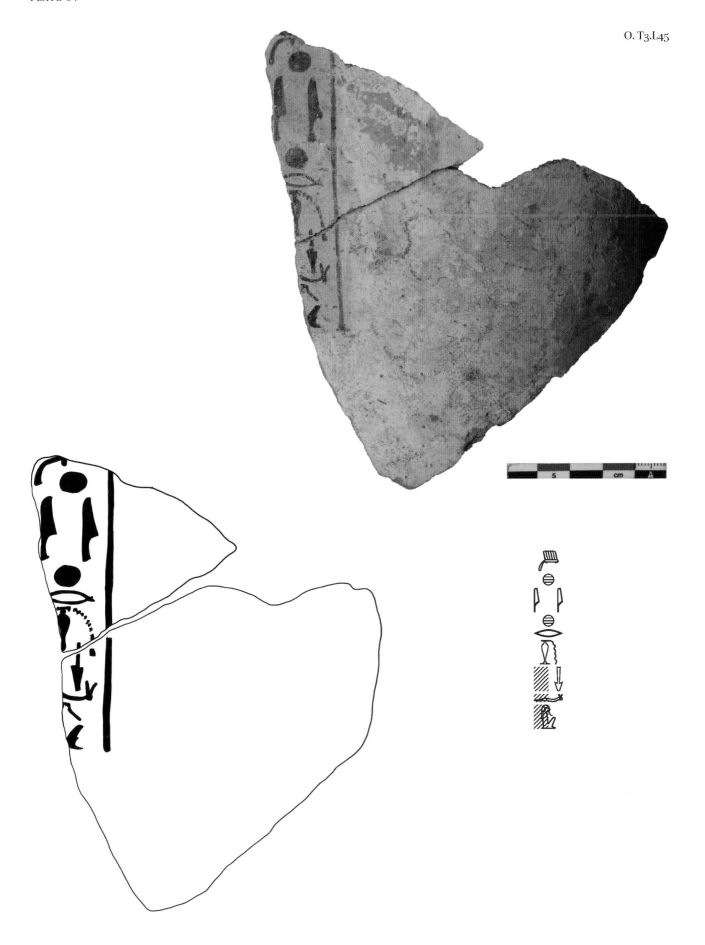

PLATE 85

O. T3.L46

O. T3.L49

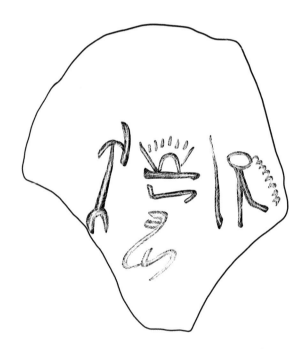

PLATE 86

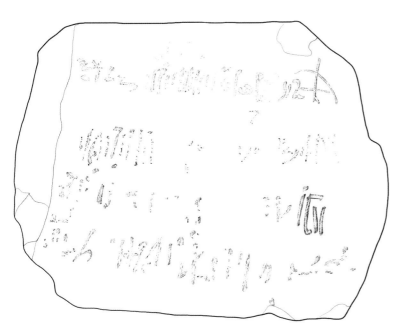

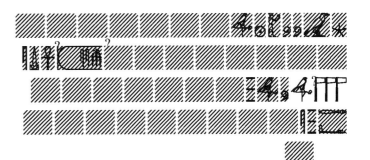

PLATE 87

PLATE 88

O. T3.L50

O. T3.L51

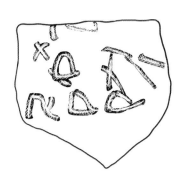

O. T3.L52

PLATE 89

O. T3.L53

O. T3.L54

O. T3.L21

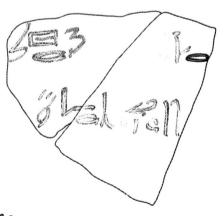

PLATE 90

O. T3.F02

PLATE 91

PLATE 92

O. T3.Fo3

O. T3.Fo5, rto.

O. T3.Fo4

PLATE 93

O. T3.Fo6

O. T3.Fo7

O. T3.Fo8, rto. (left) and vso. (right)

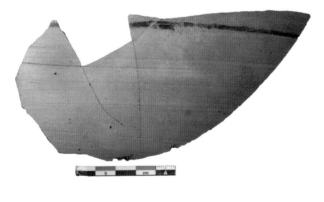

PLATE 94

O. T3.F09

O. T3.F10

O. T3.F11

O. T3.F12

PLATE 95

O. T3.F13

O. T3.F14

O. T3.F15

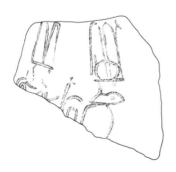

PLATE 96

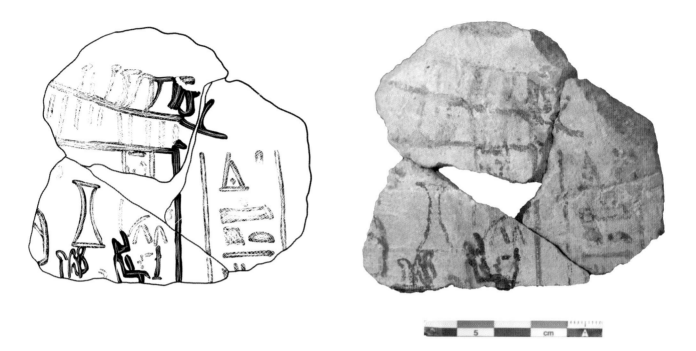

O. T3.F17, rto. (right) and vso. (left)

PLATE 97

O. T3.F18

O. T3.F19

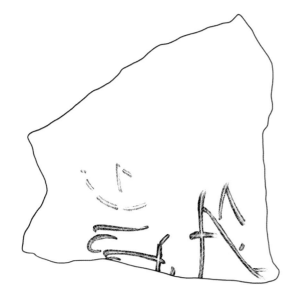

O. T3.F20

PLATE 98

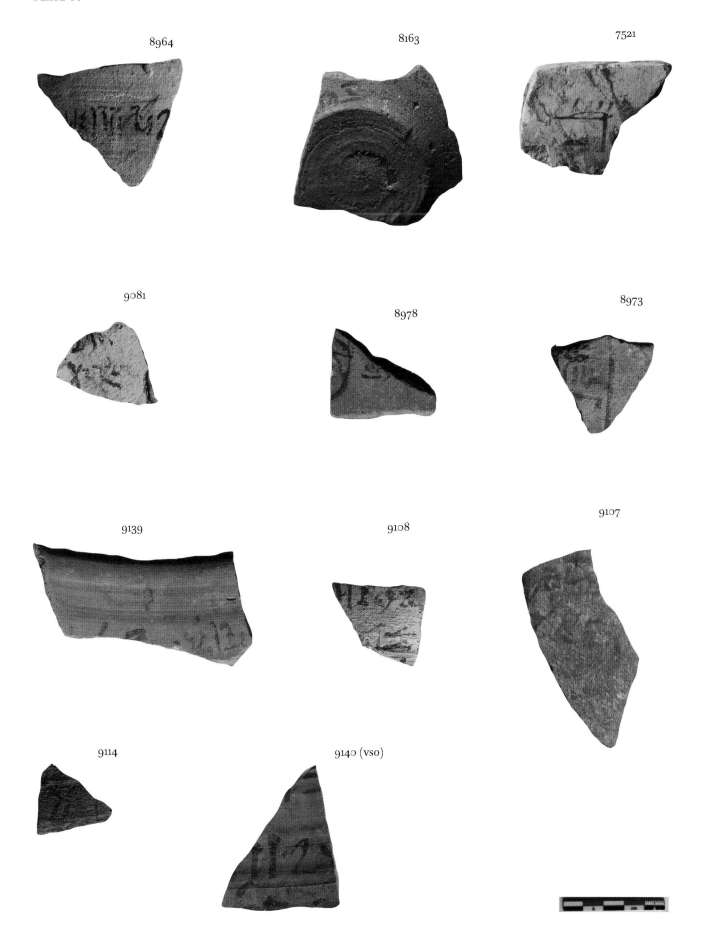

8964

8163

7521

9081

8978

8973

9139

9108

9107

9114

9140 (vso)

PLATE 99

9449

9381

9379

9216

9491

15061

15013

15121

15193

15467

20053

20048

15512